ADOPTING

of related interest

The Secrets of Successful Adoptive Parenting
Practical Advice and Strategies to Help with
Emotional and Behavioural Challenges
Sophie Ashton
Foreword by Bryan Post
ISBN 978 1 78592 078 3
eISBN 978 1 78450 340 6

The Unofficial Guide to Adoptive Parenting
The Small Stuff, The Big Stuff and The Stuff In Between
Sally Donovan
Forewords by Dr Vivien Norris and Jim Clifford OBE and Sue Clifford
ISBN 978 1 84905 536 9
eISBN 978 0 85700 959 3

No Matter What
An Adoptive Family's Story of Hope, Love and Healing
Sally Donovan
ISBN 978 1 84905 431 7
eISBN 978 0 85700 781 0

Preparing for Adoption
Everything Adopting Parents Need to Know About
Preparations, Introductions and the First Few Weeks
Julia Davis
Foreword by Hugh Thornbery
ISBN 978 1 84905 456 0
eISBN 978 0 85700 831 2

Parenting Adopted Teenagers
Advice for the Adolescent Years
Rachel Staff
Foreword by Hugh Thornbery
ISBN 978 1 84905 604 5
eISBN 978 1 78450 069 6

Keeping Your Adoptive Family Strong
Strategies for Success
Gregory C. Keck and L. Gianforte
Foreword by Rita L. Soronen
ISBN 978 1 84905 784 4
eISBN 978 1 78450 028 3

Love and Mayhem
One Big Family's Uplifting Story of Fostering and Adoption
John DeGarmo
ISBN 978 1 84905 775 2
eISBN 978 1 78450 012 2

ADOPTING
— Real Life Stories —

ANN MORRIS

Foreword by Hugh Thornbery

Jessica Kingsley *Publishers*
London and Philadelphia

Note: All case studies have been taken from Adoption UK's magazine *Adoption Today* and from the Adoption UK forum, except in the case of birth mothers' stories and one of the case studies in Chapter 9. All names have been changed, except where there has been a request to keep a real name. Occasionally a case study has a double asterisk **, which indicates that it appeared in Ann Morris (1999) *The Adoption Experience*. London: Jessica Kingsley Publishers.

First published in 2017
by Jessica Kingsley Publishers
73 Collier Street
London N1 9BE, UK
and
400 Market Street, Suite 400
Philadelphia, PA 19106, USA

www.jkp.com

Copyright © Ann Morris and Adoption UK 2017
Foreword copyright © Hugh Thornbery 2017

Library of Congress Cataloging in Publication Data
A CIP catalog record for this book is available from the Library of Congress

British Library Cataloguing in Publication Data
A CIP catalogue record for this book is available from the British Library

ISBN 978 1 84905 660 1
eISBN 978 1 78450 155 6

Printed and bound in Great Britain

CONTENTS

FOREWORD

It has been a real pleasure to read and to be asked to write the foreword to this book. As Ann states in her introduction, it's around 20 years ago that Adoption UK asked her to write her previous book, *The Adoption Experience*.

This would have been at the time of Adoption UK's 25th anniversary. I am thrilled that we now have a brand new book which gathers together experiences of adoption today and that once again many of Adoption UK's wonderful members have given generously of their time to share, through Ann, their personal stories. Adoption is important; it changes some of society's most vulnerable children's lives for the better and it enriches families, but it can also be a tough ride at times. Adoption UK's members are one of the best resources available to those who adopt: a strong, vibrant community of interest and a movement that brings change.

It's easy to reflect on the changes that we have seen over the last two decades. I could list a whole series of legislative, policy, funding and practice developments, but I won't. What I will do is reflect on the fact that two ex-Prime Ministers personally took an active interest in adoption.

It's easy to be cynical about political initiatives but, whilst recent adoption policy developments have not solved all that needs to be corrected in a fractured adoption system, they have both brought a welcome focus upon the needs of adopted children and others with similar histories. Most importantly, they have made tangible differences to the arrangements for supporting adopted children and their families. We are also seeing a much more positive interest in the development of support for adopted families in Northern Ireland, Scotland and Wales.

These developments are important because in a world that changes so rapidly some things do not change. We see historically high numbers of children in the care system. The need to protect children from serious harm through abuse or neglect does not go away. Many of these children are able to go back to their birth parents with the right support, others remain in care and a steady but relatively small proportion are adopted.

Consistently around 70 per cent of children adopted from care have experienced abuse and neglect. Too many of them will have had to move placement while in care and others will have experienced delay. We know these last two issues are in themselves harmful. The legacy of what has occurred before a child is placed with an adoptive family affects children in different ways. One significant change over the past 20 years has been our improved understanding of how children are affected by these experiences and what needs to be in place to help them. Getting the support for children right helps adopters to achieve what the international research on the outcomes of adoption tells us: that adopted children generally do well – they catch up.

As well as forming an invaluable network of support for adopters and helping children to find families, what Adoption UK achieves through the power of our membership is to have the ability to persuasively influence policy initiatives so that, step by step, we raise awareness of adoption issues, improve the understanding of policy makers and inform practical developments on the ground that make a real difference. There are many more steps to take but progress is being made and sustained, even though resources will always be stretched.

What Ann does so well in this book is to bring the experiences of Adoption UK's members to others joining our community of interest. There is nothing that can replace the knowledge and experience of those who have trod the path ahead of others and, whilst everyone's experiences will be different, hearing about the highs and lows of others, the twists and turns they may have encountered on the way, and how they got through the stormy times provide invaluable insights into the challenges and rewards that lie ahead.

The Adoption Experience provided essential information for many families over the years and I am certain that Ann's new book, *Adopting,* will go on to help many adopters and prospective adopters for years into the future – I thoroughly recommend this book.

Whether you are starting out on your adoption journey, or are some way along the road, do join or stay with Adoption UK; this excellent book shows you the strength and value of our community.

Hugh Thornbery CBE
Chief Executive, Adoption UK

INTRODUCTION

Adoption touches almost everyone. Even if we are not personally involved in this extraordinary human triangle – adoptee, adopter, birth parent – most of us have friends, family, neighbours or colleagues who are.

Nearly 20 years ago I was asked by Adoption UK to compile a book about adoption – a book of real stories from real adopters, members of Adoption UK who had shared their experiences in the hope of helping each other along the rocky road of parenthood. *The Adoption Experience*, published in 1999, recounted those experiences and was read by thousands of other adopters, potential adopters and professionals. This book is essentially an update of *The Adoption Experience*, relating the experiences of today's adopters in the context of the changed and changing face of adoption.

Adoption has evolved over the past 20 years: laws have been significantly revised and society has developed different parameters of acceptance. It's hard to believe how almost impossible it was in the 1990s for same-sex couples or single parents to adopt – and if they did get through the system, how they were often given the roughest deals, the toughest children. They still make up a minority of adopters but they are now an important and accepted minority. Odd to think that foetal alcohol syndrome was little talked about and that adoption with any contact was rare. Extraordinary to remember how complicated it was for your child to trace his or her birth parents and how the explosion in social media has leapfrogged those carefully set restrictions on tracing, making them meaningless. How do adopters and their children deal with these challenges?

Parenthood is probably the greatest adventure in life any of us undertake, a rollercoaster of often unexpected experiences – and for adopters the peaks can be higher and the lows lower.

The decision to adopt creeps up on people, an embryonic idea which quietly grows, gets discussed as it takes shape, until finally the research gets serious. The aim of this book is to help in that research with no-holds-barred real experiences of adopters and adoptees.

On adoption websites gap-toothed grins from freshly washed children scream out their 'take me' appeal. The agencies are often shameless in their sales pitch: Lucy loves *Peppa Pig*, James makes friends easily, Sam sings along to *Frozen*. On the surface they need families who will wipe away their tears, tuck them safely into bed, make sure they are well fed and comfortably dressed, and make them laugh. Underneath they need families who will hold on fast and do everything they can to heal their broken hearts, put up with their tantrums and nightmarish traumas and whatever else each adoptive child has to deal with that other children never have to face.

Adoption with all its joy is something parents-to-be need to be well prepared for, not only by well-versed and experienced social workers but also by other adoptive parents who know only too well that theory and practice are two very different things.

The experiences in this book come from adoptive families: these are the people on the front line – adopters of every kind who have shown what unconditional love really is about; adoptees who, with their new family's help, have struggled out of the darkness of their past, and a handful of birth mothers whose stories reveal how much they were victims of circumstance.

Almost all the stories in the book come from families who are members of Adoption UK, the charity providing support, awareness and understanding for those parenting or supporting children who cannot live with their birth parents. It's a community of more than 11,000 members and is the largest voice of adopters in the UK.

Their experiences often describe a moment in time, although some take a more long-term, reflective look at adoption. All names have been changed except where the writer has requested that their name be used.

The aim of this book, as with *The Adoption Experience*, is not to underestimate the joys of adoption, but to reveal the challenges honestly: to give potential adopters a bird's-eye view of the road ahead, so that they take on a child with their eyes open, mentally if not emotionally armed to deal with whatever comes next.

Adopting is not for everyone, but we hope this book encourages those thinking about adoption to consider it more seriously and those who are adopting to stick with it.

THE FACTS

There are more than 93,000 children in care in the United Kingdom (2015 statistics). The majority of these children are in the care of the state due to abuse or neglect and are from white British backgrounds. Approximately 6000 children are adopted annually, the vast majority under the age of five.[1]

---

1   Adoption UK (2015) 'Adoption facts and figures.' Available at www.adoptionuk. org/press-media/adoption-facts-and-figures, accessed on 3 August 2016.

Chapter 1

SO YOU WANT TO ADOPT?

It's a life-changing decision – whether you adopt or give birth, nothing will ever be the same again. Parenthood is more exciting, more terrifying, more joyful, more absorbing and more time-consuming than anything else you ever do.

With over 90,000 children in care in the United Kingdom alone, many families thinking about adopting might believe that their decision to adopt is the hard part, and that getting approved as an adopter and finding a child who is already looking for a family will be easy. It's not.

The first hurdle is finding an adoption agency or local authority willing to take you on. One problem is that many adopters apply to become adopters to one child under the age of two (so social workers can pick and choose from the application forms) but not enough are ready to consider siblings or children over the age of four.

'You will get further, faster if you have a flexible approach to the process,' said one successful adopter.

A good starting point is to attend an open informal information meeting about adoption. Most local authorities hold these meetings regularly and you can look up when and where they are held on the authority's website. It's an opportunity for potential adopters to meet seasoned adopters and adoptees as well as social workers who can tell them about the sort of children in their care who are looking for families.

Agencies and local authorities differ both in their recruitment criteria and in the way they take you through the process – there is no real joined-up thinking at this point – so it is often worth attending several meetings in several different areas. Prospective adopters soon find that there are no hard and fast rules to the adoption process.

'It all seems really illogical that all these authorities and agencies are doing their own thing,' wrote one frustrated potential adopter.

'I feel really shocked at the negative response to our enquiries,' wrote another. 'We've waited eight months because there were no "free" social workers in our area to take us through Form F,' wrote a third.

'Overworked social workers need to find families for the children in their care. Despite the number of children looking for families, as an adopter you have to learn to be incredibly patient,' said another adopter.

The next hurdle is the assessment itself. This necessarily time-consuming process involves an in-depth appraisal by a social worker, usually over several months. It often starts with group sessions with other potential adopters, and graduates to home visits and the central part of this process, the completion of the standard Form F. This involves a large amount of self-analysis, which can and should be an educative and illuminating experience, helping potential adopters to discover and understand the special parenting skills they have and will need to offer to a child placed for adoption; but for some the experience of assessment can be nerve-racking and intrusive.

But it's necessary. This is a lifetime's commitment.

Claire was adopted when she was six years old; now 19 she has strong views on adoption:

> I think it's important people think about what the child has gone through and how they might feel to have to go and live with people they don't know when they've had to do it before… when they've already lost parents.
>
> If you want to adopt, I think you need to realize it's not easy and will take a lot of work. But if you really want to give a child a family, don't make them think they've got one and let them down because you can't stick to it – make sure you can beforehand. Otherwise you're just going to mess them up more.
>
> Adoption isn't just about people having and helping kids because they think it will be nice. It's about what the kid needs too.

Having waded your way emotionally through the process, you will hopefully find yourself on an approved list of a potential adopters and it is time to wait.

The last and final hurdle is finding the child who is looking for you. There is no limit on how long you have to wait between being approved as a potential adopter and being linked with a child or children looking for adoption. For many this is the most frustrating and often upsetting time: children gaze out appealingly, longingly from agency websites or the Adoption UK *Children Who Wait* magazine, but sometimes it seems that none of them are meant for you and calls and letters are fruitless. Many agencies will interview two or more sets of potential families for a child and then choose the adopter they perceive to be 'the best'. Being told, often with little compassion, that you are not quite right for a child or children can be a devastating blow to your self-esteem.

'You begin to hold back. You don't jump around with joy every time a social worker calls to discuss a child,' said one adoptive mother who wrote over 100 letters before her children 'found' her.

Every person's experience of finding an agency that will take them through the approval process and then to the child or children waiting for them at the centre of the adoption maze differs enormously.

Bringing me home

Ten-year-old Cam is the eldest of three adopted boys. He was inspired to write about his life for a BBC children's competition.

In the first picture my mum ever saw of me I was pulling myself up the sofa in my foster carers' house. I was only ten months old and I don't remember a bit about it, but from the pictures Mum has shown me I had lots of fun!

My foster carers were an awesome family, really great. It was a month later when my mum and dad first saw me there. Mum says that as they walked down the garden path their knees were knocking and their hearts pounded really loudly. I'd heard the doorbell ring and crawled into the hall. I looked right up at Mum as she came in the door and she knew at that moment that I was the one. That feels lovely.

That was a long time ago. I've done so much since then. We still keep in touch with my foster family – they nicknamed me Vinnie because I loved football. I still do. I guess some things just stay the same, whatever. I don't remember coming to my real home.

I've felt how exciting it was collecting my siblings from their foster families, so I imagine it was the same for me. It's strange to think of going to meet your new brother for the first time and I remember feeling excited and nervous all at once, more so the first time I did it. Would he even like me for a start? Would he enjoy the same things that I did? What if he hated me? Would we still be brothers then? The journey was really long and tiring, but when we finally arrived everything just fell into place.

I saw him looking through the sitting-room window. He looked just like his picture but better because he saw me and did this huge grin. I jumped out of the car to get to him first. He ran out and straight to me, gave me a big hug and said, 'Hello! You're here!' It was weird because we'd never met each other before but there was this great big feeling like we'd always been together. After all my worry it was me he wanted – I guess we were meant to be together after all.

It used to upset me that I didn't come out of my mum's tummy, but she'd hug me and say it didn't change anything. Mum always says that it doesn't really matter how we get to earth; what's important is that we find the people we love. We're all lucky that it didn't take us long. Last night we sat together looking up at the stars. It's funny that our star constellations are all right next to each other. Mum says that love glue has always tied us together, even before we were born. She says that there was a big plan written somewhere, like a map, that led us to each other. It was just meant to be, a bit like her meeting Dad. I think that we're different parts of the same puzzle. Sometimes it takes a while to fit those pieces together, but, as Mum always says, you've got to believe in magic!

Square pegs round holes

We adopted two boys aged two and a half and three and a half years old 20 months ago – they had been in foster care for 21 months. I read articles about disrupted placements and failed adoption, and looking back I can see the hit-and-miss nature of adoption.

- How can social workers tell if you are compatible as a family?

- How do social workers know the true character of each child?

- How much do social workers see of the children in a family environment?

- How much do social workers know about the history of the children?

- How much is fostering a holding zone for kids?

- Who makes adoption a success?

I know the answer to the last one. We do: the kids and parents in the new family as we change shape to accommodate each other. If this sounds a bit bitter, it shouldn't, as I would struggle to find another better way to prepare for adoption and I don't know how social workers could find out more. We, the adoptive parents, take a huge leap of faith just as the placement team put a huge amount of trust in us.

I have been around adoptive parents who tell me they fell in love with their child(ren) the first time they saw them – I didn't. The first time I saw our two I was shocked that their development was so far behind.

I wonder if we say we love them so early in the placement because we want to be like any other family, because we don't know what we feel or because we are encouraged to feel this way. So was what I felt wrong? Well, we are not like any other 'normal' family because 'normal' families only have their own history to contend with, not at least another two, the birth family and foster family.

These 'normal' families do not have to explain 'what happened' to their kids later in life without lying or making them feel abandoned. We are not 'normal', and for that matter who would want to be? I was at an education seminar recently and heard that the figures for children who need some sort of intervention in their school life is 80 per cent. So the perceived normal are the 20 per cent who don't – it turns the perception of normal around.

Through adoption we have been given a rare opportunity to see part of human nature in the raw and to learn how and why a child attaches to its parents. I have watched two very confused boys grow and develop. The initial change was very quick and marked.

Learning how to bond with our children, we understand ourselves a little better – and we learn to take nothing for granted.

Finding my child

As a fresh-faced teenager with a wild urge for freedom, it was an immensely strange and completely 'out there somewhere' concept to ever consider having children and becoming a parent. If I had known then what I know now, I would have drunk less, sobbed less and got out of bed more often in the morning.

I married my lovely husband Neil when I was 28 – nine years after we first met. I guess I thought I would become pregnant quickly. But Nature has a crafty way of sticking her foot out and she caught us both in the proverbials. The ratio of struggling couples was then around one in four and I believe it is the same today. When you are confronting this difficulty, you walk to the paper shop and count every fourth house as you go, imagining the crying and hand-wringing that must be going on within. You feel isolated, gutted and angry. Why does every teen you see get to push a pram whilst she clearly ignores her failing, flailing baby as she chats fervently on her mobile? It's not fair. Not bloody fair. How could I want something so much that I had never thought I wanted before? Infertility does that to you, though, and I know because I was there, in that dark lonely place. For a long time.

My story is actually one of such huge and immense joy that now, aged 42, I have gone back to dancing and skipping around the kitchen as I wash up, making up ludicrous lyrics to songs and performing them to no one in particular.

This miracle of joy – this momentous event that I never even knew I wanted so desperately until I couldn't have it – is the advent of a bundle of gurgling joy sitting happily before me, chewing my fingers and dribbling. To be quite exact he is my third wonderful bundle of dribbly joy through adoption. Even now I have to take a moment to reflect on what it's like being the happiest mum on earth.

I guess it's true that suffering makes you appreciative. The pain and the misery really is an interim period. For anyone reading this story who is still at the dark, sad and interminably long other-end of the story, then please, I beg of you, take heart. Things do change.

I appreciate that daily life doesn't always inspire faith, but I've learnt to appreciate that it is how you see things that counts – learn to ignore the doubtful expression of the person next to you and listen to your heart.

Adoption is about kids' needs too – an adoptee's story

I think adoption is an amazing thing and I'm really pleased it gives children the life and family they deserve. I have good parents, a good life, brothers and sisters I love, and I've had the best upbringing possible.

When I was little, I'd imagine another me on the other side of the world wishing for my life. I'd always think I should be the other girl without the family; that I should be the one wishing for one. And I'd always feel bad because I felt I had what someone else should have, not what I deserved.

I still don't feel like I deserve this family yet.

My mum helps people when they adopt. When they are finding it hard. She's talked to me about some of the things people do. And from what I can tell, people don't always think about what they're doing.

You might – I don't know. But I think it's important people think about what the child has gone through and how they might feel to have to go and live with people they don't know when they've had to do it before…when they've already lost parents.

I was a perfect child for the first year I was with my adoptive parents, before they formally adopted me. It was because I was scared if I did something wrong they wouldn't want me. When I was adopted, they were my parents and my God did I change! So did my brothers and sister. We pushed them; we tested them; we wanted to know how much it would take for them to get rid of us.

But they stuck to it. They kept us and taught us how to behave – even how to play and talk. It took a long time and it was hard for them, but it paid off. In shops, people would say that we were all so well behaved. They took us to nice posh restaurants, I was nine and my mum would happily take me anywhere. And I realized that I finally had parents who would keep me.

If you want to adopt, I think you need to realize it's not easy and will take a lot of work. But if you really want to give a child a family, don't make them think they've got one and let them down because you can't stick to it – make sure you can beforehand. Otherwise you're just going to mess them up more.

Adoption isn't just about people having and helping kids because they think it will be nice. It's about what the kid needs too. Either provide it or don't.

Older children will know what's been happening. And they will have no reason to trust you or believe that you're kind and will keep them. You gotta prove it first. Can you do that and take what the child throws at you?

When my parents adopted me, I was seven. And the best thing they ever did was tell me I was adopted. They told us they didn't give birth to us, so my sister would hide up our mum's top and pretend she was in our mummy's tummy.

I guess my point in writing this is to try to get people to think about what a child is feeling when they are being adopted. So please, please, if you want to adopt, please make sure you can do it and won't give up. Make sure you can handle it.

Adoption – the challenges you should be prepared for

Usually when I sit down to write, I do so as a psychologist. This time it is different. My wife and I are adoptive parents.

People in Britain are being urged to adopt children from what we call the 'care' system. To be inspired is good but it is not the same as being prepared. People who take children from 'care' need to know what they may face. Posters advertising for adoptive parents typically show children playing happily or looking adoringly at the camera. The reality can be very different. Here are some questions that I would ask potential adopters:

- How would you cope if your adopted child physically attacks you for no apparent reason?

- How would you react if he or she hits one of his or her siblings?

- How would you deal with stealing or refusal to go to school?

- How would you address inappropriate sexual behaviour?

- How would you cope with a child who is constantly angry for no obvious reason?

- Could you cope with urinary or faecal incontinence in a child of junior school age or older?'

This is just a short list but, as you may have gathered, adoptive parenting can have its challenges. Other problems may include dealing with the judgemental attitude of others. Adopted children may look the same as others but behave very differently, often through no fault of their own.

Imagine this situation. You are out shopping with your newly arrived child. He has had a number of 'placements' before coming to you. You need a cake and decide to buy one at the supermarket. When the child sees you take the cake off the shelf, he thinks it is in preparation for a going-away party. He thinks he is going to have to face yet another move. At this moment he is overcome by sheer terror. He starts screaming so the whole store can hear. You try to explain to the child that he is your child now and that he is not going anywhere. The child, however, is too distressed to hear this. A passer-by tells you, in a voice loud enough to be heard by others, that you should 'Make that child behave himself! He just needs some discipline!' (At this point you may be tempted to put the cake in the passer-by's face, but this would not be very Christian and could get you arrested.)

Some adopted children can appear to be well behaved at school or in church but be extremely difficult at home. It is easy in this situation to point the finger at the parents. Reactions like this can lead to a parent who may already be exhausted feeling utterly demoralized. The reality probably is that the child is less secure at school, or anywhere outside of the home.

Sometimes an adopted child appears to relate well to one parent but not to the other. Again it can be very easy to jump to the wrong conclusion. The fact of the matter is that some children from severely disrupted backgrounds can only form a close attachment to one person. This can be emotionally draining for the parent with whom the attachment is formed and very difficult for the other. What both parents need is support. It takes stamina to be the only caregiver for an extremely needy child and emotional maturity to cope with constant rejection.

These are just some of the issues that adoptive parents can face with their children. It can be edifying to sit and listen to adoptive parents talk about their encounters with schools, hospitals and the caring professions. Again there are questions that I would ask of those thinking of adopting:

- How would you cope with teachers who see your child as 'misbehaving' when in fact he or she is actually frightened or reacting to some past trauma?

- How would you cope if the same teachers simply saw you as making excuses for your child's supposed misbehaviour?

- What would you do if you come to the conclusion (after much thought and reflection) that your child would be better placed in a special school but your education authority refuses to agree to this?

- Could you cope financially and emotionally with taking your child's case to a tribunal if necessary?

- What would you do if civil servants or others assume that because your child has learning difficulties you must have similar problems and speak to you in a simple, patronizing manner?

- How would you cope if, having endured all this, someone says, 'Adoption is a win/win situation. Children get the homes they need and you get the child you always wanted. Now your family is just like any other!'?

In view of all this, what might help? Allow me to make a suggestion: encourage those who are thinking of adopting to talk with as many adoptive parents as possible. Suggest they ask what services are available locally.

Finally, we need to do the most important thing of all – that is, to pray. Pray for the adopted children, their birth parents and adoptive parents. Pray for the churches of which they are part and pray for a nation where writing this article has been necessary.

The pain of the matching process

Unable to conceive, adoption was something I thought about for years and years. I was in relationships, but as they broke down it heightened my desire to adopt.

Over the last five years I started thinking about it more seriously. I am now hoping to adopt as a single adopter. In the middle of February I had a meeting with the adoption organization Coram and they started me on stage 1 and stage 2 of the process, which went fine – although there was a problem with my medical as I have had to have half of my thyroid removed. The agency and my social worker were brilliant. The approval process was as they described – it took about six months. It was enjoyable and smooth and not unnecessarily intrusive. The questions felt relevant as part of the process.

I was approved for a child aged 0–5. My choice would be preferably a girl but I will consider a boy. I live in a two-bedroom house so I didn't think it could be a sibling group. After I was approved I expressed an interest in some children and was approached by a social worker. A little girl had just come into care. She was about to be four and had a care order in place. I was told that if I pursued this, it would potentially be a lengthy process and could end with no result. I exchanged profiles with the social worker and said I would be interested in her.

A potential date was set to put her forward for adoption and, although I was told this might never come off, social workers told me, 'We're going to pursue you for this child, so let your worker know and stop looking elsewhere for children.' I was asked to stop looking and decline other interested enquiries. They said there would be a matching panel four months later, but the date was put back and then adjourned before a long-term foster care order was granted for the child. I felt so frustrated. I was annoyed they made me stop looking at other profiles. It meant three to four months of waiting and not looking elsewhere.

Of course, I'm pleased this little girl got long-term foster care as it means she stays with her siblings. But the process is quite insensitive to would-be adopters. They had me hanging on in the background. But I'm determined and this is just part of the challenge. I missed opportunities because I waited, but I'm quite pragmatic. I speak to my social worker every other week. I hear some stories from other prospective adopters who don't hear from their social workers for weeks. I was adopted myself and so was my mum, so I know it works.

Child's play

We were approved to adopt nine months ago, and although we knew we might have a long wait, as we have birth children to consider in making the match, we haven't found the waiting easy.

You hear a lot about finding the right match; four times we have believed we had found it, but the children's social workers placed these children with other families. All the children were from outside our local authority, and what made it worse was the lack of communication between the children's workers and ours; we once waited ten weeks only to hear the children's social worker had left, we had been overlooked and they had been placed elsewhere.

So when we were invited to an adoption party recently, we were interested but understandably quite nervous. We were worried that the children would feel they were being 'shopped for' and that prospective adopters would be competitively trying to find a match while other children were left out. However, the communication and support we had from the party organizers both before and since has been really great.

At the briefing beforehand it was explained that the kids are told that we are there to learn how to be parents, and they are there to have a fun party with their carers. We were told to play with as many as possible so no child thought you were promising anything. In one room there was a sort of disco party which some children liked, with spacehoppers and balloons, and in another room there were lots of stickers, masks and things to colour, etc. The spacehoppers were a good idea as the children bounced around manically grinning and then calmed right down.

There were 25 children between two to six years of age and one ten-year-old. I played with some lovely little boys, all about five years of age, for a few minutes, with each moving off when their attention turned to something else. My husband was doing the same, but with the older children. You never thought you were in a room with 'hard to place kids'; they were so ordinary and having a lot of fun. The crafts were a great idea as it gave us all a chance to sit quietly with a few children and talk/swap pens in a more intimate way. Those aged three and under, of course, mostly preferred to just run or to lick the icing off the cakes rather than sit down and speak to anyone. But that didn't prevent us from seeing them as 'real' people, rather than paper profiles.

It was really very helpful to meet some carers; they were inspiring people. I think all the unknowns can be a little scary for adopters. This event made us feel part of the process – we are lucky to have every confidence in our wonderful placement worker, but, even so, the long gaps when she has nothing to tell us can easily make you feel like you've been forgotten. Here, we could see the children for ourselves, and also see how prospective adopters around us were reconsidering their age band on the spot – many of these lovely children were only four or five but already 'old' in adoption terms. Best of all perhaps was seeing several couples seemingly find their match at the party, as if they had suddenly fallen madly in love, but were trying not to show it...and that maybe we have too.

If we had read the profile of those two without meeting them, we may well have been put off by their challenging history, but seeing them, and talking to their very wise carer, was incredibly encouraging. We contacted the party organizers first thing the next day and within minutes had a response, which led to a flurry of emails and exchange of profiles. Whether or not we have found our match this time, we thought this event was brilliant. We came away feeling that every prospective adopter should attend one as part of the assessment process, and before they fix an age range/sex for their match, and that they should be a regular event, especially as they were open to would-be parents from outside the region. (Sometimes it's hard to place children merely because it's impossible for them to stay within region.)

We both went from feeling very apprehensive to extremely positive, and the children really looked like they were having a great time. If all that results in a few more matches, especially amongst the harder to place children, it's certainly something to celebrate.

With hindsight

I'm a relatively new adopter as my son Jack has only been with us for five months, but my biggest piece of advice to prospective adopters is to get hands-on experience with children – not just reading to them or playing with them but the 'normal' stuff such as changing nappies or feeding.

We had a great foster carer who showed us what to do, but in some ways that made us feel even more inadequate! We've found our way and our son's doing very well now, but we spent so much time reading about attachment and other difficulties that adopted children can have, we didn't make time to read, learn about or experience day-to-day parenting.

Chapter 2

FIRST MEETINGS, FIRST MONTHS

Nothing can really prepare you for the first meeting with a child who is about to be a major part of your family. Dreams of what it will be like, which have absorbed you for days and nights, disappear as reality takes over.

'It's an impossible task, this painting a portrait of another human being. It's like an arranged marriage: the parents tell their son that the girl is tall, with dark brown hair and blue eyes; that she likes music and her eggs hard-boiled and is a dab hand with a needle. "Yes," thinks the bewildered youth, "but what is she like?" It's the same with a child. No one can ever tell you what it will be like to meet and still less live with him or her,' says one seasoned adopter.

It is at this 'arranged marriage' stage that a good social worker, with an innate understanding of what makes people tick, can make all the difference, ensuring you know as much about the child as possible and that the child or children are well prepared to meet you.

It is well to remember that the local authority that places the child with you is responsible for assessing your adoption support needs for three years after adoption. After that it becomes the responsibility of the local authority where each adoptive family lives.

Research findings show that post-adoption depression is just as common as postnatal depression.

'I found the first year the most challenging by far. I had been on courses, read many books, and thought I was prepared. Nothing, and I mean nothing, can prepare you for living with a traumatized child,' said one adopter.

'Adopters need a huge amount of support in the first few months, and not necessarily from social workers; quite often they need to check things out, reassurance that they are doing the right things,' said an experienced social worker.

A survey by Adoption UK asked adoptive families what advice they would give to themselves if they could travel back in time. They all said that they would tell themselves not to be so anxious and to trust their gut feelings about their children and what they needed. They mentioned the feeling that they were being watched by social workers and by other family members, and found themselves parenting in a very self-conscious way.

All adopters find the process challenging. If the foster carer has done his or her work well, the child you are about to take on is comfortable and settled in their home, but ready to find their forever mum and dad. But in creating a safe environment for the child, foster carers often become strongly attached to the children in their care – and the feeling is mutual. Adoption advice is to do everything you can to make it easy both for the foster carer and the child; promise to keep in touch, however intermittently, and hope that the foster carer won't burst into tears as you take the child home on the final day of introductions.

The adopter is, in every case, at least the third family a child has been expected to become attached to. Even the smallest children wonder if you will really want to keep them. It can take children weeks, months or years to trust you and to believe that you are not just a temporary fixture in their lives.

As you bond as a family, make sure you have support on three different levels: a partner or family, a fellow adopter or mentor, and a professional who understands the complexities of adoption…and be prepared to parent the child you adopt at their emotional rather than their chronological age.

The introduction weeks are emotionally and physically exhausting as you get to know as much as you can about your child, from the foods they like to their favourite toys and their night-time fears. Send pictures, make lists of questions to ask and try to create a positive relationship with the foster family.

One adopter suggests you plan a holiday before you adopt – in preparation for the physical and emotional challenges of adding to your family – and another holiday within weeks or months of your adoptee's arrival – time out creating your first 'family memories' that can sustain you when things get tough.

Adopters don't just need to offer commitment and unconditional love; they need to give PURE love: love with Patience, Understanding, Resilience and Energy.

In this chapter adoptive parents recount some magical and not so magical meetings and first months, and how they got through them.

Caring can make it difficult to let go

I adopted my daughter Chloe at the age of four. I was a single adopter and had been approached with a possible match after a year of waiting following approval. It was a very exciting time but also a very stressful time.

My daughter had been living with her foster carer for over a year and was very settled there. We started introductions and everything seemed to be going well. However, after the initial few visits I was told that my social worker needed to see me. She told me that an allegation had been made against me by the foster carer. I discussed this with my social worker and, luckily, they did not believe the allegation and it transpired that they had had concerns about the foster carer, who they felt had previously 'sabotaged' adoptions for the other child she was looking after.

A meeting was held and I was told that they would like to speed up the introductions to avoid any potential problems. As you can imagine, this situation made my relationship with the foster carer difficult at a time when I felt under scrutiny from everyone with regard to my parenting skills. However, at the same time, I was well aware of the importance of the foster carer to my daughter and that she had done a fantastic job of looking after her for the past year, giving her the love and security she needed at such a vital time. I completely understood how difficult it was for her to let go of this funny, cute little girl who had been an important part of her family.

The day I went to pick her up from the foster carer's home for the last time was so difficult and emotional as I needed to focus on my daughter's needs but also was well aware of the heartache the foster carer must be feeling.

We kept in touch over the phone and my daughter spoke to her as I knew it was important for Chloe to know that the foster carer was still around. We then arranged to meet up in a 'neutral' space and it went well. We had a couple of meetings all together and then about a year after I adopted Chloe I received a telephone call to say the foster carer had recently died.

I had known that she had been ill, but it still came as a shock. Looking back, I can understand why she found it so difficult to let go. It is so important that foster carers have an attachment to the child, but this inevitably makes it hard for them to move children on. This can be even harder if the adoptive parent lives a long way away or has a different lifestyle to the foster carer. However, I believe that foster carers and adopters need to put their differences aside in the best interests of the child or children involved. I know that my daughter's foster carer really loved my daughter and wanted the absolute best for her, and who can blame her for that?

Since adopting Chloe eight years ago, our lives have changed considerably. I met my future husband and we married a couple of years ago, with Chloe as our bridesmaid. She is now 12 years old and enjoying life to the full. She is still that funny, cute little four-year-old but has also matured to become the loveliest daughter anyone could wish for. I want to thank her foster carer again for giving her a warm, loving home at a time she really needed it, to help her on her way to her new life.

Stripping back the layers

Daniela was 40 when, because of her Polish heritage, she and her partner decided to adopt two-year-old Dominic from a Polish orphanage.

Dominic had experienced gross neglect, alcoholism and abuse as a baby which is why he was taken into care at ten months of age. He had suffered a lot of trauma in his short life, compounded by institutionalization and little therapeutic care. Handed over to me without ceremony by the children's home, he saw me as his abductor and as a consequence he hated me with a passion. From morning to night he would hit me, punch me, bite me, scratch me and spit at me. There was I with all my maternal hormones racing, love issuing out of every pore of my body, willing to do anything for this poor tortured soul, and all he wanted to do was to hurt me.

I was ruing my inexperience and shortcomings, and at the same time becoming self-pitying and exhausted, but I was determined to rectify this behaviour. Nightly, I scoured the internet looking for clues and there I began to find the information I needed: attachment disorder; effects of trauma on the brain; therapeutic parenting; research into institutionalized behaviour. The words flew past my eyes and the scales fell from them. I realized that what I had to do was to re-parent Dom, not expect him to conform in ways in which he had no experience. It was down to me, not him, to fill in the missing gaps. So I thought I should start from the beginning.

I resolved to do something positive. So I took all my clothes off. I stood in the middle of the flat starkers, hoping that no one would knock on the door and disturb my experiment at re-parenting. I went into the kitchen and picked up a Tippee cup and filled it with warm milk, then I went into the bedroom where Dom was smashing up some toy or other and I picked him up. I think he tried to bite my shoulder as he usually did, but this time the feel of my naked skin somehow stopped him in his tracks and he looked at me quizzically. I took off all his clothes and cuddled him close to me. I can't say at first this felt comfortable, because for all my English reserve, my somewhat prudish approach to nudity, I felt an utter prat. 'God, if someone could see me now, I would die of embarrassment,' I thought. I sat on the sofa bolt upright, trying to imagine what an idiot I looked, saying over and over to myself, 'Just do this, no one can see you, just do it.' I cradled Dom like an oversized newborn.

He looked into my eyes, perhaps for the very first time, and he took the Tippee cup like a baby taking a bottle. He sucked on it contentedly and I felt my body begin to relax. He relaxed. We both relaxed. The feeling of skin against skin in such a way was new to both of us. We both had to experience those first feelings of connection, of birth, motherhood and parenting. I could feel his little body snuggle happily into mine and we sat there together for ages. Eventually, he fell asleep and I popped him into bed. I looked at him, this tiny body in this large bed, and I really did utterly love him.

The next morning there was a definite change in his behaviour. Only a slight change, but a change nevertheless. We finally had something good to build on. There was more laughter, more fun and a lot of happiness.

Four years on, Dominic is an extremely healthy, sporty and intelligent child. He has exceeded all our and his teachers' expectations. We tell each other we love each other every day. We cuddle, we kiss and, of course, we still have our crabby moments. We are attached, bonded and complete. I know he loves me and my husband with all his heart.

The professionals aren't always right

When she discovered she was infertile, Jane and her husband Peter decided to adopt.

Jason was the first child our social worker talked to us about, and he seemed to fit us, so we went ahead and arranged to meet with his social worker and then with his foster carers. We went to matching panel and were approved. I can't describe how I felt when this happened; it was so hard to believe that soon we would have a son. But I admit that I struggled from the very beginning when we met Jason. I was so overwhelmed. This two-year-old boy would be moving into our house in nine days, and he would be ours forever.

I feel now that from the start we were not supported properly. There were two pieces of advice that were given to us that I believe were completely wrong. The first was that Jason was to have no contact at all with the foster carers. This was traumatizing for him. It was as though his emotions and connection with his foster mother didn't matter. For weeks Jason would ask for her and felt heartbroken. Think of this as an adult with your partner. One day they are there and the next they are gone, but no one explains why.

The second piece of advice was that we were not to introduce Jason to anyone else and we were not to leave our house for the next two weeks. This is a technique called funnelling, used for changing from one caregiver to another, and the new caregiver doing all of the caring tasks so that the child learns that this person is their main carer. I cannot express how alone and isolated this made me feel.

I was anxious and so was Jason. Those initial two weeks were so hard and the isolation only compounded my anxiety about wanting to get things right. My need was to have my mum close to support me. If I was supported more, I felt I would be a better parent to Jason – how could this not be putting our needs together?

Of course, his difficult behaviours continued, and I struggled. I expressed my concerns to his social worker and she questioned me about whether I liked Jason and whether this was the right placement for him. As a consequence we were told that the professionals involved in Jason's placement would meet to decide what support they could give us and whether our family was the right placement for Jason.

We were not allowed to attend the meeting or given a report but told that we would be allocated a social worker and given six months to get our relationship on track with Jason.

So we did what most parents do when threatened with their child being taken away: we lied. We told the social workers what they wanted to hear: I was bonding with Jason and everything was going OK. We put in for the adoption to become legal so that we could get the social workers out of our lives. Was it OK? No. Did it get worse? Yes. But I finally did what my social worker should have advised me to do in the beginning: I went and spoke with my GP. She encouraged me to go on anti-depressants. I did, and they didn't work perfectly but they did stop the anxiety and I started to deal with life and become a better parent.

All I want is to be a good mother and for Jason to do well and be happy. And I do love him and adore him; he still drives me crazy at times but he is beautiful and funny and caring and very precious to me.

Here's Daddy and...

I'm writing this listening to the sound of my son Adam, upstairs, supposed to be asleep in bed, but most definitely not asleep and not in bed.

My journey started like so many others, making the decision to adopt. I wanted to adopt all of the children that we saw – my husband was the voice of reason and we decided to try for a match with a little boy. Before a matching panel we met our son's nursery, paediatrician and foster carers. I was a little taken aback by the foster carer as she wasn't that warm, but I brushed it off, thinking she may be nervous, shy or just coming to terms with this next step as he'd lived with them since birth and he was now two.

Matching panel came: a unanimous yes. We were delighted. The council where our son lived had rented a cottage for us for our two-week stay during introductions, which turned out to be the most difficult and gruelling two weeks I have ever experienced.

We were to meet our son for half an hour on the first day. We were nervous, we didn't know what to expect and we had no idea how this would change our lives forever. Until you go through this it's hard to put into words the feelings you experience. At the house, we rang the bell and waited, took a breath and let the next chapter of our lives begin. There at the window was our 'son' and his foster carer. It was the strangest feeling – our son – we knew him so well but didn't know him at all. The first thing the foster carer said to us was 'He can say Daddy and point to Daddy in the photo album.' (We'd sent a photo album of us.) 'But he doesn't know Mummy and can't point "Sarah" out in the photo.' From then on until the day we came home I was known as Sarah and my husband was Daddy. My world fell apart. Our son was gorgeous, my husband fell instantly in love and my son adored him instantaneously; me, on the other hand, I had a hard job on my hands and it was only going to get harder.

Our son had a very strong attachment to his foster carer and called her Mama. He had been visiting his birth parents in a contact centre every week. He had several 'mummy' figures and so looking at me he didn't need another one.

The foster carer was going through her own turmoil and grief of our son leaving and didn't give our son 'permission' to let her go and to let him attach to me. We discussed my feelings with our social worker. Looking in from the outside, you'd say discuss it with the foster carer and sort it out, but when you're in someone else's house and 'taking' her foster son away from her, it felt like another hurdle I wasn't able to jump, so we kept quiet.

Our two weeks went on like this, trying our hardest with the foster carer, my husband enjoying our son and me just being there but feeling inadequate and not forming a bond with our son. We got to the house at 7am every morning and didn't leave his side until he went to bed at 9pm. The relief of going home was unbelievable, but the challenging times had only just begun. I felt scared and out of my depth.

Our son has found the transition very hard. It was a traumatic experience and has had a lasting impact on him for which we're now receiving Theraplay. Two and a half years on, he is settled and doing well but needs constant reassurance from us. He has also made big leaps in his development and learning. Luckily, I now have a fabulous close bond and relationship with my son but it has been hard work.

Taking the scenic route

The day we brought our son Damien home was hideous. We drove away from the foster carer's house with him screaming and shouting.

It didn't last long (he was successfully distracted by Jessie J 'Price Tag' on my phone) but it was heart-wrenching and I still weep at the thought of it. Starting a family with so much grief erupting in front of you is no easy task. This goes some way to explaining my reaction when we got home.

As I hung up the remaining few clothes removed from his familiar bedroom at the foster carer's house into his new wardrobe in his new bedroom, I fell to pieces. I had to sit down quickly for fear of falling. My heart was going too fast and tiny flashing lights crowded my vision. Thoughts were racing, my hands shaking, and the tears came fast. Everything was out of control. There was a small stranger downstairs who needed me and I had no idea how to look after him. The enormity of the task we'd undertaken was utterly overwhelming.

The next week was excruciating. I was mostly debilitated by anxiety. My chest was constantly palpitating and tears were never far from the surface. My constricted stomach and throat would not accept food, and I was light-headed from hunger and losing weight rapidly. My husband was amazing. He mostly dealt with our scared and disorientated little boy while I was hiding away somewhere, trying to pull myself together.

I spent that week locked away in my own head. I couldn't just be in the moment and functioning. It felt like there was a war raging in my head.

It was an amazing feeling when I caught myself being present in the moment and enjoying my new family, or at least feeling a part of it. Each day the noise in my head died down a little earlier and I became more able to function. On day eight of being a family, I woke to the sound of little feet running through to our room; he scrambled into our bed and on top of me and I smiled. There was no noise, no fear and no dread. It was lovely.

First year home

Like most mummies, I don't *think* our daughter Sasha is perfect, amazing and wonderful, I know it!

She has changed our lives in every way for the better. I told someone that she's adopted earlier this week and they nearly fell over with shock. 'You would never guess,' they said, 'not with the attachment she has to you.' That's a lovely thing to hear because, a year ago, our daughter was not too chuffed to have me as her mummy.

After a three-week introduction period we removed our daughter from all she knew. She had been with her foster family since she was a baby and grown up calling the foster carer mummy, so to come to our home and leave what was, in effect, her mummy and her foster family behind was not her idea of ideal.

In the early days she spent a great deal of time trying to push me away; the words 'go away' were said a fair bit. She would play with me, but would always choose my husband first. When he went back to work, she was pretty cross as it meant she had to put up with this 'new mummy', but gradually we made a routine together. At first it clunked along but the moments of connection grew and grew.

Still the tests, still 'I don't like you' was yelled at me and I would say, 'I don't mind at all, I love you and I'm staying right here!' Sasha would repeat herself, only louder. I would say I loved her again with an even bigger smile. That may sound counter-intuitive, but this little girl was on her third mummy in as many years. She was terrified, and if I was going to let her down, then she needed me to get on with it. That doesn't mean I didn't have a good cry after Sasha had gone to bed.

But I had read the adoption gurus ahead of placement. These kids are hard-wired for stress and need a different kind of parenting. The traditional kinds of discipline just don't work on a child who has a history of neglect and abuse and who doesn't feel so great about themselves. I had rethought how I would parent and I believe that making changes in my thinking and behaviour has made a big difference to the strength of the relationship I now have with Sasha.

A year in, I still get the questions: 'Are you keeping me, Mummy? Do you still like me, Mummy? Do you love me, Mummy?' There is still a doubt there, but these questions are asked less frequently than before and Sasha is more ready to accept the 'YES!' I yell in response. Actually, I grab her and shower her in kisses and shout, 'YES!', which makes her laugh.

We now know each other well. I know the things that can trigger her anxieties and am now more able to help her cope with them. Sasha still finds it hard if she cannot physically see me. She struggles with any separation.

Many adopted kids are fine to go to nursery; we were advised not to send Sasha. It was the right call and we feel that had we ignored that advice, the strong attachment roots we have started wouldn't be as strong.

This has been a hard year but also the most rewarding one ever. I gave up a well-paid job and my financial independence, and I've seen my husband glow with pride at seeing his daughter grow and develop, and I've never been as happy or fulfilled. Would we do it again? Yes, definitely.

Dos and don'ts

Having adopted three children, two sisters and a young boy, Judy gives her top tips for the handover period.

Before introductions:

- Make a list of what to ask the foster carer when you first meet them: from the child's likes and dislikes to the size of their shoes.

- Make a list of all the things you don't know about your child/ children and would like answers to, particularly anything related to their health and insights into the birth family.

- Give the foster carer inexpensive presents for the kids and a photo album and even a DVD for introductions. We were amazed at the effect that these had on our children before we'd even met them.

- We were very conscious of the association of smells. We sprayed the cuddly toys with the perfume I wore when we met, and found out what washing powder the foster carer used and started to use this.

- If you can, take time out before introductions start. It will probably feel like the last thing you should be doing, but you need to fill your batteries up and be fully charged for the weeks ahead.

- Ask the foster carer to write down a list of all the significant 'things' your child owns. Where did they come from, who gave them to them, and why.

During introductions:

- If you already have children, make sure they are involved in the introductions process, but also make sure you as the new parent(s) have time with your new addition(s) before introducing your existing children.

- Take photos of you and your child on your first day of introductions (send to extended family), and of the foster family and their home (useful for the child's life story book).

- Find out as much as you can about what your child is used to in the daily/weekly routines in their foster placement. Take a notebook with you everywhere and write things down. You will forget: you're only human.

- Ask the foster carer to sit down with you and plan a typical week's menu for your first week at home with your family.

- Ideally, see where the children sleep, put them to bed during the introduction process and help them pack up to move to your house.

- Moving day is always difficult. Be prepared that the foster carer will probably be very emotional.

- Don't panic when things get hard during introductions. You cannot underestimate the emotional tension involved in the transition of the care of a child between foster carers and adopters.

When your child comes home and your new family really begins:

- Help your child with the loss they will be experiencing for their foster carer and reassure them that it's OK to miss their foster carer. Send a card/photo to the foster carer sometime during the first two weeks. If your child is old enough, get them involved in this. Make a plan to meet your foster carer again on neutral ground after a month or two.

- Take time to unpack and put your child's things away in their new room with them. Don't leave packed bags in their room.

- Eat as a family, making meals that are familiar to the child/children.

- Plan what you are going to do each day and for the next week. This will help you and your child to know what is happening today and helps to remove some of the uncertainty of life. Build some memories.

- Put strategies in place to keep significant visitors at a distance until you are ready and have built some initial bonds with one another (our children met their grandparents after six weeks).

- Encourage friends and family to call you when the children are in bed. You do need to share how things are going; it helps to keep people involved and part of your journey.

- Keep your child out of nursery or school initially if at all possible in order to build a closer attachment.

- Don't be afraid to go with your instincts and do what you feel is right.

- Finally, don't underestimate the impact that bringing a new child into your family will have on you or any existing children.

What people say in the playground

We have only had Pip, our little one, for a few months and here are just a few of the gems so far from the playground:

- 'Oh, I would have adopted, but my husband was worried I'd get too attached.'

- 'Oooh, look at him looking at that bus – were any of his daddies a bus driver?'

- 'Shame that they couldn't have found one that looked like you.'

- 'So can you send him back if you need to?'

I could go on, but, to be fair, people I barely knew before have offered me help I didn't know I needed, listened in patient and non-judgemental ways and offered so much support generally…you just have to sort the wheat from the chaff.

Letter to my daughter's foster parents

Dear J,

You were my first contact with the little angel who is sleeping in what used to be my spare room. I read the report you had written and your words showed me that this little girl was already loved and cherished in your family and that I could do this too. I was also reassured that her start in life might not have been the best but she was in safe hands for now.

And then I met you. I think from that first time I knew we could work together to make things OK for her. I say OK because I expect no miracles. We both know the little angel can be the exact opposite when awake and when circumstances create the monster that I am learning slowly to deal with. You showed me a video of her. I fell in love. I never put it into words at the time but I knew. I think my best mate sitting beside me knew too.

During the months it took for the boxes to be ticked, we talked and you helped me get to know my little one. You never pretended it would be easy, you never promised me anything, but you answered every question and query with kindness and patience, and slowly

I got to know her through your eyes. You also never made me feel as though I were intruding on your time with her because it was running out.

Guiding me through the introduction process, you made me welcome in your home and part of your family. When I needed to cry, you hugged me and helped make it better. You showed me, by example, how to do all she needed and then stepped back to let me do it. Most importantly, you praised me when I got it right.

Oh and cups of tea…you made me loads of those. When most mummies bring their baby home, they have their own mummy to help. Being a single adopter is incredibly isolating, but you stood in when my own nearest and dearest could not be there. You do know that your family are now my nearest and dearest too, don't you?

And then you let her go. Your wonderful family stood in a circle after saying your goodbyes and said, 'She's yours now, Mummy.' If she were not there needing my strength, the tears could not have been stopped. I hugged the first man who had taught her what daddies do and told him when our baby gets married he will be invited.

I looked at your lovely, kind, gentle young men and knew she had a good grounding in how to be treated by the ones she chooses to share her love with in future. And I thank whoever put her in your arms when she needed you most.

You continue to be there now, almost a year on. You are one of the first people I want to share her joys with and I know you love hearing the little things. When I am at my wits' end, I come to you for advice and sometimes it is just enough to know I can call. It has been a while since we have spent time with you all, but we will do again before too long. We will pick up just where we left. You will marvel at how tall she is, how her reading has come on, her new teeth and all those tiny little things you notice. She won't have finger nails, though! That's one battle I'm just not ready to fight.

Thank you for giving her those amazing role models so she knows not all men are violent and angry. Thank you for being on my side and making sure with your words and deeds that she was ready to love me. Thank you for not being her mummy but for doing everything her first mummy failed to do. Thank you for pretending it was easier to let her go than it was. Thank you from the length and breadth of my heart. I have no idea where people find the strength to love a child as you loved my little one and then let them go.

— Chapter 3 —

ADOPTING BABIES AND TODDLERS

It used to be the adopter's dream: a baby looking for a family. For many of us, babies are almost irresistible: hands grasping, legs kicking, skin as soft as butter and eyes wide and wondering.

But there are far fewer babies or toddlers coming into care and looking for adoptive homes than there are older children. And it is wrong to think that the baby you carry into your home will have a life without problems associated with its adoption, or that you will find it easy to accept this little loveable alien into your home and into your heart.

Many prospective adopters have decided to create their family through adoption after years of treatment for infertility. 'I have all this love to give,' explained one infertile mother looking for a family. But adoption is not the same as giving birth: 'This baby didn't know us and we didn't know him. We called ourselves Mummy and Daddy but we were strangers playing at this family thing because we were so desperate to have it,' said another. Overwhelmed, she spiralled into the self-despair of post-adoption depression but, with good support from understanding social workers, health visitors and her doctor, recovered within weeks and bonded with her baby.

The same adoptive mother says:

Each person will have come to the adoption process for a different reason, but for many it will have been a painful journey. That pain can be easily buried when there seems to be new hope. However, the reality should never be denied. There is a grief attached to never being able to have a birth child. Pretending that adopting a child will take that away is unrealistic if understandable. We thought we had listened and we thought we had understood but we didn't do it well enough.

Social workers want to ensure adopters coming forward after discovering they are infertile have worked through any sense of loss. Their concern is not that adopters feel that loss, but how they are able to deal with it. How do they feel about not being genetically related to their child? How do they feel about dealing with issues around birth parents?

Another challenge is not knowing what really happened to your child before they came to you. 'A baby or toddler doesn't have the skills to articulate their feelings verbally. The child is still being uprooted but has no voice to ask why,' says another adopter. 'Easy-to-place babies doesn't mean easy-to-parent children.'

All children are in care for a reason: all have to deal with rejection at the most basic level and many babies are in care because of drug and alcohol abuse by their birth mother. The long-term damage done to the foetus by alcohol is only now beginning to be properly recognized. 'While adopters may be told about a birth mother's drug abuse or the neglect a child has suffered, alcohol intake may not be mentioned – despite being capable of causing irreversible damage to the unborn child,' said Dr Raja Mukherjee, consultant psychiatrist at Surrey Borders Partnership NHS Foundation Trust.

Dr Mukherjee has spent the past few years examining children damaged by their mother's drinking during pregnancy. Most have serious problems with learning and concentration; some suffer internal organ damage and even facial malformation. He believes foetal alcohol syndrome disorders (FASD) are still widely under-diagnosed and that many children are incorrectly labelled with 'behavioural' problems.

Whatever is known about the history of an adopted child, one certainty is that not everything will ever be known or understood. One real difficulty with the 'added layer' of adopting is the constant struggle to determine whether your child's behaviour is attributable to their past experiences, their moves in care or just a normal stage in their development.

But adopters are constantly amazed at how sometimes the most damaged children can defy the bleak outlook predicted for them and grow up into responsible and caring adults.

'We wallow in the pleasure our little boy gives us, laugh at his antics, cherish the abundant love he has to give and love him dearly in return,' wrote one parent who adopted a two-year-old. 'We give thanks that in this world full of anger, war and death, the arrival of our son reminded us of the things that really matter in life.'

Olivia's story

We almost adopted ten years ago, but after being approved for adoption we found out that I was pregnant and went on to have our birth child. Some years after this we decided that we would foster. We fostered for three years and in that time looked after three babies.

When Olivia was three weeks old, she was placed with us as her foster family. I had been visiting her in hospital for three days before she came home, and although I was excited to be bringing another baby home for us to care for, I was also sad for her parents and very aware that this was not going to be an easy placement.

Olivia was in the special care unit of a large maternity hospital for three weeks and the nurses there told me that she was the worst case of a drug-withdrawing baby that they had ever seen. The medications they tried didn't help and so Olivia had to withdraw 'cold turkey'. She cried almost constantly, and although the nurses did their very best, inevitably they could not give her the one-to-one attention that she needed because they had other sick babies to care for. In the three days that I visited Olivia, I sat and held her very tight and the nurses were amazed because she stopped crying and she slept.

That was the beginning of two months of holding. Olivia needed swaddling and holding very firmly for two months day and night before we started to be able to put her down at all. She fed little and often, and although she did have many periods of crying, she did also manage to sleep. My husband had to reduce his work to one day a week and we developed a routine where I would sleep 7pm till 2am and he would sleep 2am till 9am and we would sit through the day and the night in a dimly lit, quiet room.

Olivia has changed our world and that of our eight-year-old son. Olivia hated loud noises, bright lights, and once she started to cry it could take hours to calm her down. Olivia had been exposed to high levels of alcohol and a cocktail of drugs in the womb including crack cocaine, heroin, methadone and more.

When we heard that Olivia needed an adoptive family, we knew that we wanted to be that family so we once again started the arduous process of assessment and getting approved for adoption and then 'linked' with Olivia. Recently, she was officially 'placed' with us for adoption.

Olivia was tiny (below the bottom centile on the growth charts) and unwell from birth, but much to everyone's surprise she improved steadily and started meeting all her developmental milestones. Now at 14 months she has started walking and is starting to communicate with a mixture of sounds and signs. She is sociable, very happy in character and into everything, and we adore her. But we are not going into this with our eyes closed. It is very likely that Olivia will have some effects from her early exposure to alcohol and drugs. We have read books and attended conferences and got to know other people with children suffering from foetal alcohol spectrum, and know that the road ahead may not be an easy one.

It's hard not to worry about Olivia's future. Sometimes I worry that we won't be good enough parents and that maybe another adoptive family would have been better than us. I feel guilt that we are seeing all her firsts rather than her birth parents and I feel a huge weight of responsibility as we have been chosen to look after her rather than them. I also feel a huge amount of joy and happiness that we get to be Olivia's forever family. It's hard to keep the balance of enjoying her as she is now while being prepared for the likelihood of issues in the future. We are only at the beginning of this adventure and we look forward to it with equal measures of excitement and trepidation.

Oh baby

An adoptive father tracks the steep learning curve he and his wife took on when they adopted a nine-month-old baby.

Monday: Well, this week is much like last week…the learning just keeps on keeping on. Little Person (LP) gets up about 6.30am, enjoys some time on the toilet then takes a light breakfast of Aptamil followed by porridge and then fruit of the day. A period of frantic play ensues leading to a 'Nana Nap'. This is pretty much repeated throughout the day until it's rubber duck play time in the bath.

Tuesday: Much excitement in the household as LP reportedly said her first proper word. My money was on 'dog' or perhaps 'dad'. Great sadness befell me as apparently, or should I say allegedly, 'mummy' was uttered by LP. This was further corroborated by our niece, who, with the absence of a lie detector, I shall have to believe. I do hope LP's first sentence will be 'Cousin Vicky's a wee fibber'. I'm not bitter, though.

Wednesday: Yummy Mummy (YM) and LP attended their first Mother and Toddler Group this week. YM advised that LP had 'been a wee rascal' and chucked baby porridge on her jeans which went unnoticed until YM and LP were greeted by the Chapter Leader who was, of course, immaculate in a Mumsie kind of way. YM who was by now a tad frazzled and oat-encrusted reported that the baby porridge was now semi-hardened to resemble weeping pustules. LP had a blast, though, and LP resembled a *very* young Geri Halliwell. Despite initial hiccups, YM and LP will return although Boogie Babies is trying to sway YM's resolve with the offer of 'yummy tray bakes'.

Thursday: There are things you should not Google and then there are things you *really* should not Google. Sometimes when you Google stuff, it is interesting to see how quickly Google fills in the search term for you. Try typing in the phrase 'baby poo'. Not only is there a handy description but, to my horror, pictures too!

Friday: We are currently capitalizing on a number of items, which we lovingly call 'baby prison'. Ever wondered why Mothercare and Babies R Us are full of fold-down travel cots? It's not because parents are planning a holiday. Let's face it, holidays are a thing of the past anyway unless you are willing to sell a kidney, which I no longer have to spare as I lost it on the baby gate. The *real* reason people buy travel cots is to imprison their small person. Oops, I meant to say keep the little angel safe while those charged with their care try to undertake regular tasks like consuming coffee, maintaining personal hygiene and scraping embedded semi-puréed foodstuffs, which defy description, off the carpet. We like baby prison. We have a few: a Disney bouncing one, the travel cot and the vibrating, reclining one favoured by YM. LP likes the bouncy one.

Saturday: Here are some tips I'd like to share with you:

- Do not on any account make eye contact with a baby when they wake up in the middle of the night! It's like amphetamine to them. Just say nooo! Simply soothe them and pop the little angel horizontal, tiptoe backwards out of the room and hope you get another half hour's kip.

- Baby monitors allow for some weekend shenanigans. Sneak into LP's bedroom. Blow a raspberry. Await YM dashing to LP's aid with industrial strength nappies, gauntlets and coal tongs in anticipation of a code brown.

- Be 'really bad' at changing/dressing/feeding LP for five out of seven days. This allows for two days to feel useful and slightly smug while avoiding most of the tasks which involve either 'business end'.

- There should be a mathematical formula to measure the disproportionate relationship between ironing baby clothes, the size of baby clothes and how long they will stay clean, or indeed in fashion. I know this as I spent 20 minutes ironing a dress for LP's evening engagement only to be informed by YM that the dress was too 'summery'.

Sunday: Important things that I have learned this week:

- If you squish a rubber duck on the bottom of a bath it will stick for a wee while and then pop up randomly.

- Baby prison can be easily downgraded from category A to category C with the addition of a few hundred balls.

- I have not yet acquired the skills to change nappies in the complex and indeed compact environment of a caravan.

- Getting waved at for the first time by LP as I leave for work irritates my eyes.

- Putting toys away at night is about as futile as wearing a clean T-shirt these days.

- The term 'family car' is purely a marketing ploy. Two adults, LP, the hound, buggy, Go Bag, etc. make an A-Team transit van feel like a Fiat 500…I should imagine.

- LP cuddling into my chest is a wonderful experience…until I realize she just wants to rub her runny nose on me.

This baby didn't know us

Adoptive mum Alice went through a series of failed IVF treatments before deciding to adopt.

There we were, Mike and I and our baby, a family. But this baby didn't know us and we didn't know him. We called ourselves Mummy and Daddy but we were strangers playing at this family thing because we were so desperate to have it.

I couldn't understand why I didn't feel anything for this baby that we'd craved. A mummy loves her baby. Why wasn't I overwhelmed by a feeling of at least some affection for a baby that was now ours?

We went out; played, walked and showed this baby our world. We looked like the perfect family, but I was trying to suppress the immense panic inside me growing into a blazing fire. Finally, I broke down…I couldn't do it. My family arrived to find a shadow of the person they knew. Our little boy sat in the middle of the living room whilst I sat on my dad's lap and sobbed. 'This isn't my baby. I can't love him.' No amount of soothing words could soothe my panic.

In the meantime my husband's life continued. He was going back to work as a teacher that he loved. His world went on; mine had ended. The cry came. I answered it: bottle, breakfast, wash, clothe. My baby looked at me; I couldn't meet his gaze. I set out toys and waited for his nap. And so it went on, the longest week of my life. I longed for my life to return, cursed the fact that I had thought that I could replace the baby I couldn't conceive with someone else's and felt the shame of feeling these things. As the days bled into each other, my whole body began to turn itself inside out. I thought about how I must not lose sight of this baby; he was an innocent, gorgeous example of human life and he deserved to have kisses and cuddles and to have his eyes meet those of someone who wasn't afraid to love him.

I had to get help. I telephoned our health visitor. We decided that social services could provide the best support. Very quickly, two social workers arrived and an emergency appointment was made with my doctor, a psychologist contacted and a massive amount of support given. They never judged, not once. And to our huge relief our baby was not removed.

My doctor prescribed some anti-depressants and diazepam and sleeping tablets. I was grateful. I could feel nothing else because I had never been so afraid in my entire life. My mum came to stay and fed me soup.

Two things happened that made me believe this nightmare wasn't forever. We were visited by a psychologist. I told her of my guilt that I didn't feel able to love this baby. She showed me that I was not some evil mother figure but a human being experiencing very human feelings and that it was all right. The magic of those simple words should not be underestimated.

At the same time I began to have short bursts of time when I could play with our baby as well as look after his needs. I picked him up, tickled him and blew raspberries on his belly. This would pass but I'd had the moment; the house heard laughter again. Slowly the time spent playing became longer; the time spent curled up in bed holding my body in case I fell apart became less and less.

I will never comprehend my reaction to our beautiful boy. I think being a parent to an adoptive child is different. Each person will have come to the adoption process for a different reason but for many it will have been a painful journey. That pain can be easily buried when there seems to be new hope. However, the reality should never be denied. There is a grief attached to never being able to have a birth child. Pretending that adopting a child will take that away is unrealistic if understandable. We thought we had listened and we thought we had understood, but we didn't do it well enough.

Today I love our baby in a way that surpasses any feeling I have ever known, but this has taken time. We are lucky with our little boy. However, we are his third family and he's not yet two! He is our child and we are his mummy and daddy, and our love is unconditional. There may be issues as he grows up, but like any other parent, we will be his rock, his safe place – always.

We couldn't get his picture out of our head

The children you first think you'll end up with are not always the child you end up with in reality! You go through a tick-list asking questions such as 'Would you consider a child with foetal alcohol syndrome?' to which we replied, 'No,' but we actually ended up with a child from an alcohol-related background.

We saw a picture of our son in an issue of Adoption UK's *Children Who Wait*, and while it was not 'love at first sight', we felt a connection. The first thing we noticed was his eyes. We couldn't get the picture out of our heads. We knew he was considered harder to place, because of the potential risk of foetal alcohol syndrome, but it was our opinion that he needed exactly the same as any other child; it had just taken longer to find him a family.

We went to a Foetal Alcohol Syndrome Support Group meeting which was quite scary as you find out about the worst-case scenario – but we still decided to declare an interest in adopting Freddie.

We got a reply within weeks and were interviewed by his social worker who wanted to meet us and make sure we knew the risks of adopting a child like Freddie. We then went up to the Midlands to meet Freddie's foster carer and the paediatrician, and proceeded to complete the relevant paperwork. And eight months ago Freddie was ready to join our family!

At that point you don't know what sort of parent you'll be – you can only speculate. It's nothing like I thought it would be. In reality you get nothing done! Freddie's turned our lives upside over – but it's hard to imagine our lives without him now.

I wasn't sure how my husband would take to fatherhood, especially nappies, but he's taken to it like a duck to water. He's a smitten kitten. He wouldn't swap Freddie for his own birth child now.

I'm a stay-at-home mum so it's really important for me to have a support network made up of other parents who've adopted, some of whom I met through Adoption UK. It really helps to know you're not alone, especially in the beginning.

Freddie doesn't look like us as we're both dark-haired and I'm mixed-race while he's got blond hair and blue eyes, but he's already adopted some of our mannerisms. Everyone knows he's adopted;

we're proud of it so we're quite open with people. Some people say to us, 'Oh, doesn't Freddie look like you!' and we think, 'Mmmmm...'

We've met Freddie's birth parents and grandparents. It was a very emotional process but I'm glad we did it. The picture we'd built up in our heads of what they'd be like was very different in reality. We have written contact with them once a year. We're now Freddie's parents and he knows us as Mummy and Daddy, but that can't take away the fact we are not his biological parents. When Freddie's 18, if he wants to meet them we would support that, although it won't be easy.

Effects of being denied in the womb

I am interested in the effects on our adopted children of being denied in the womb. I have three adopted children (not related through birth) and they were all concealed pregnancies and relinquished for adoption as babies. I have always believed that the impact of being concealed and possibly unwanted must have an effect on the unborn child.

Generally with concealment comes lack of the birth mother taking care of herself in respect of nutrition, so this must surely impact on the growing baby? But, as experts in this field have pointed out, the mother's denial of existence could have an emotional impact on the unborn baby, with them feeling 'abandoned, unwanted, insecure, sad, angry and unable to trust'.

My eldest daughter is now 19 years old and these are all words that describe how she has felt during her teenage years. This is despite her being our daughter from seven months old and her always appearing to have good attachment with both me and my husband. My younger daughter is 14 and was placed with us aged eight months old, and whilst she is better able to mask her feelings and manage her behaviour, she too has a fragile sense of self, again despite having a good relationship with us. My son is 12 years old and was placed with us when he was four months old. He is more like his older sister and he finds it difficult to regulate his emotions.

Whilst we have provided unconditional love, security, stability, understanding, reassurance and more, our children struggle with these feelings and do not fully trust that we love them still. What helps most is having an understanding of where these feelings come from.

I just sat with them on my lap and cried

Rachel and her husband have adopted a two-year-old girl and twin boys aged 20 months.

We could not believe our luck when we adopted our three children. Wow: all and more than we ever dreamed possible. I was really surprised when I started to suffer days and days of real lows, having never had depression before. Sometimes I was so overwhelmed with all of my new tasks, feeding, changing, cleaning, clothing and dealing with naughtiness, that I would just sit in front of the TV with the kids and do nothing apart from feed and change them.

I was totally shocked. I had all I ever wanted, so why was I unhappy! Always being house-proud, my house resembled a bomb site.

I think it would have helped had there been someone to talk to; if someone could have said it was OK to feel like this. Social services did not seem to bother with us after placement. I had lots of trouble with the twins' sleeping habits, which really told on me as I am not good on going short of sleep. One morning the boys were up early and crying and I could not figure out why, and I just sat with them on my knee and cried with them.

I don't know how I coped, but to be honest it just gets easier. I have a really great husband and my mother is also really great and comes to visit whenever we ask. I still have the odd low but now I don't worry about the house so much. And we got the children each a toy Hoover and we share the housework which is great fun.

An adopted child's inheritance

All adopted children come with baggage as well as blessings. My daughter Addie is no exception. I adopted her as a single mum after I got divorced.

Before I adopted Addie, I made a point of meeting her birth parents, Annia and Christian. Addie was in care because her parents could not manage to keep her. They didn't have an income or a suitable home for a two-year-old. They were in poor health. They were alcoholics. When I met the couple, I immediately liked them and guessed that I would probably like their daughter. So, with some trepidation, I made the biggest decision of my life and adopted my adorable daughter.

Twenty-four years later I can tell you: I made the right decision. Like all children, Addie has taken her mother on a unique journey with lots of surprises. As a toddler she had delayed development, problems eating, speaking, counting and learning. I assumed these difficulties were due to her complicated start in life. Then, when Addie was 11, I attended a conference for adoptive parents and, for the first time, I heard about foetal alcohol syndrome (FAS) and foetal alcohol spectrum disorders (FASD). Bells went off in my mind! It seemed that the speakers at the conference were describing my daughter. They talked about how alcohol changed the brain before babies were born. As a result the brain of an alcohol-affected child is smaller than normal which often causes the head circumference to be smaller.

When I heard this, I made a connection. I had been to all the local bicycle shops in our neighbourhood and none of them had a children's bicycle helmet small enough for my daughter's head. It was difficult to believe that Addie's birth mother's drinking during pregnancy had given Addie this lifelong disability.

I took Addie to Great Ormond Street Children's Hospital and she was diagnosed with foetal alcohol syndrome (FAS). I went into shock. How would I give my loveable daughter a normal life now that I knew she had a disability. But what is 'normal'? Is anyone normal? We are all different. Now, with an 'identified' disability, we (Addie and I) had powerful information. Having learned what we were dealing with, we learned to navigate around some of the pitfalls. We learned to build positive bridges. We found practical strategies and got positive results.

When Addie was a toddler, before I knew she had a disability, I gave her horse-riding lessons. She became confused and couldn't follow instructions. After I got Addie's diagnosis, I moved her to Riding for the Disabled (RDA) and everything improved. The instructors understood that she had a learning disability and gave her appropriate support. Addie gained confidence and a passion for horses. She participated in the Special Olympics and won two bronze medals and one gold medal. Addie's diagnosis changed the course of her life and mine for the better. Her diagnosis explained her confusing behaviours and helped us to better understand her actions and helped her to understand herself.

Chapter 4

ADOPTING OLDER CHILDREN

These are the children that are hardest to find homes for and the biggest group languishing on adoption registers around the UK.

Talking, walking little people, they are aware more than any baby or toddler that they have been cut adrift and rejected. They are emotionally traumatized and tagged 'hard to place' by professionals floating in and out of their lives. Having spent their short lives being uprooted and let down, they instinctively trust no one. They are old enough to have clear memories and confused loyalties. Abuse and rejection have resulted in a chronic lack of self-esteem, and these children carry a heavy load of emotional baggage that will be unravelled in the years to come on your living-room floor and that you and they will have to sort through.

Care of these traumatized small people can be counter-intuitive: they need time in when they do something unacceptable, not time out. They don't need to be told to 'grow up' and be a big girl or boy when they fall over literally or figuratively, they need to be allowed to regress to the early days they probably never had and learn how to accept a hug, and sometimes they need to be taught how to 'play'.

> 'I can't remember specific instances of cuddling and comforting my birth children, but the day our adopted son first allowed me to comfort him is fresh in my mind,' wrote one adoptive father. 'He'd been with us for around seven months and he fell off a chair. For the first time ever he snuggled in for a few moments when I picked him up. The "Aww" factor was enormous.
>
> 'Even better was the day over two years into placement, when he asked if he could give me a hug. At last this hurt, frightened, alienated little creature was able to do something that comes so naturally to most children.'

Adoptions of older children are those most likely, except in certain abusive circumstances, to be open adoptions where the children the adopter is trying to nurture are constantly reminded, sometimes for good and sometimes not, of their birth family, at the very least by letter contact and for others with regular arranged meetings. For some, despite all the love and support offered by an adoptive parent, they suffer from a divided sense of loyalty, wanting against all the odds and all the abusive evidence to defend the parents who gave birth to them.

But those who have adopted older children successfully say that the unhappy awareness of their circumstances is not always as much of a disadvantage as it is perceived to be. 'Harder to place doesn't necessarily mean harder to parent,' said one adopter. The longer road to finding a stable, secure, forever family can also result in an active willingness to make an adoption work.

If adopters and adoptees are well matched, the rewards for all can be enormous. Children blossom and grow, physically and emotionally, and begin to take pride in themselves where once they had none. Transformations of all kinds can and do take place.

Hard to place?

My son Simba is 11: this Saturday is our fourth anniversary. He was rising eight when he came home, so quite old in adoption terms and considered 'hard to place'. We didn't have any great difficulty bonding, but I think that's partly down to us being a very good match; we have lots of similar interests, for example, and had lots to share. One advantage of adopting an older child was that he understood more and was very ready for a mummy.

So what is our life like? In many ways it's fairly average. Simba is doing well, holding his own in a small mainstream secondary. He has made some nice friends. He adores his nanny and grandad, and they think the world of him. He goes to Scouts and Woodcraft Folk. He has tennis lessons, is a member of the athletics club, he swims like a fish. Yes, he is sports mad! Yes, he likes his iPad and Wii as well. He helps on the allotment. In the last four years we have been every year on holiday to Cornwall, we have camped in Gambia, ridden camels in the Sahara in Morocco. We go to the theatre, cinema and concerts. He loves a party and a boogie.

So why was he hard to place? He was seven when I saw his profile, he is a boy, he has ASD and a mild learning difficulty. He is dual heritage. After I expressed an interest in him, the local authority put him in *Children Who Wait*. In three months there was not one single enquiry about him. My gain: I have an amazing son.

I do think it was important that, although he was at school, when he came to be part of my family I took a full year of adoption leave. The long summer holiday together was really important. I didn't have to use any childcare. I was available all the time after school and at weekends. I was able to attend every single event at school. This helped bonding and gave me lots of time for that positive influence stuff because I wasn't running around frazzled between job, housework, shopping and him. We spent literally hours just cuddled on the sofa in the evenings, or whole days at the weekend playing board games and doing jigsaws, because I could, knowing I had the weekdays free to do all the other stuff.

And now? It's not all roses. Simba is very anxious; there is a deep underlying grief and sadness. His behaviour can be very 'challenging' as they say. The ASD means all those holidays and trips need huge amounts of preparation. We don't do surprises. He likes his routines. I am single but I do work three days a week and it's just about manageable. Thanks to the Adoption Support Fund, we have just started fairly hefty therapy which will take a year.

Chances are that many people looking for young, easy-to-place children are going to end up with many of the issues we have anyway. I had the advantage of being fully aware of his issues. He arrived with a diagnosis, a statement and in receipt of Disability Living Allowance (DLA). Many people who adopt babies and toddlers will end up having to fight for these things.

I'd really encourage any prospective adopter to look beyond the labels, at the child that lies behind. I wish the description 'hard to place' could be banned. My son is no harder to parent than many of those easy-to-place children.

The right match is key. For both of us, it's been the right thing. I have a wonderful, amazing son, and he isn't languishing in long-term foster care. Despite all the challenges, we have built a good life. We are happy, we are a family. Which, after all, is what this is all about, isn't it?

Never give up?

Kyle is a kind, funny, articulate and creative young man. I was told it was 'too late' for him academically at five years old because he had missed so much in his early years. He has just completed the first year of college and left school with 10+ good GCSEs. He wrote this poem about some of the things he still finds very challenging – feeling safe, secure and at peace – and how troubled his mind is when he struggles to switch off in order to eventually get some sleep.

NOTHING AND EVERYTHING

Like thousands of unsettled butterflies they float around,
Dodging thought clouds and overcoming any thought
of sanity or salvation,
Things that have not been told, things that are never thought
drift across my now sleepy state,
The guard has been given up and the foes
are attacking the mind.
Glass shatters and the shards reverberate
inside my now hollow head,
This continuous loop of breakages perplexes
my now wide awake mind,
And how can the night make subtle thoughts unbearable?
Everything breaks up in a dreamlike state,
Immense worries become thousands of fluttering creatures,
Whereas the smallest inkling of negative thought
grows and increases till it breaks,
And the loop of broken thoughts starts again.

Looking back – an adoptee's story

Having met my adoptive family at the age of seven, there are some things that I wish they had known. These things may apply to all adopters too.

One of these things is that I don't like change; I was in and out of care from the ages of three to four and again from five to seven, until I was finally adopted officially at age nine. This, for me, makes it almost impossible to trust adults and their decision-making skills. Another effect of this is also making secure and long-term attachments with the adults that are my parents.

Another thing is that I didn't like sharing attention. I was adopted with my three siblings. We are still a family unit, but in trying to get my parents' attention, I'd usually revert back to silly behaviours, such as climbing on things, slamming my door, shouting at my siblings and general rudeness. I wouldn't mind how I got my parents' attention, just as long as I had it.

Third, when meeting my adoptive extended family, it was really weird meeting them, because as far as I was aware, I might be moved at any moment. I love my grandma, grandad and all my aunts and uncles and cousins and step-grandparents but, meeting them, I was overwhelmed at the prospect that this was my new family, and that I wasn't going back to my birth mother.

One thing that I found useful was the service from Family Futures. This therapy really helped me with my relationships with my parents and to realize that I am not going back. One particular thing that helped me most of all was the video of my biological mother answering questions that we (my siblings and I) had sent her. She lied consistently throughout the video, and I realized how much of a waste of time she really was. She will always be the one who brought me into the world, so my feelings towards her will always be very complicated.

Of course there will be stressful times, but among those there will be times of immense happiness. I am now 15 and struggling with all the normal things that teenagers have to deal with, as well as the legacy of my past. When you grow up in a traumatic household, it actually affects your ability to plan ahead. I don't make excuses for myself, but these are reasons why I find it hard to understand consequences. In our family, we're struggling through a really tough time at the moment. I have returned home after 12 weeks of Section 20 care and am adjusting back into family life.

In those 12 weeks, I learnt that every family has different ways of functioning and coping with everyday life, and you know what? I think I prefer my family just the way it is. What I would like adopters to know is that it's going to be tough, but love makes a difference. I was doing some creative work in a therapy session, and then I thought of this: 'Love lifts off masks we fear we cannot live without, but know we cannot live within.'

Keeping on the right track

When I adopted my beautiful daughter, she was eight years old. She is feisty and a bundle of issues, but it was a match that surprised us both with the closeness that would develop over time. Ever since the adoption day, we have marked each year with a special time together, exchanging gifts and cards and having a day together.

Each year I would have a message or a letter in the card. These became increasingly loving and thoughtful as we became closer and closer. But I have to say I was absolutely blown away when I received this poem for the last adoption day. I am in awe and feel particularly humbled by the way my daughter was able to express herself with these beautiful words just for me. However bumpy times get and however tricky things become between us, I still carry this poem around with me – I think I will always carry it around. I find it hard to read it aloud and on the occasions I have shared it, I will usually cry. See what you think:

POEM FOR MUMMA

There comes a time in every life when trials fill the soul
And all around no help is seen as heartaches take their toll.
Nowhere it seems (that) can she escape
whose life is plagued with hurt
And the pains that fill that life of gloom, no joys can come to avert
When all around on every hand only struggles can be found
And through that life would like to sing,
the heart seems chained and bound
Downward ever falling, that life would soon lose hope
Distresses seem to hang that life at the end of no small rope.
But in that time I rebelled, when my heart was cold and black
I seemed to feel a loving touch, t'was a hand upon my back
And when I looked to see whose hand was extended in my aid
I saw a loving woman with no profits to be made.
The love of life reached deep within and made my heart anew.
I honestly don't know why you picked crazy wild me
Out of all the different girls that you did see
Mature, simple, kind
But you never did seem to mind
So I thank you now mother
For sticking with me these past eight years
Even though you tend to smother
You always seem to deter my tears
Now that I'm regrown I can understand
Why there is such a high demand
To adopting kids
Because all the parents want to be like you
They want to rescue kids amid all that trouble
And be their knight in shining armour
Live life with no regrets,
Now thanks to you, now I will

The light of our lives

David was adopted when he was seven years old after a traumatic early childhood. When he was 17, friends and family nominated him to be at Olympic torch bearer.

Although the rain barely let up and coats and jeans were the order of the day, David looked the part in his white sporting outfit as he walked down the stairs of the little hotel we stayed in before his run. He made a good job of showing off his outfit round the local punters who admired his gear and he was busily telling them that the whole thing was luck. Hmmm…

In a moment of sun, I nipped out with him to remind him that his run was far from luck. People chose to nominate him and he got picked out because he got mentioned a lot and because he had such an inspirational story. David looked down and shuffled his feet a little. 'He doesn't feel worth it even now,' I thought. I twigged. I gave him a £2 coin for a snack just in case (food is number one on this lad's list when he gets anxious – starvation has a long legacy…). I began to worry once more if this was just a step too far for David. Could he hold it together? Would he run off and his post-traumatic stress disorder be triggered?

We got in the car, found a vantage place and waited. After two hours David and the procession came by. To our delight, David's adopted sister came along to see him too and we all cheered and waved excitedly despite the rain. When he went past me, I can hardly describe the feeling of overwhelming, powerful love that came over me. David's dad and his grandparents, aunt and friends all came to support him despite the foul weather and the wait – but it was so worth it. Such an achievement for him. Such an achievement for all of us.

Last year, David got into the county trials and at the age of 16 missed the nationals by one place. Being a traumatized youngster, rejection hits him extremely hard.

'When I'm running, well, the thing is I feel alive, truly alive and nothing else matters then,' says David.

He had several months of difficulty following the trials, but being such a sporty lad, having done so well from not being able to hold a pen to a handful of GCSEs and presenting so well, numerous friends and family nominated him to be a torch bearer.

His big day was his chance to show the nation that a young lad with a poor early start is really someone rather impressive. We are so proud of our lad and were so honoured to share his chance to shine.

Celebrating

We adopted our daughter Emily three years ago when she was four. Now aged seven, we know that as well as a severe attachment disorder she has attention deficit hyperactivity disorder (ADHD).

I have type 1 diabetes and have had this condition since I was a child. Over the years, I've explained to Emily what it means and that I have an insulin pump, but she hasn't taken much notice of how I deal with things. She has seen me eat sweets and have low blood sugar, but she has never appeared that interested. We've also explained that she should dial 999 if I'm in a bad way – for example, if I'm sleepy, shaky or if I faint. Again, probably as part of her severe attachment issues, she's dismissed it and doesn't seem to want to know.

In March I came home with her after school and told her I didn't feel very well. Unfortunately, when my blood sugar goes low, I get very confused and don't know that I need sugar, and I can often argue and refuse help. I went upstairs and collapsed into convulsions and don't remember much else until I eventually came around with my daughter shoving sweets into my mouth. She had a bottle of Lucozade too and kept shouting at me, 'Wake up, Mummy, don't sleep…' Sleep is exactly what I shouldn't do! I drank the Lucozade and she helped me to eat the sweets when the phone rang. I was too weak to get the phone, so my daughter picked up the receiver and said, 'Yes, my mummy is talking and awake now.' She had phoned 999 and they were calling back to see how things were and to say that the paramedics were on their way.

I have tears in my eyes as I write this. My dear daughter is a lot younger than her years. She is a child with a disability who struggles every day of her life to cope with the stresses of school and everyday living that we all take for granted. I feel sick to the stomach that I put her in that awful situation…another trauma. She remembered everything we had told her, she found sugar and she called for help. She is terrified of the police and ambulances from previous experiences, so to call them was remarkable! She is a star and I am very proud of her!

Memories are made of this

Jamie was almost eight years old when he joined our family. At that time he was unable to read so we have been helping him to read and write. To help improve his literacy skills, we often ask him to write a page on a certain subject and on this occasion my husband suggested he write about a particular memory.

When I read what he had written, my own adoption journey became so worthwhile, and if it helps someone who sometimes thinks they are on a hard road, then it would be a bonus.

MY FAVOURITE MEMORY – JAMIE AGED 12

My favourite memory was the day I was adopted because I knew I would be loved forever.

When we went to the court I was really disappointed that the judge didn't wear a wig.

When my sister Sarah and I were adopted we were given a certificate. Afterwards we went on a boat trip down a river!

I was so happy I had a family again.

I had to be adopted because my mum died of cancer and my birth dad couldn't look after me and my sisters properly. I was nine years old when I was adopted. I have five sisters and live with two, Sarah and Jane.

I have had lots of memories over the years such as going to an aqua park, building a new house, moving house and lots more, but being adopted is my favourite one. Lots of people are adopted and keep it a secret because they think people might say horrid things about them.

My eldest sister is called Karen and is 18 years old and has got a child of her own.

Remember, don't feel shy about telling people you're adopted.

Finding Mary

Our daughter, Mary, was placed with us just a few days after her eighth birthday. Her arrival marked the end of a two-year wait to be matched with a child and six busy weeks of introduction. For Mary, it marked the end of 18 months in foster care. For all three of us, life changed forever.

Six years on, our daughter has grown into a tall, poised 14-year-old who enjoys sleepovers and shopping trips with her friends and who actually listens to us when we ask her to turn the music down on her iPod!

She has just started her GCSE syllabus and is studying hard for her exams. In addition to the compulsory academic subjects, she is studying for a BTEC in Hospitality, Travel and Tourism, which, if she does well, could offer her a vocational route into the sixth form.

Although Mary's difficult start in life had affected her learning, by the time she left primary school it was clear that she had a talent for writing. With support and encouragement from her secondary school English teacher and from us, this talent has grown. She frequently writes poems and notes to express her feelings, whether happy or sad. The following poem was written by Mary when she was thinking about her past, separation from her birth family and being adopted.

It is an honest account of how she feels and, I believe, an indication of the progress she has made over the past six years.

I KNOW HOW YOU FEEL

People say to you, 'I know how you feel.' But I know
They don't because they have no idea about living a life
Knowing you may not hear or see your blood related
Family again.
Many people are lucky; they have a family since birth
Who love them and care for them. Lastly a family who
Will never let go of you.
Now I live with a family who do that for me. It's not
The same but it's close enough for me. I know
They love me and I know I love them
So I thank them for finding
ME

Did today just happen?

Did today just happen? Just watched my youngest adopted son at his army passing-out parade. He looked so handsome, so grown-up, I felt so emotional I had a little cry behind my sunglasses. Was that really my angry, hurt, abused little boy who trusted no one and lashed out at everyone? I was so proud just had a permanent lump in throat all day.

To top it off, I also met my oldest adopted son's girlfriend who was very lovely and polite to me. She told me he has turned a corner since going on probation and that he now has a job and they have a little flat in a better area. For first time in months we met and he came straight to me and we had such an emotional cuddle. Asked him to keep in contact, he promised he would.

Still feel quite choked up, a surreal day, one I honestly thought I would never see.

I didn't fancy a baby

Eleanor Bradford, BBC Scotland's health correspondent, and her partner, Ross, adopted two brothers, William and Edward, who were aged seven and four when they were placed with them.

The interesting thing about the start of my adoption journey was that I didn't fancy a baby as I had friends who'd recently given birth and they all looked so miserable and exhausted! I had always been keen on adopting an older child, as had my partner.

We thought we would be waiting a couple of years, at least, but before we went to panel our social worker hinted they had two children in mind. They came to see us the next day and asked us if we'd like to see photos of two brothers, William and Edward. The boys were aged seven and four, and the bizarre thing was that they were living around the corner from us with their foster parents so they were using the same supermarket as us.

We met them within a few weeks. We made up a book for them, all about our lives, so they could get used to us. We were told that when William, the older boy, got the book, he slept with it under his pillow. Edward was more suspicious as he'd only ever known his foster parents, but William knew he had no mum and dad and so he was excited about getting a new family.

The introductions went smoothly and by the end of November they were with us and we were preparing for Christmas! Because they lived so close, they stayed at the same school, kept the same friends and saw their foster parents around – which, at first, we were worried about, but in actual fact they have taken on the role of grandparents as they're in their sixties.

We were very worried about things breaking down, but, in hindsight, as an adoptive parent to older children you know exactly what you're taking on, whereas with babies they may have disabilities or attachment disorder, and the adoptive parents don't always know what they're taking on.

The number of children out there in care is a hidden problem for society. If people knew how many children were out there, what they've been through and how rewarding it is to look after them, I'm sure thousands of prospective adopters would come forward.

Would I recommend adopting older children? You can't pick them up and swing them around like a toddler, but you can have even more fun with them like we do with our boys when we go camping.

We've found with our children that they're so grateful because of what they've previously gone through. I'd definitely recommend adopting older children and I'd say the more the merrier. We were warned that parenting older siblings would be challenging, but our charming, cheeky boys have made it easy. There have been challenging moments, of course, as these children have suffered terrible neglect in the past.

It's a shame there's a myth with older children that 'the damage is done', because that's not our experience at all. They're *amazing* characters and happy children.

It's different

One thing is obvious to me through my own experience and observation of others: adopting a younger child is a completely different experience to adopting an older child. I personally put the threshold of younger and older at five years old.

Adopting an older child has its advantages: no nappies is the obvious one! The children can speak and communicate what they're thinking (if they choose to). They're over the terrible twos (although maybe not emotionally). They have some sort of understanding of their past, remember being in care and look forward to being adopted.

But their trauma level is high. I see it in adopters' get-togethers. I hear it from fellow adopters.

I follow other adopters' blogs: many of those where an older child was adopted didn't end well. I know of two where the placement disrupted. Others went offline, and I never knew their fate. Some still report huge struggles many years after the children moved in. If you adopt an older child, you don't only become a parent, you become a therapist. You are 'on call' 24/7. You're not allowed to make mistakes. I'm not saying, 'Don't adopt an older child'; I'm saying, 'Be prepared.' And if you think you're prepared, think again. Read more. Talk to people. Make sure you've got the full picture. Get support in place.

Saved by Thomas the Tank Engine

It is the intensity of the children's needs that can be frankly terrifying in the first few months. My son was six when he moved in and he would barely leave me alone for a minute at a time – with him the only space I got was the length of one Thomas the Tank episode when he could sit still and watch it. So he watched lots of episodes of T the T across each day.

I would advise anyone adopting an older child that, aggravating as it is, the more you can keep them close, the better in the long term. Because they are at school, they are already (in their eyes) spending a lot of their time away from you so will want to reconnect as much and as soon as possible when they are at home. The more 'available' you can make yourself (and pretend to be happy about it!), the more they will relax over time.

It has also been worth working on the permanency side by talking about and preparing for things that will take place in the future. Gardening is great for this – sowing seeds and talking about how they will grow, what you'll do with the harvest – growing a pumpkin for next Halloween! Measuring my adoptive son and making marks against a wall and guessing how many years it will be before he is as tall as the light switch/bookshelf. Doing things that reinforce the idea that they will still be there next week, next month, next year.

Talk to your social worker about therapeutic support like Theraplay. The government has recognized that children who are adopted often have needs far beyond the love and attention of devoted parents and has provided some funds to provide additional help.

In the immediate term after placement, concentrate on having as much fun as possible. I found the best way to distract my adopted son from poking/prodding/squeezing the life out of me was tickling him!

Chapter 5

ADOLESCENTS

Adolescence is a breathe-in-and-hold-on moment for most parents as their child or children start to ask the question 'Who am I?' and stretch their fledgling wings towards adulthood.

For adopted children, finding their own identity opens up a Pandora's box of horrors: supressed memories of abuse, loss, drugs and abandonment that are hard to digest and yet are often an integral part of their psyche.

Many feel out of kilter with their peer group, isolated and unable to engage in the day-to-day demands of any formal education system. Some hit out in despair; sinking into the darkest, dankest corners of their memory, they react by lying, stealing, fighting, drinking, taking drugs and being promiscuous as they seek to understand who they are — and then sometimes they risk potentially dangerous contact with their birth families.

The adoptive parents are at the sharp end. They get attacked from every side: the out-of-control anger of their adolescent child is blamed on their poor parenting by schools, friends, neighbours and even members of the extended family.

'Sometimes you find yourself dealing with people who just don't understand,' said one adoptive parent. 'They regard you as the problem and your child as simply the product of your poor parenting.'

And the attacks keep coming. Most parents will be told, 'You just don't understand me' by their children on a regular basis during adolescence. For adoptive parents it's an accusation that cuts deeper, a slap across the face of all they have done, all the work they have put into giving their child a secure, safe and happy family.

As the adolescent storm rages and builds, parents have to show not just unconditional love but absolute commitment, resilience and determination. The emotional toll on adoptive parents cannot be underestimated, nor can their need for support as they face a situation layered with complexities as the emotional age of an adopted adolescent is often well below their physical age. You can't easily pick up a teenager and cuddle them on your lap for half an hour because they are upset, although a cuddle may be just what they need and want but don't know how to ask for.

Adoption UK trainer Jane Mitchell says:

> Communicating with adolescents can be an area fraught with tension in many families with good reason. During adolescence, neurological development is prominent; also hormone surges and massive bodily changes are taking place, affecting the young person's perception and reaction to the world around them. At the same time, others' reactions towards them are changing. This has the potential to create self-perpetuating negative feedback where the young person's physical changes, fears of becoming an adult and reaction from the world at large confirm their worst fears – they are unloveable, unloved, rude, ugly and going nowhere quickly. Add to this the complex issues in an adopted child and you have a very challenging situation. The underlying emotion is fear.

Adoption UK has come up with a ten-point guide to handling teenage adoptees:

1. Believe in the long-term effects of early trauma. Even if your children seem fine as youngsters, don't be complacent. Sometimes everyone around you thinks you are fine, but you have niggling doubts at the back of your mind. Adopted children have coping strategies which involve not letting anyone into their internal world and that includes their adoptive parents. They over-compensate and can be incredibly people-pleasing and compliant so you won't turn on them like others did. But this behaviour often changes in adolescence when the compliant child suddenly erupts.

2. Educate yourself about early trauma and therapeutic parenting. Not all adoption preparation courses cover this comprehensively. Make sure you understand the effects of early trauma so you can put your child's behaviour into some

sort of context. Using traditional parenting techniques can make matters worse. Being stricter doesn't work.

3. Surround yourself with like-minded people. Often this means other adopters, but it also means professionals who understand the effects of early trauma. Sometimes adopters are keen to leave the world of adoption behind and become a 'normal' family in their local community. The problem is that other people don't understand the effects of early trauma or the challenges adoptive children are facing. It's OK to be a part of the local community and still keep involved with the adoption community.

4. Harness the power of any special needs/special educational needs your child might have.

5. Choose schools carefully. You need a school from the onset in adoption which will be responsive to an adopted child's needs if and when the need arises.

6. If your child is diagnosed with ADHD or ADD, consider trying medication. Children sometimes need the chance to calm down to take advantage of therapeutic parenting.

7. Talk openly about adoption and their birth family. They have another family out there somewhere. You might find the birth family's lifestyle distasteful and can't believe it would attract your child, but they might think differently in their teenage years. Social media has enabled unrestricted connections to be made between birth families and their adopted children.

8. Have a dedicated adult, preferably a parent, around all the time. Don't aim for early independence. Don't assume that because everyone goes abroad with their mates at 16 your young people should do the same. Always take their particular capabilities and attachment needs into account when making any decision that involves time away from the family.

9. Use therapy and other interventions wherever possible. Don't assume that any unwanted behaviours/attitudes will get better on their own. Seek help early.

10. Self-care: Look after yourself and make sure that you are strong enough both emotionally and physically to be able to cope with parenting these children. Living with trauma can be debilitating. It can cause a downward spiral as you don't see your friends and family as much as you used to, and maybe when you do, you end up feeling judged and criticized.

Above all, try to hang on in there. This is a critical time within adoptive families when adoptions are most at risk of disruption.

With good understanding and knowledge from the start, there is every chance you and your adoptive child will sail through the stormy waters of adolescence with reasonable ease...and only the occasional trauma – but that is completely unpredictable.

My teen 'angel'

I don't want to speak too soon, but do you know what, I'm really proud of my boy Brad. He's just turned 14 and we are in the midst of the dreaded teen years I had been anticipating with more than a modicum of fear. But so far so good.

OK, he's on a 12-month conditional discharge from the court for theft, but he hasn't been in trouble since that short sharp shock dealt out by the magistrates. Could it be a turning point? That's the trouble with the parenting business: you never really know if you've turned a corner and just as you sit there feeling self-satisfied something is guaranteed to smack you in the face.

But I will have to admit I am looking forward to this summer. I enjoy Brad's company and he is able to look after himself and entertain himself far more than he has ever been able to in the past. Some days I hardly see him as he is out on his BMX with friends. That probably helps. It just seems so normal. It doesn't seem that long ago when he was under my feet every moment of the day, complaining about something or threatening to do something to me or some household item.

He does smoke, but it could be worse. I've decided that is a battle I'm not going to get into – except when he stubbed out two cigarettes on the sill of my new front windows. That was a step too far! But we didn't get into an argument. I just banned him from smoking in the house and guess what – he's stuck to it.

What is the most heart-warming is seeing in him my own values and beliefs about treating people fairly, about not bullying anyone different, about ignoring bigots and turning your back on them. I am amazed each time he says something which I've been drumming into him over the years. Amazed he has listened to me and amazed he now believes it himself. It makes me proud of him and proud of myself. If he goes on like this, he's going to be a wonderful, happy, caring adult: the one thing we all want our children to be. That seemed impossible at one time when he was so wound up in his own self-hatred, insecurity and loathing that he would lash out at everything – mostly me!

If I was to say to anyone what had made the difference, I would say time. It takes an awfully long time to undo that feeling that they must be inextricably bad in some way to have been rejected by their birth parents – whatever the reason they were removed. It also takes a long time of pushing you away physically and verbally before the penny finally drops that you are not going anywhere. You are in it for the long haul because you do actually love them – and yes, they are loveable.

And, guess what, he loves me too. If I let him know something upsets me or makes me unhappy, I can now see genuine remorse. Not that flippant 'sorry' that used to trip off his tongue because he didn't want to miss out on a bag of sweets and that I found so irritating. He has also shown that he has finally got another of my messages I've drilled into him: 'Don't tell me you are sorry, show me' and 'Don't tell me you won't do it again – just don't do it again.' Perhaps some parents might think he is on to a good thing. But you have to remember the journey we have been on. To have an out-of-control child who you couldn't keep safe and who you actually feared turn into a funny, insightful and reflective teen is incredible.

I am far more laid back and in control of my own feelings now and that helps too. I am still quick to feel stress because of our past history together but I don't react inappropriately (well, most of the time). I am also better at providing some structure to our weekends so that he knows where he stands – at the moment he has a sleepover on Friday, I take him somewhere on the Saturday and he entertains himself on Sundays. That has removed the stress from our weekends when I needed to have some time to myself and not always be tied up ferrying him all over the region.

We still have a lot of battles ahead and I know I have to keep my expectations in check. But at his last school review when he declared he wanted to study design at university, I couldn't quite believe my ears. He has always been great at art and is very creative, but to have thought it through into a career path is more than I could have hoped for.

He knows I went to university, but we have never talked about it together. I thought he might go to college to get a clearer idea about the job he would like, but this came as a complete surprise.

I know next week he might want to be a rock star or a sports player, but he is thinking ahead about his future and about getting a job and that is great.

My teen is definitely no angel, but how he has developed in the past 12 months has given me such hope. To think at one time my ambition for him was to keep him out of prison; now it looks like I won't be able to stop him going to university. Fingers crossed!

Exhaustion, commitment and surviving the teen years

I want to give you a flavour of what life has been like with Tom, our adopted teen.

Teenagers in general get a bad press – they are a modern folk devil. Adopted teens, bringing with them a huge amount of internal distress externalized in a variety of alarming ways, very easily become the embodiment of everyone's fears. When I drop my son off to spend the evening out on the streets with friends, I see how other people may see him – hood up, baseball cap pulled down to his eyes, large, swaggering, smoking. Scary.

There is an element of truth in this. He is sometimes scary. When overwhelmed with pain, fear or anger – and it's hard to separate these out – he has gone on violent, destructive rampages. I once spent part of a night in my polytunnel because I was too afraid to be in the house with him. He has twice been excluded from educational provision because staff felt too unsafe to work with him.

For some years we had a reasonably good relationship with both sets of next-door neighbours. But since we've had several visits from the police – on one occasion the end of the road blocked off by police cars – along with the frequent sound of raised voices and breaking glass, and sundry dodgy-looking teenagers visiting the house, they've asked for their spare keys back and built high fences so that they don't even have to see us. A large part of that is because they're afraid.

Our son has been in court four or five times (I've lost count). The first time I talked about his early life and its impact on him. That made the magistrates a whole lot more sympathetic, but he was mortified and tearful to hear his story made public. It was awful for him to hear me describe in brief and rather bold terms the neglect and abuse he had experienced. Although he knows about it, he doesn't like to be reminded of it, and particularly doesn't like it to be told to people other than those of his choosing. He would rather be seen as tough and bad than as vulnerable. The world is, of course, happy to oblige him with this.

The next time, Tom said he'd run from the court if we made any mention of his history. Fearing what that might lead to, we remained mute, were clearly seen as hopelessly inadequate parents, and were assessed for a parenting order. Of course, we were then able to give a full account of our son's history and all that we were doing in our attempts to help and contain him. A very affirming report was returned to the court and no parenting order was made. Despite that, I couldn't help feeling shamed and humiliated by the whole experience. For the subsequent court appearances we got smarter and supplied the solicitor with a detailed written history and various reports prepared by professionals over the years.

We've had every single internal door in our house kicked, punched and head-butted in. I've just counted them and, if I include a cupboard door, that's 11 in all. We've had every glass and every bit of crockery in the kitchen broken, along with some expensive Scandinavian double-glazed windows. When only one pane of glass has cracked, we've left them as they are, and have become used to the pretty patterns they make. We've found ourselves hoovering the flower beds (broken glass) and pruning the furniture (wicker, jumped on). We now acquire domestic goods differently. Freecycle has been wonderful for replacing smashed televisions and most of the kitchen stuff has been replaced from charity shops. We've come to prefer our minimalist style of (lack of) ornaments and pictures. Genuinely prefer it.

We have at various times had seven (I think) of our son's friends living with us, for periods of up to three months each. He continues our adoption habit by adopting his homeless friends.

During his mid-teens his sleep pattern and our carefully constructed and maintained lovely bedtime routine went to pieces with the onset of adolescence. I would get out of bed to watch a DVD with him, this large teenage boy with his head on a pillow on my lap as I stroked his back so that he felt safe and soothed enough to fall asleep. The link between toddler and teenager was never clearer to me than at those times. I was able to adjust my hours of work and those midnight hours were a precious experience.

Family holidays became a thing of the past when Tom, at 14, shredded the tent during a particularly bad episode on a campsite.

I've had a black eye and my husband has had a cracked rib. I realize that many other people would have given up by now, would have done what many people have advised us to do and said, 'Right, young man, that's enough, you're out of here,' and certainly some of the people we know have thought we're mad not to have done that.

I've been stubborn in my refusal. I couldn't bear my son to repeat his birth mother's teenage death. He's now 19 and has already lived longer than she did. That in itself feels like an achievement, although I don't take it for granted. He still sails close to the wind, but I'm more relaxed about it than I was. When he went out with mates at the age of 14 or 15 and failed to come home or be contactable, I lay awake for most or all of the night. Now I may worry only briefly before I tell myself to go to sleep, and do.

For years we responded to middle-of-the-night calls to pick him up, in order to keep him safe. Now we don't, even, as happened recently, when the temperature was sub-zero. I did lie awake for a while then, but parental exhaustion means it's time to draw that particular line. It's an ever-changing line, trying to balance his needs with ours as best we can.

One thing I've learned – support doesn't necessarily come from where you expect it. At dance camp a young woman, naked apart from the towel she was clutching in front of her, appeared outside our tent late one night asking if she could help when my son was alternately shouting and sobbing his heart out. I still think of her as a naked angel. The staff at our local Blockbuster have been more consistently helpful than social services have in the task of managing our son's needs. CAMHS (Child and Adolescent Mental Health Services) have apologized for their inadequacy in providing a good service, as did, in a Sunday afternoon phone call, a senior education official. The appalling lack of understanding and, especially, failure to listen to us on the part of most of the staff at our son's secondary school remains a very painful memory.

Some friends have listened well – most times that's all that's needed – and some haven't. Some, in wanting to protect me, have had punitive responses to my son. As I love him dearly, that doesn't help me. For a while I went to a support group for parents of adopted teens run by a local adoption charity. At times it was helpful, but it hasn't been the most helpful thing.

We've had an absolute lifeline of mutual support with another adoptive parent we met initially through Adoption UK... At times the exchange of hair-raising, despairing, hilarious emails with her has been the one thing that has kept me going and certainly the only thing that has made me laugh. We've been doing that for six years now.

In our efforts to parent well in an impossible situation, my husband and I have attended workshops with experts and we've read a lot of books about trauma and brain development. All of that has been hugely helpful in informing us and helping us to find our own answers.

'You must give him boundaries,' some people have said. We always have. The interesting thing is when he can't keep within them. Then it's a sign of too much stress, internal or external, to be able to manage. As some of my guiding lights have said, when parenting a teen we're better off going for influence rather than control. To be able to influence, we have to maintain a close relationship. My preference has always been to do what I can to nurture the relationship, rather than take a more behaviourist approach.

So where are we now and where do we go from here? Looking back over five years, my husband and I can agree that things are much better than they were. We now have many evenings when we sit peacefully by the fire, like any other ageing couple, whether our son is in or out.

Our son is nearly 20, but that just means we go from parenting an adopted teen to parenting an adopted adult. He is still living at home. He and we agree that he would not be able to manage on his own. Supported housing works for some, but our son would experience fear and the huge sense of rejection that is always just below the surface if we went in that direction, and because he still has outbursts of temper he'd probably get thrown out anyway, as many of his friends have.

Tom still finds disappointment, frustration and boredom very hard to handle, and life involves a lot of all of those, but he can handle them better most of the time.

Since he was permanently excluded from mainstream education at the age of 13, we've patched together an intermittently good stream of alternative provision, but seem to have run out of that at the moment.

He can't manage regular college – there was a recent failed attempt – and getting or holding down a job is currently beyond him. When he was younger, a couple of child health professionals described him as having developmental delay of about three or four years. At nearly 20, he's still functioning like someone younger. He has some good, consistent friendships. I worry about his binge drinking and the desperate mental state he gets into when drunk. He doesn't remember it the next day, so has no motivation to change. However, he had a few lost weekends last year on a nasty drug that left him paranoid and delusional, and he decided not to touch that one again, and hasn't.

There have been minor skirmishes with the police, but no court appearances for three years now. Most importantly for us as his worn-out parents, the destructive outbursts are fewer and smaller, and violence towards us seems to be a thing of the past – that's the one thing that would now be a bottom line. A couple of light switches have been punched in recently and the bathroom door still has holes in it. But the other doors are replaced and intact, and my husband and son together have repaired most of the damage to his room and redecorated it.

In the absence of work or training, we're focusing on other living skills, so he now often cooks for himself, does his own laundry, helps with communal domestic tasks and is making some efforts to manage money better.

Our son has always been loving, loyal and respectful, between storms, and as the storms subside, life under the same roof starts to feel more tolerable. Quite where all this will go I don't know. Living in the present is one of the things we've learned to do. We can relax in a way we couldn't even think about a few years ago, but we can't relax completely. I still work part-time and I've managed to add in some things that are just for me – meditating, swimming, growing vegetables, singing.

The thing I'd like to finish with is this. Love may not be enough – we need masses of understanding and skill, unlikely as well as likely support, things we do to nourish ourselves and a grim sense of humour – but in my experience love is the most important thing.

I enjoy teenagers immensely

Our adopted daughter Lucy is nearly 13. She joined our family at nine with a brother of four. I have absolutely no regrets in adopting older children. I'm proud that we adopted older children, and it has been very rewarding. To focus on my eldest, I'm sad that we missed her being younger and so is she. But in a way that adds to our bond – and if I'm honest, our bond wasn't that quick – but she is understandably avoidant, so it has been a long process. Having said that, we are very much a family and we all love each other dearly.

I'm enjoying this phase of my life with her – I enjoy teenagers immensely and feel like we have seen massive, positive changes in her, and she recognizes them too. At the moment she's no more difficult than she was at nine, although I'm aware that could change! In many ways she is still nine, younger even. We do see her hormones at work – but we just roll our eyes (out of her sight) or have a secret chuckle. She is much more opinionated than she was, but I see that as a positive, for one so compliant. She is also much more into material things – but as someone who cared about nothing when she came, her naming six things she wants for her birthday from us is brilliant!

On the theme of age being no indicator of 'unknowns', we have had a different experience to others. Although Lucy was known to social workers for pretty much all her life with her birth parents, we have only recently had some learning disabilities identified that were never investigated by her foster carers, social work or her previous schools – it was just put down to her treatment with birth parents and missing school so much – and, of course, we went with that received wisdom. In the past few years, we have slowly been 'unpacking' some of her difficulties at school and in life. I think she may always be a very vulnerable girl, but I hope we can help her find her way into adulthood successfully. I must admit, I feel very maternal towards her – my need to protect her is overwhelming!

Update 2016: A year on from this, our daughter is a flourishing 14-year-old. She makes mistakes, is incredibly disorganized and forgetful, can't work money very well, ignores homework as a concept, and her maths is still at middle primary school level. However, she is happy and has some (non-academic) ambition for her life, which is more than we had hoped for at this age!

Having continued to investigate her additional support needs and other issues, we now suspect she could have been affected by alcohol *in utero*, but we have no way of proving it. But at the moment a diagnosis wouldn't really give her anything more than she has, so we just continue to parent the amazing teenager we have in the best way we can.

Therapeutic parenting – a reconstruction job

Before our two adopted children, Jaymey and Harlee, arrived I contemplated, in a superficial kind of a way, what sort of parent I would be. Calm, I decided (as I rarely lost my temper), patient (I've always been patient), fun, sensible (no faddy eaters allowed here), practical (let's all learn to tie our shoelaces, tell the time, boil an egg). These were things I knew to be true about myself. I was wrong.

Ten years ago our two bemused, energetic, funny, distant, angry children moved into our home and they weren't the only strangers who arrived. Someone hijacked the old me and replaced her with a shouty, short-tempered, knackered, impatient harridan. I didn't recognize her and I didn't like her at all. Almost everything I thought I knew about being a good parent, haphazardly gathered together from the experience of being parented myself, from observing parents around me and watching back-to-back *Super Nanny*, either escaped me or failed. And on top of that, much of my parenting 'style' was completely unconscious; it just fell out of my mouth.

Early on, when our two children were little, I began to realize that methods which worked with the children of my friends and family were not working with ours. A flaky boundary would immediately be spotted and bulldozed, and chaos was never far away. I started having to be firmer and stricter than my friends were being. I found I had to reassure much more often and that sometimes looking fine and feeling fine were very different things. Tantrums were more explosive and prolonged. Insults came in full technicolour. We struggled along for a few years, me learning as I was going along and delivering 'good enough' parenting while our eldest child raged and our youngest child withdrew.

I thought I was a therapeutic parent and I certainly got more proficient. I went on some courses, watched some DVDs and read some books. But therapeutic parenting was something I bolted on to the unconscious methods I was importing from my own childhood.

When our eldest child entered the early stages of adolescence and the end of primary education loomed, there was a sudden escalation in behaviours: it was like being hit by a nuclear weapon. My 'good enough' parenting was no longer fit for purpose in the face of those behaviours which we thank our lucky stars we never see, until we do and then the world caves in. Suddenly, the rages were much more frightening and destructive, the language could break window glass and we saw all the behaviours I'd always felt grateful we'd escaped, the socially unacceptable ones that you can't tell your friends about. Apart from the rages and the swearing, there was lots of sneaking around and suspicious noises, money disappeared, scratches appeared on precious items, mouldy food turned up in unlikely places, things which should only be found in a toilet were, well, I will spare you that detail.

As is common with reformed characters, I turned a corner only when things got appallingly bad. Every single moment of every single miserable day was a battle. Rob, my usually solid husband, declared that he couldn't carry on. My stoicism collapsed. Our younger child, burdened with her own trauma, was wilting under the pressure. Things felt desperate. I don't know if there was a light-bulb moment, but with some good support from our social worker, some revisiting of the books, a course or two and some coaching in therapeutic parenting, we realized, at a much deeper level, what we had to do and everything began to make more sense.

We had to let go of our horror at the behaviours we were experiencing and see them differently: as an expression of trauma, something which wasn't being enacted on purpose. So when our son said that he didn't know why he lost control of his temper or took money, he really didn't know. We had to take away opportunities to fail: lock away money, get out of bed in the morning at the first signs of life, practise close and constant supervision. We had to relax over certain behaviours and not sweat over the small stuff so that we weren't nagging the entire time. We had to stop being shocked and start turning on the empathy.

We had to pause and think before any words came out of our mouths so that negatives were expressed positively. 'Can I go to the park now?' was followed by 'How about we go in the morning?' rather than 'No, it's getting dark'. Language became very important. 'I can see you are finding that difficult' rather than 'That was naughty'. A punishment is a consequence. And we've really had to think hard about the consequences which work and those which don't. Mostly the consequences which make Rob and me feel better actually make things worse. Sometimes we tire of having to parent so consciously and Rob will say in exasperation, 'Why should we have to live like this?' We both know the answer.

It has taken me ten years to 'get' trauma, and I am still learning and improving. After faking it for a while, it feels more natural now, and both our children have started to relax. Of course, certain behaviours have worsened as our parenting has improved. Shouting and throwing are good ways of escaping pain and loss, both of which have now risen to the surface. But at least now we can journey through those together. Our son in particular has shared some powerful insights into what it feels like to live with trauma, and this has allowed us to make great progress.

A big part of my 'shaping up' – and I'm not quite there yet – has been to shed received ideas of what it means to raise a successful family. Measures of success, whether they are associated with academic achievement, sporting success, musical prowess or a vibrant social life, do not apply to us because we have to set different priorities and live life differently. I fought against that for a long time and to accept our lives as they are has taken much self-examination. I still deliver an occasional 'I would never have spoken to my mother like that' and other vintage classics, but on the whole I'm getting there.[1]

Hitting out

Our adopted son Owen has displayed challenging behaviour since his placement with us at 14 months old.

By age 12, our son was getting increasingly aggressive both verbally and physically. We also have an adopted daughter who thought it was 'normal' to have a brother who couldn't control his mood swings. She didn't blink an eyelid at living in a house where all the doors had holes in and most of the walls were marked from things being thrown at them.

When a three-year-old has a temper tantrum and throws his teddy out of a car window and takes two hours to calm down, it's challenging. When a 13-year-old throws his mobile phone at the car windscreen and cracks it so it's undriveable, and *still* takes two hours to calm down, it's a lot more challenging!

For years we tried to hide things 'behind closed doors'. In public, our son usually presented as well spoken, intelligent and loving, and rather hyperactive. I wore long sleeves to hide my bruised arms. It all changed one Christmas Eve when, in despair, I went on to the Adoption UK forums for some advice about what to do about a particularly painful injury I'd received when my son attacked me as I was driving. Another parent told me to (a) go to the doctor immediately so it was recorded and (b) tell my husband. I did both and, although the bruise was still there, I realized we couldn't keep things a secret any more.

After Christmas we went along to an Adoption UK support group where we met several other adopters who were experiencing similar situations. We realized for the first time that it probably wasn't just our parenting skills (or lack of them) that were at fault and that however many courses we willingly attended about managing teenage behaviour, the problems we were facing were far more deep-seated than coping with a rebellious teenager.

---

1 Sally Donovan is the author of *No Matter What: An Adoptive Family's Story of Hope, Love and Healing* (2013), London, Jessica Kingsley Publishers.

At the support group, we were able to unload and share what was happening with other parents who really understood. Some of them had older children and spoke about how family life carries on as these challenging young people reach adulthood. At times we used to think, 'That can't possibly happen to our family,' but as the years went by and things did get even more difficult, we were able to reflect on how others who'd walked in our footsteps had coped.

I joined an adoption panel in my capacity as an adoptive parent. That was where I first heard about non-violent resistance (NVR). One of the other panel members had attended a course and over coffee told me how he thought it might help our family. Our son was 16 years old by this time and life wasn't getting any easier. He had some outstanding support from a psychotherapist funded by the local authority for about 18 months. We are sure that this support managed to keep us together as a family and get him through his GCSEs.

We knew Owen was likely to have one of his epic meltdowns on GCSE results day, so we ensured we were out of the country, somewhere where we wouldn't be hearing news bulletins about 'best results ever'. When we phoned the school for his results, we were jumping for joy that he'd managed to get ten A–C GCSEs, but sad that we couldn't share our joy with our son because it would all have just been too overwhelming for him. He didn't 'do' birthdays, Christmases or any other celebration very well. He didn't even ask us about his results until the day was nearly over.

At age 17, in the middle of A level studies, our son threatened his father so seriously that we had no other option but to ask him to leave home. He managed four months with his grandparents before we found him a place in a supported house.

Eventually, he became looked after under Section 20 of the Children Act. We thought long and hard about whether this was the right decision. But his problems were likely to be long-term (after all, they'd now been going on for 15 years already) and he'd be more protected if he became looked after under S20.

He is now 20. Over the years, in order to maintain some sort of family life, we have gathered a group of people around us into our NVR 'support network' – teachers, social workers, psychologist, neighbours, family members, close friends, even some of our son's friends and the local police – and worked out roles for them all. One of the most helpful things we did was come up with our text code system as part of our 'campaign of concern'. When we could sense that our son was going into one of his meltdowns, we would text our code word to a neighbour or close friend. They knew to turn up as soon as possible on the pretence of dropping in for a coffee or borrowing a DVD. The presence of a different face often helped to de-escalate situations. Things weren't a secret any more.

We'd learnt a huge amount from reading Dan Hughes' books, hearing him speak at an Adoption UK conference and borrowing Bryan Post's *Great Behaviour Breakdown* book.

We need to come out the other end of this journey and still be a family. Although our son is not living the sort of life we would have hoped, he is living life in the only way he knows how to, 'for now'. Do we wish we'd done anything differently? Well, perhaps it would have helped to be more open, much earlier on, about the struggles we were experiencing behind closed doors.

And what about our teenage daughter? She's now 16. She isn't our son's birth sibling and thankfully she's had none of the same challenges. She misses her brother being at home and regularly sends him little cards and gifts to maintain *her* presence in his life. We recognize that 'for now' this is all we can do.

Chapter 6

ADOPTING A CHILD WITH A PHYSICAL OR LEARNING DISABILITY

Almost all children coming into care have special needs of one sort or another – many take time to recover from the hurt of rejection, others suffer from an inability to attach, many are on the edge of the autism spectrum and find it hard to communicate, and the vast majority of older children are well behind in meeting their educational goal posts.

But there also many children in care with a physical or learning disability: Down's syndrome, spina bifida, cerebral palsy, a variety of life-threatening congenital heart diseases and others. Their trauma is a physical one. These are the children most likely to languish in care, who are rejected by their birth parents because of the kaleidoscope of demanding physical and mental challenges they present and that their parents will have to deal with, in their sometimes short lives.

However, they are first and foremost just children looking for love and a family of their own. Adoption agencies urge prospective adopters to look beyond any physical or mental disability to the child within who has the same emotional needs as any other child.

Adopting a disabled child is demanding, but it is also hugely rewarding. 'Yes, there are challenges. Of course there are. It's hard work and no doubt it's different for everyone as a parent depending on the type of disability. But I know from experience that children without disabilities are hard work too,' said one adoptive parent of three disabled children who first had three birth children of her own.

Adopters can't do this on their own. These children may not tax you as mentally and emotionally as other adoptees, but they will drain you physically. Their physical and learning needs are paramount and always come first – for them and for you; they need huge support and adopters need to have the persistence and energy to put that support in place, from finding good special education facilities, medical and social care to finding a way to give themselves very necessary occasional respite. These are essentials both for the adopter and for the child they adopt.

'It can be one long battle to find everything from the right school to the right shoes,' said one adopter.

These children are looking for families who are prepared to fight for them because they can't fight for themselves. For these adopters, adopting a disabled child is the right option, not a second choice, and brings as much joy as the adoption of an able-bodied child. Many describe the instinctive feeling that they have that they can help one particular child, however severely disabled.

'We all have disabilities of some description – who and what is normal?' said one successful adopter.

The delight for these adopters is in the happiness of their children and the physical progress they achieve, however small. One adopter has drawn up a list of musts for parents of a child with a disability:

- Accept life as it is.

- Laugh at situations when others might cry.

- Give until it hurts, even when you get no response.

- Never give up, even if you seem to be getting nowhere.

- Put achievements before failures.

- Help your child to accept himself/herself.

- Teach your child to love and always give him or her a lot of love.

Leaping into the unknown

Everyone says adopting is a bit like stepping out into the unknown. Adopting a child with a disability, or no clear prognosis, is like leaping

head first into an entirely unknown place. But, as time has gone on, things have become clearer and I realize that I wouldn't have had it any other way. It isn't easy, but I don't think any adoption is – adopting a disabled child just brings a different set of unknown factors into your life, and I wouldn't change Chloe, my little one, for the world.

I knew right from the start that I wanted to adopt a disabled child. I had worked in social care since leaving school, so had a good idea of what I was getting into.

Waiting for a match was the very hardest part. I found my little girl at an exchange day – after many weeks of waiting by the phone and searching family-finding websites. As she had complex needs, the agency wanted me to meet her before we went ahead and, to be honest, there was no sudden rush of love, but I knew she was the one.

When we got to panel, the first question was: 'This child can't do x, y or z and has all these problems – why do you want to adopt her?' The red mist came down, as I couldn't believe anyone would ask such a silly question about a beautiful little girl with so much personality and potential. In that moment I realized two things: that I absolutely adored her, and that we would both have to spend our lives fighting to get people to understand.

I would say to anyone thinking of adopting a disabled child: think incredibly hard about matching, before you start seeing profiles – honestly, it is a lot easier when there aren't real children involved. Think about exactly what needs you can meet: specific behaviours, sleeping patterns, whether you can cope with having to insert tubes, which body fluids you can clean up. What can you actually manage, every single day for the next 20 years – at four in the morning, when you have flu, or when your support network have all got a bit bored and you realize you are completely on your own?

I made a huge yes/no list before adopting and felt bad ruling out some issues, but it is the right thing to know your limits. I also had to decide if I could adopt a child whose disability was caused by their birth parents – and if I would be able to explain that to them when they ask me.

Only you know what you can do.

Mark and James**

After endless discussions about what sort of child we could cope with, we concluded that they must not be above eight years old or mentally handicapped; anything else fine. With hope, we set off.

Endless phone calls and letters came to no avail. Then the Adoption UK journal came out. We planned to phone for details of the children of our choice the following day. The only child in the journal in our age range was a three-and-a-half-year-old boy with Down's syndrome. Although we felt this was a handicap with which we couldn't cope, we decided to apply. The social worker wanted to meet us and we kept the appointment thinking to ourselves, 'You never know, he may know of other children.' After long discussions we agreed to meet Mark, but we were pretty sure he wouldn't be coming to live with us.

We met Mark. We couldn't believe our emotions that day. We liked him and he appeared to like us. Perhaps the mental handicap wasn't as bad as we thought. We returned a week later, and on this second meeting the fact that he was mentally handicapped had flown out the window for us. We were too busy getting to know our son and making arrangements for him to come home.

The joys he has brought us are unbelievable. We have never regretted that decision to visit the little boy we didn't think we could cope with. Now we cannot imagine life without him! Each milestone he reaches brings us the greatest joy. The tears I shed before Mark arrived were of sorrow and sadness. Since his arrival the tears have been of laughter and pure joy. Two years later we saw James, who had a physical problem. We all took to him straight away. Now we have two loving, boisterous, mischievous little boys which is more than I dared hope for at the beginning.

Surely we all have disabilities of some description! If my sons are disabled, then I am the proudest disabled mum you are ever likely to meet. Yes, our boys have problems, one intellectual, the other physical; with both it's uncertain what they will achieve academically and physically. But I am confident in the knowledge that, with love and patience, our boys will grow to their full potential, no matter how great or small that may seem to others. To the four of us, every single achievement will be a wonderful thing.

Once a bruvver, always a bruvver**

To the social workers he was a multi-jeopardized, stateless, ethnic minority refugee with a learning disability, adopted by a racially naive white family. To the nasty bullies on the bridge who taunted him he was ching-chong-Chinaman-yellow-skin-slitty-eyes-no-brain. To my parents' former friends he was odd, possibly unsanitary and certainly daft.

To me he is my bruvver. He is absolutely my bruvver.

There was only ever one moment when I doubted whether he should have become part of our family. He'd been living with us for about a year. I was desperate to ask my mother a question about my homework, but my brother was in a particularly demanding mood, kicking the table and rocking from side to side. It required all our mother's energy to keep him engaged with a story book. She couldn't break off from devoting her attention to him without running the risk of him getting furious or sulky. In my instant irritation at him for monopolizing my mother, I suddenly saw him as others did. I could hear the questions asked of me by those curious friends of my parents.

'Do you mind having a disabled brother?'

'Do you actually like him?'

'It must be frightfully difficult for you normal children.'

And I understood the ignorance and hostility behind them.

Apart from that disloyal moment, he has always been a brother. He does all the things most brothers do. Sometimes he needs looking after, like when he got the shingles when our parents were on holiday. Sometimes he needs affection, like when he is remembering that he was handed into an orphanage and wondering about his first parents of whom he knows nothing. Sometimes he looks after me, like when I was very depressed and he would suddenly hug me and say, 'I hope you be better soon.'

Sometimes he does brilliant jokes, like on New Year's Eve in a country pub after hours, when all the villagers were dancing to the juke box and one of our brother's favourite rock tracks came on. Having been ambling back from the toilet doing up his flies, he suddenly recognized the tune and flung himself into a knee skid, coming to a halt in the middle of the brick floor. He then performed an air guitar solo to the amazement of other drinkers and the delighted hilarity of his siblings.

His turns of phrase have passed into our family's collective vocabulary like 'Splash you' when someone has sneezed, instead of the more usual 'Bless you'. His difficulties with reading or counting are the least important things in a description of what sort of a person he is, but to many caregivers what they call a 'learning disability' is his defining feature. As I see it, he doesn't have a problem learning things, it's just that he forgets them again immediately. The discomfort that our society feels when dealing with slow people shows in what they are called; there are so many convoluted terms which we use in order to distance ourselves from the moral judgements and overtones associated with calling someone stupid. People who can't write, talk, count or think very well are assumed to be morally or emotionally inferior to those who are literate, numerate, articulate and quick-thinking. And as fast as new terms are invented, old connotations catch up, rendering the new work insulting as well.

People like my bruv don't need any new phrases to describe the things which make their lives difficult. He and we need sufficient support so that we can all get on with the discovery of our abilities and pleasures of family life.

First put on your oxygen mask

'Parenting is hard work but so rewarding' and 'You'll be such a great mum; what a lucky boy' were the two commonest responses received when I told the families I was working with that I was taking adoption leave. Having worked for 15 years as a children's occupational therapist, I had witnessed from afar the 'hard work' of parenting.

I described to my husband the 'super parenting' required for many of the children I worked with and how I suspected parenting an adoptive child may be on a similar level. After the first day of our adoption course our desire to have two children reduced to one. During the second day of the course we muttered to each other that perhaps we should adopt a dolphin instead! Our eyes had been opened a little to the potential challenges.

'Sam' came to us with the label of delay but has gone on to receive diagnoses of being on the autism spectrum and dyspraxia. This is my bread and butter and I know theoretically how to help him. And to a very large part I have done and continue to do so. Our first winters together were very cold ones. When the temperature hit the balmy +7 degrees, we were the ones at the park, Sam flying on his tummy on the boat swing, developing his prone extension and giving me lovely eye contact.

The downside is that the high expectations others had of my parenting ability were mirrored by my own expectation of self.

I am learning that it is one thing knowing what to do and quite another doing it as a parent – our emotional investment makes the relationship so different. So too, however, can be the strategies. One mistake out of ten spellings this weekend by my perfectionist boy led to the typical flare-up. What worked on this occasion, however, was tickling him until he laughingly conceded it was OK to make mistakes – not a tactic I would use as a therapist!

However, the hardest lesson to learn has been the need to look after the self.

On a recent course, the oxygen mask analogy began to make sense to me: how can we put survival gear on our children if we're unconscious? However, it took a personal experience for it to finally hit home. Sam and I were swimming in a pool that is unstaffed and we happened to be the only ones in. He'd recently learnt to swim and could swim in the deep end, but as a precaution I ensured he was next to the side while I swam along the other side of him. Of course, his instinct on beginning to flounder was to grab me, not the side, at which we both went under the water. We had a scary few moments before I was able to haul him up and sit him on the side. Since then, I swim next to the edge. There I can reach him and hold the side to keep us both afloat. So, that's the challenge for us all. What is our 'side' that keeps us afloat while helping our floundering kids to stay above the water?

While I was looking for a pre-Christmas treat for our son, my mum suggested that instead my husband and I should go away together. I was aghast! How could we do that instead of taking our son to see Santa? The reality is, of course, that what we think is a treat for our children sometimes isn't. I thought back to two years earlier when parents and grandparents were photographed sitting on Santa's sleigh while our little boy stood expressionless, keeping his distance. After end-of-term parties, fairs and performances, perhaps a quiet day mince-pie making with Nana wouldn't be so bad. Our indulgence of self, and, as importantly, of each other, charged our batteries for Christmas. On returning home, I had a lovely bear hug from my happy son (my husband had a punch, but hey, that's lads and dads!).

We need to regularly check our capacity for this super-parenting by ensuring we and those we share this journey with are topped up with oxygen and are always within reach of the side.

The hardest time of the year

As I open the door, I send up a silent prayer that my neighbour won't ask me, 'Did you have a good Christmas?'

It is good to catch up but, as we sip our coffee and finish up the last couple of mince pies, I feel that familiar hollowness inside. I force a happy voice and put a spin on things but, if I told her what our Christmas had really been like, there would have been an awkward silence, a change of subject and an early exit. I know this because I have been honest with 'friends' before, and they don't stay friends for long after the initial expressions of sympathy.

Our child is adopted and has Asperger's syndrome, which means that he is on the autistic spectrum. He is ten now. When we adopted him, we were so looking forward to celebrating his first Christmas but, instead, Jack was really poorly with a chest infection, causing catastrophically broken nights and stressful days. Relatives went home early.

Christmas has continued to be an extremely difficult time of year. The preparations for Christmas that we usually enjoy can for him be unbearable, given the change of routine, noisiness, large hot halls and churches filled with people, singing, different food. All of these things and more are very challenging for our son, especially when combined with illness.

In Year 3, he had the sickness bug just before Christmas and, after persuading him to return to school, his anxieties became so high that we were called in before the carol concert to support him.

He was unable to take part or, indeed, complete the term. He spent Christmas itself pale and uncommunicative, rocking on the sofa and refusing to eat.

This year, weeks beforehand, just as the play rehearsals began at school he became ill again, and every time he picked up and went back to school, the anxieties began again and illness returned. By December 29 we had visited the doctors six times (no easy thing with an anxious child) and missed days at school, being ill for 12 weeks off and on (but mostly on).

Of course, most children become ill at some point at this time of year; coughs and colds are everywhere. Jack, however, has always been more prone than most and this year exceeded all records! The anxiety and panic attacks that came with the illness were the worst part. He suffered from the sort of anxiety that completely debilitates. He could not/would not leave the house; he was constantly convinced that he might be sick. He had to be surrounded by certain items to feel safe – an inhaler stick, water bottle, cuddly toy – a bit like a sad version of the conveyor belt on the *Generation Game*. And, preferably, he had to have the TV on 24/7 – to provide distraction and background noise. He flapped, hyperventilated and couldn't sleep. It was taking him up to three hours to go down, even after having taken melatonin, and then he would wake you up repeatedly in the night: 'Do I look pale? I feel sick.' We had to co-sleep at this point because Jack needed constant reassurance.

Thank goodness, we have an extremely patient and understanding team around Jack at school. His classmates love and accept him for who he is, and he has good friends, both at home and school. He is a loveable, attractive and determined child, and when we can help him to overcome these difficulties, he will continue to succeed and make his way in life.

Jack couldn't take part in the school play, Christmas carol concert or parties. He couldn't eat his Advent calendar chocolates. He couldn't go to the town Christmas Fair or visit Father Christmas. But on Christmas Day, he did tuck into a huge dinner with his extended family and go out proudly on his new BMX bike. We could all breathe a sigh of relief – until next year!

You can hold a conversation with someone who doesn't talk**

David is quadriplegic: he can only move his head and needs total care. The only person to really try to stop his adoption was his paediatrician, who was concerned that ordinary people couldn't look after someone as disabled as David.

When Davie first came, he screamed all night and also screamed if he couldn't make us understand what he wanted or if we weren't doing things quickly enough. He once screamed for three hours solid at a very posh wedding we went to.

We had to learn to ignore people staring at us, and remarks made to us such as 'You must get paid well' or 'Children like him should be in a home' and so on. We have learnt who our real friends are.

Having three teenagers in the house is great fun! Of the eight children born to us, only Iain and Anna remain at home. Iain and Anna have been very good with David. Having him with us has been a big change in their lives.

In his own way David has taught people that they can hold a conversation with someone who doesn't talk and that he doesn't choke too easily if they feed him. He has a wicked sense of humour and he very aware of what is going on around him. He goes to a very good school and is learning to communicate through computers. Things are getting easier; this year's holiday was much better than last year's. Most of his problems were the result of living in a home. After two years with us, he has put on weight and seems to have matured. But it is still very hard to know what age he is at – sometimes he is like a small child, whereas sometimes he is like a stroppy teenager.

With a child like David, if you follow your own instincts and stand by them – sometimes against the experts' advice – you can generally overcome problems. For instance, we felt that David wouldn't want a room of his own; he loves to share with Iain. David was cuddled like a small child when the nights were at their worst. Above all, David likes to be treated as much like the other children in our family as possible. We have done lots of things the wrong way round. We have learnt to decorate a room with a child watching every move from a large wheelchair. David has had to learn that it's not funny when someone hurts themselves, that the same people who are up all night are also up all day, and that if you don't like someone they don't go off shift.

We don't know what the future holds for David, but we do know he will always be loved and cared for by his family. All our lives have been so enriched by David being part of our family, and we are so pleased that he loves being one of us.

Proving them wrong

Adoptee Hannah writes about how she feels being adopted and having autism.

Hello my name is Hannah. I am 16 years old. I have one brother who lives with me and one half-sister who still lives with our birth mum. My brother and I were adopted when he was three years old and I was two years old. When I was nine, I was diagnosed with an autism spectrum disorder (ASD) – NLD, that stands for non-verbal learning disorder. Having autism makes it difficult for me to understand some forms of communication.

My mummy and daddy are called Carolyn and Phil. Bryn (my brother) is 16 years old too. He was born ten months before me. He also has an ASD as he was diagnosed with Asperger's syndrome last year. My brother and I generally get on quite well but sometimes like most brothers and sisters we do fight over things.

Mummy and Daddy think we are both very special, not just because they adopted us but because we are the ones they love and care about very much. I think my brother and I are very special because we were both diagnosed with an ASD and have survived so much since we were little and we have come through it all together.

When we are at home, Mummy and Daddy say that Bryn and me are the best things that could ever happen to them because they couldn't have children of their own.

Our autism means that sometimes we act younger than we are and people don't always understand us. Sometimes we can just tell people we have an ASD and they don't need any more information than that, but sometimes we need to explain a little more about what kind of help we need.

When I was little, Mummy and Daddy thought I would never be able to write in a way other people could understand and I have proved them wrong. After a lot of practice for years and years I have managed to learn to write to a legible standard which everyone including me can read without any difficulty. I still need some support in drawing graphs and reading mathematical stuff like charts and tables in school but that's alright. It doesn't make me mad or stupid, it just means that I need some help like everyone else does at some point in their life.

ASDs are sometimes a good thing in some ways. I still haven't worked out what the good things are yet, except for the fact that I can make people smile in the most annoying and scary situations which is a good thing. I might have impaired social skills but I and everyone else with autism or any kind of ASD are amazing no matter what!

Autism does not mean that I or anyone else diagnosed with an ASD are 'mental' or 'insane', it just means that we are different in a good way and have a disability. Some people like Bryn and myself have mild forms of autism but other children can have very high forms of autism. I'm not sure if mild and high forms are the rights sort of words for what I am trying to describe, but I don't know any other words for it so it will have to do.

I do not think there is a cure for autism but that doesn't matter. I am happy the way I am, no matter what other people say.

Some people think me and Bryn and other children and young people with autism or other ASDs are 'retarded' or 'thick': they are wrong. I am very good at some things and so is Bryn. Sure, I may be rubbish at science and exams but I am good at English and writing stories, IT and cooking. Bryn is good at art and science and he could be good at maths if he ever put his mind to it.

Please do not hate me because I am autistic or have NLD. I am very special because of it.

Every moment is exhausting, wonderful, crazy and precious

We adopted Callum, a three-year-old boy who suffered a serious brain injury at four months old and now has complex additional needs.

After several miscarriages, I couldn't face continuing to try again. I had always been interested in adoption, but my husband had been less keen. When we arrived at First Thursday, a monthly adoption agency open evening event for those wishing to enquire about adoption, I didn't know what to expect and was pretty apprehensive. My husband can be fairly shy and certainly would feel awkward in a situation like this.

We needn't have worried. I've rarely felt so welcomed, by everyone. Each member of staff made sure they came and said hello. They were warm but also sensitive to how we might be feeling. This has continued throughout the process, from phone calls to letters. Every attempt has been made to make the process less overwhelming.

Within ten months we were approved adopters and a few months later we had met our wonderful boy.

The matching process was challenging and a very emotional time. At the time the numbers of children who were being 'approved' for adoption had dropped by nearly 50 per cent, but there were still so many children waiting to be adopted. Lots of them had additional needs, and most adopters, including ourselves, decided that their needs were just too great. However, I felt constantly drawn to these children who would wait and wait for forever homes. I would read their short descriptions and try and convince my husband, who is the cautious one in the relationship, to at least read their profiles.

We had attended several activity days and profile events without success when our social worker suggested we go to an activity day for children with additional needs. The idea being that meeting these children would give us a much better idea of the practicalities and see beyond their often overwhelming profiles that can prevent you from finding out more. That is certainly what happened! Within minutes my husband and I had completely fallen in love with our son. Yes, we had to make sure we could manage his needs and find out a lot more, but having met and played with him in person made it easier to imagine him in our lives.

When we rang our social worker to express our (rather strong!) interest, she got straight into arranging opportunities for us to meet with the various health professionals involved in our boy's life. This was vital to help us make a considered decision. Every effort was made to ensure we knew as much as we could about our son's health needs. It was very important to our agency that we weren't rushing into anything blindly. There were additional meetings to ensure we weren't making the decision without thinking it through but also lots of offered support. From pairing us with adoption buddies who had adopted children with additional needs to support groups and websites, our agency advocated for financial help for us and insisted that the health professionals involved started work on the transfers.

Since our boy has been placed with us, the support has felt like a steady stream. When we have asked for support for the smallest thing, our agency have made it their mission to provide the advice or point us in the right direction.

Callum's brain injury resulted in a visual impairment. We can't tell quite what he can see: it's more that the neurological pathway to the brain is damaged and he can't interpret what he sees. He has a squint in one eye and poor peripheral vision with lower field vision definitely a problem, which means he trips over things left on the floor. He has sensory processing disorder and global developmental delay. He walked at two and a half and is beginning to talk now at nearly four years old. He is just beginning to put two words together.

He is displaying some autistic and ADHD features, although he shows himself as quite socially aware. His behaviour can be quite challenging with head banging, pinching and biting and repetitive screams to get attention. He has quite a lot of specialist equipment.

He did charm us with his smile and laugh, which is incredibly infectious. Also the way he interacted with his foster carer and social worker and ourselves. I have had a very challenging morning with him; however, I can say in all honesty he is very affectionate and just delicious!

We have our family and every moment is exhausting, wonderful, crazy and precious.

I'm so proud of how far both our little ladies have come

At the beginning of June 2016 my husband and I receive word that our adoption orders had been granted. It has only been nine months and one day since we came home with our two beautiful little ladies and it feels odd. Odd because nothing has changed – we were already a family – and yet simultaneously everything has changed. We are waiting for our celebration day and all the official paperwork so we can start to legally change everything at school, at the hospital, the bank, the dentist. It's a long list

really. Especially when your daughter has additional needs, a rare chromosome disorder that requires specialists in a variety of fields. She is amazing; over the last ten months since we met her, she has surpassed everyone's predictions for her and continues to thrive.

I'm so proud of how far both our little ladies have come. Especially our eldest. From the shy rage machine that would kick and punch and scream with a smile that never reached the eyes. She now has less frequent meltdowns that result in massive heartfelt sobs as she tries to find the balance between no rules, too many rules and finally a home where she can just be five, where the love is unconditional. She now has big belly laughs where her face creases up in a smile as she screams in delight. I know there are families out there that haven't got to this stage, families that might never get to this stage. We were lucky and we have worked very hard with our girls to give them their sense of identity and self-confidence. I thought child-on-parent violence was something other people would have, not us. I thought it would be easy not to sweat the small stuff.

Only yesterday I was chatting with our social worker on the phone and I used a film analogy for adoption that she said was very accurate. I likened it to going through the process believing you are going to get the Disney version of adoption and then finding out you've got Tim Burton's *Nightmare Before Christmas* version. It's not all bright colours, singing and loveliness, but it's a pretty awesome adventure with lots of interesting characters and well worth seeing it through to the end!

It's been quite quick really from start to finish, though at the time it seems to take forever. I remember how it felt and now I look back it's like it went in the blink of an eye. We had setback after setback the whole way through, including when we finally got a hearing date for the adoption order, but it is more than worth it in the end.

Chapter 7

ADOPTING AN EMOTIONALLY, PHYSICALLY OR SEXUALLY ABUSED CHILD

A recent survey by the NSPCC revealed that one in five children has experienced serious physical or sexual abuse or severe physical or emotional neglect at some point in their short lives.[1]

These are the children for whom your nightmares have been a reality. The horror of what has happened to them will probably haunt them in some way for the rest of their lives, however much care and love their adoptive and foster carers give them.

They are the innocent victims of evil behaviour. Their past is often so deeply buried in their subconscious that they don't understand why certain everyday events, sounds and words can trigger panic and make them shiver with fear. One foster mother of an abused child recounted how her child screamed every time she turned on the Hoover.

Though desperately in need of understanding, appropriate love and care, abused children often find it hard to accept love and respond appropriately to it. Those who were supposed to love them most and teach them how to love were also those who abused them.

'Caring for children who have been sexually abused can be a daunting task for the most committed carer. Because of their horrendous previous experiences some of their behaviour can be so

---

1   NSPCC (2016) 'Domestic abuse facts and statistics.' Available at https://www. nspcc.org.uk/preventing-abuse/child-abuse-and-neglect/domestic-abuse/domestic-abuse-facts-statistics, accessed on 5 October 2016.

extreme that placement can disrupt at an almost alarming rate,' said the director of a residential project caring for grossly sexually abused children. Mistrust of almost everyone, a need to feel in control and an eerie watchfulness can dominate their behaviour.

These children need very careful handling. House rules must be clear, but care intuitive. An old-fashioned bear hug from dad is probably off the agenda permanently. 'They have to be shown how to love appropriately and to understand what love is,' said one seasoned adopter.

Many adopters take on an emotionally, sexually or physically abused child without realizing the depths of what they have been through. Social workers often don't know the full horror of what they have been through. It's like a time bomb waiting to go off. And at an unlikely moment, perhaps when a child is suddenly feeling secure, the horrifying truth of their past comes tumbling out.

There is no universal remedy. Some need to regress to their earliest childhood days which passed them by in a blur of abuse; others don't. A combination of personal traits and circumstances makes each child unique in his or her ability to cope and come to terms with their past. However, recent research published in the *Journal for Abnormal Psychology* shows that even the most resilient child will remain vulnerable throughout their lives if they were severely abused as a child, even if they are taken out of their problematic environment and raised in a loving, caring family.[2]

A lot of support and understanding for the child and for the adopter is needed. Adopters of these children need counselling for themselves as they try to come to terms with the terrible truth of their child's past.

To adopt an abused child, a family needs a double dose of emotional strength and determination. But the rewards are enormous. One adopter of an abused child who was 'frozen' (she flinched if anyone touched her and she touched no one) remembers the sudden breakthrough. 'Something had really upset me and I was standing in the kitchen shedding a few tears when she came up to me, quite spontaneously, and put her arms around me and she gave me a cuddle. I knew then that we would win.'

---

2   J.B. Kaplow and C.S. Widom (2007) 'Age of onset of child maltreatment predicts long-term mental health outcomes.' *Journal of Abnormal Psychology*, *116*(1), 176–187.

No regrets

I do not regret adopting Robbie. OK, it hasn't quite turned out the way I hoped it might, but he's my son. Some people have children with disabilities, or children who suffer from terrible illnesses. We have a child full of trauma. But also a child who's capable of loving, most importantly, and many other wonderful things. I love him more than words could ever communicate.

We have a lot of work ahead of us. But it'll all be worth it if Robbie learns to make and keep friends, is able to hold a job (I frankly don't mind if he gets a PhD or stacks shelves in a supermarket as long as he's happy), manages and keeps a relationship that is not abusive and eventually has children who won't get hurt, therefore breaking the circle of violence that's been going through his family for generations. For that he'll have to learn to trust others, to love himself and let go of the past. We'll be there for him as long as he allows us to. We're not giving up.

Keeping watch

When Jane's daughter Louise was struggling at school with a new teacher who had no idea of her abusive background, Jane wrote the teacher a letter from the viewpoint of her daughter. This is an extract.

I can't remember much but I do remember I had an older brother and sister. They played with me and I miss them. Don't know what happened to them? Are they OK? Are they dead? Are they still with Mum? Maybe they weren't bad like me?

There was shouting, I don't like loud noise. It means hurt is going to happen. I don't like it, but I don't realize that it's not supposed to happen. I'm often hungry, sometimes we children are left alone. The neighbours called social services once. They told Mum and Dad things had to be different. Nothing really changed.

Mum had another baby, a little girl. Does that mean I am not Dad's princess anymore? Will he touch her now instead of me? Shouting, hurting, touching, hurting.

We all go to visit my granddad, Dad says he's taking me and my little brother to the shop for sweets. We drive a long, long way. There is no shop. From now on there is no mum. That was the last time I ever saw her. From now on there are no older brother and sister. That was the last time I ever saw them. What about my baby sister? ...

I am four years old. I think I am bad inside but I don't tell anyone. Now things are different. I really am Daddy's little princess. I don't have to go to nursery, I stay with Dad, we watch programmes together, we sleep together. He seems to like it when I dance for him. He smiles and holds me. I need to make sure to keep him happy because otherwise he might go too.

Sometimes we are hungry and cold but we have worked out how to climb out the window and ask the neighbours for food. Sometimes the way my dad shows me I'm special hurts me inside, underneath. I go to hospital a few times because I have pain underneath and when I wee. I don't tell about what Dad does.

Dad brought my little sister back today. Where was she? She is funny! She sleeps with the dogs sometimes, she likes that. She's not Dad's special little princess like me.

Last night a lady got us out of bed and put us in her car. She was kind, she gave us blankets. She had yellow hair. I didn't know then that I would never see my dad again. Now I know I had stuff, my toys, not many but they were mine, my clothes, they may be dirty and not fit well but they were mine, my bed, my house, my dogs, my dad... All gone forever... I decide from now on I don't want stuff, what's the point?

They take me to a house with other children but they don't leave our little sister with us. Now I've lost her too. Once Mum finds out she'll get us, won't she? I scream, I cry. Nice people, nice to us, only because they don't know yet that I am bad. I watch their faces waiting... Waiting for them to see I'm bad... Waiting for them to shout and hurt... I try to make the grown-up man (foster dad they say) like me, maybe I can be his special princess? I don't mind if it hurts a bit... But he looks worried and cross when I dance for him or try to touch him... I don't understand... I must be really bad...

But I have learned to watch. I watch all the time.

There is so much food. A few times I have eaten till I was actually sick. I try my best to learn things like reading and stuff but I can't really because watching keeps me very busy, and I have learnt that watching is the most important thing. I watch faces so that I can work out if I am doing OK and they will let me stay, I watch conversations so that I won't get any nasty surprises, I will know before the car comes to get me, I watch for the day when the hitting starts, I watch the food, I don't want to be hungry again. I watch, I watch, watch, watch... I watch for my dad to come and get me.

My teacher doesn't know about me, I think my teacher knows I am bad and might tell my mum. She thinks that it's kind to pretend I am just like everyone else. I may appear that way to her but that's because I am trying hard to. She likes the pretend me, this makes me sure that the real me is bad. She doesn't get that I am different, different because, as I said before, I know stuff, stuff about hurting, stuff about losing, and stuff, a lot of stuff, about watching.

It's because I love you

My son Ben is an emotionally vulnerable child and would like to be spoilt. He wants the best and latest mobile phone. He wants the latest Xbox. He wants the freedom to go to the street corner and 'hang out' with his mates. He wants the freedom to come and go as he pleases.

However, because we don't allow it we are mean parents. We are too hard. We are the strictest parents in class because we treat him like the much younger child he really is emotionally. We do not let him roam the streets like some of his peers. We do not even let him walk into town to buy a magazine.

I know my son has suffered terrible hardships so I would love to indulge him. I often feel that my son has this desperate desire for things and for love that will never be satisfied. He seems to carry around a black hole, and however much love or however many things I give him, it will all just be swallowed whole. It doesn't even touch the sides. This has made me realize that just loving him isn't enough. He really does need structure as well as nurture.

The fights over freedom and responsibility are the hardest. He is a good actor and even his head teacher has said, 'He can look after himself.' Unfortunately, he thinks he is able to cope too. Well, we know him better and we know he is very vulnerable child. He just hides it well, sometimes very well. But all the major issues we have had at school have been at playtime – basically unstructured time.

He finds it difficult to understand social situations, to regulate and to control himself, yet he desperately needs to control everyone else.

Sending Ben out to play on a street corner for ten minutes would be crazy, let alone for an hour. We tell him he will be able to one day but he is not strong enough yet. We have given him golden rules for when he is out in social situations like: don't try to take control and if anyone gets upset let them have time out (including himself). We also tell him if he feels upset or angry to just come and find us and hold our hand until we are ready to give him our full attention. He is now brilliant at coping with this. So we do see light at the end of the tunnel.

How old?

A couple of weeks ago our nine-year-old adopted daughter Lily was in the middle of a fairly run-of-the-mill tantrum when my husband (feeling exasperated) said to her, 'How old are you?' I replied, 'She's three at the moment,' as I led her firmly to the sofa for some 'time in' with me (as opposed to 'time out' when a child is left on their own).

This set me to thinking about all the behaviours our children exhibit that are utterly confusing given their chronological age but which can give us an insight into their developmental age, or at least give us a clue about what developmental stage they might be lacking.

Many adoptive parents complain of crazy lies and incredible stories. One of the problems is that when an older child is doing this, because they are at the wrong developmental stage, adults think they must be telling the truth. My daughter told her teacher that I was going to adopt a new baby called Lil and showed her a photo she had got from the internet and gave her a whole image history. Her teacher was astounded when she congratulated me and I revealed it to be a fabrication. I reminded her that, although she is nearly ten, developmentally and intellectually my daughter is pre-cognitive (has not developed reasoning skills) and is simply displaying normal traits for her developmental age. Although the school knew this, they had not considered its social and emotional impact.

Fact or fiction can be very blurred for children at this stage as they believe what they see in a very literal sense. For example, having watched her favourite Disney film, my daughter said how she likes Labrador puppies. I agreed with her before saying gently that she did know that they cannot really talk, didn't she? 'Oh yes,' she said. Then added, 'But those ones can!'

Her logical thinking function has not yet developed, even though at nine you would expect this to have happened.

Learning to regulate my child

From the moment my son Charlie started school he found it difficult to stay out of trouble. Looking back, I believe it was his inability to self-regulate his emotions that led to the kind of behaviour and outbursts which don't go down well in a classroom environment. His overreactions could disrupt a whole lesson, classroom and on occasion the whole school.

I can remember one day going into the cloakroom with him to try to help him deal with the transition from home to class without incident. As I looked on, my XL son had accidentally knocked two XS girls out of the way and taken off his coat in such a way that his arm clipped another child around the head. Said child then ran off complaining my son had hit him. This all happened in the space of 15 seconds. I despaired for the rest of his day and how these innocent-enough actions could escalate from him feeling misjudged and angry to all-out rages. There is not a malicious bone in his body, yet he always seemed to be upsetting someone or getting upset himself.

Since those early, bewildering days, I've done lots of reading and attended training events trying to decipher the messages contained in my son's behaviour. One central factor stemming from his early losses, neglect and abuse was the missed opportunity to learn how to self-regulate himself. This is something we all learn to do and are shown by an attentive and responsive carer, usually Mum! When you've missed this nurturing part of babyhood, it can take some time to learn how to deal with feelings and needs that overwhelm you. In fact, it explained so much about why my son felt it was the end of the world if he was told he might have to wait to do something.

When you are able to regulate yourself, much of it takes place without you even knowing. For example, our brains are continually assessing our body's needs, setting off a stress alarm when it senses something is wrong such as low blood sugar, a need for a drink or a threat that needs you to move away. When we eat a sugary snack, reach for a glass of water or run away from danger, we are in effect self-regulating. Our self-regulation matures as we grow, but if as a young child you were not helped to self-regulate, you don't learn how to cope with stressful situations.

In a healthy mother–baby relationship, a child's cries signal that they are thirsty or hungry. They are met by a responsive adult attuned to meet their needs. This cycle happens over and over many thousands of times, helping to move the child from external regulation to self-regulation. Child psychiatrist Dr Bruce Perry says, 'When a child's capacity for self-regulation does not develop normally, he will be at risk of many problems – from persistent tantrums to impulsive behaviours to difficulty regulating sleep and diet.'

I learned quickly not to make a promise unless I could keep it. Unfortunately, as you know, this doesn't always happen in the wider world when we are let down by others. The ensuing tantrums were difficult to deal with and seemed like a ridiculous overreaction to outsiders.

You have probably heard therapists recommend 'time in' for children who have experienced early abuse and neglect. This again is closely linked with the child's lack of self-regulatory skills. A time out may be good for a child who has grown up in one safe, secure and consistent home. A time out for a child who has experienced moves and feels unsafe and insecure and cannot regulate their reaction can result in all kinds of feelings of rejection and abandonment.

The few occasions I sent my son to his room, he took it as a chance not to calm down but as a chance to destroy his toys, write on the walls or bang his head on the wall. He had no idea how to deal with the big feelings inside him.

By keeping a child close, you are able to transmit your calm – of course, you do have to be calm in order to achieve that, which can be easier said than done.

Modelling how you want your child to behave and giving them the right words when they might be struggling to express themselves or using words that you wouldn't expect to hear before the TV watershed is helpful. Now that my son is quite a lot older, I still find myself trying to help him out. Over the years his inability to cope with stress has led him into trouble and making poor decisions. He still has problems with his emotions and impulses and he can still react angrily, but I know now he will calm down and we can reflect on what happened and on his response. Within ten minutes, we might be laughing together about what just happened. The change in our conversations is amazing if he feels he is being listened to and sympathized with. My advice to new parents, or some not so new, is to practise keeping yourself calm. As the much-quoted saying goes – keep calm and carry on!

Saying it through poetry

During his teenage years Ruairi was pretty haunted by his early life with his birth family. He had nightmares of what had happened to him and his younger sister. He had 18 moves of house before he was three years old and witnessed domestic violence.

It was during those teenage years that Ruairi wrote poems to help himself to deal with his feelings. Each poems focuses on a photograph included in his and his sister's shared life story book – one which offers no commentary but whose illustrations do not hide the neglect and sadness undergone by the children. He put the poems in the form of a downloadable book to raise funds to help him through university.

Ruairi's story is one of success. It travels along a winding road with hold-ups and potholes, but which gets there in the end. But most of all it illustrates the resilience of some children who are able to overcome their bad beginnings.

This poem relates to a photo which shows Ruairi and his sister (11 months younger) with their birth mother. They look ready to go out, dressed in coats, and his sister is in a baby buggy. All are looking at the camera, but only Ruairi is trying to smile. His sister looks unhappy and anxious. Ruairi remembers the buggy because they would hide under it when his parents were fighting.

THE BUGGY

I don't know if this is true
The memory is old and corrupted by time
But I think some of it must stand
The buggy, a safe haven for a child
To sit, waited on hand and foot by the family that surround them
Your mobile fortress protecting you from the world around
I sometimes found myself seeking comfort, protection and reassurance
From its cheap frame
I slipped in under it, my sister by my side
This was my bunker
This was my last defence against
The cries, cawing, curses, barks and wails
Here we could be hidden
Protected
Letting her take the beating for three
Listening to each undignified crack, thump, echoing scream
Both male and female
And after the battle had ended we crawled out
Re-entering the war
Taking in the wounded world that surrounded us after the fight.

My beautiful son

Adoptive mum Clara looks back at how life has changed for her son Caydon over eight years.

Caydon doesn't know where his name came from or why it was chosen. He doesn't know the colour of his birth mother's eyes or what country his father comes from. He doesn't know why his mother hurt him so much and forgot to feed him, leaving him in his cot, sore, hungry – his only comfort coming from his own gentle rocking motion. He didn't understand why she disappeared when he was 18 months of age and why new people looked after him.

He doesn't know why this house was always full of people, children and babies coming and disappearing, people in suits having meetings.

He didn't know why he had to go and live with another woman (me), leaving behind everything familiar. He didn't understand why he wanted to love this new lady so much but he hit her when she came close and screamed when she walked away.

He didn't know why he hurt so much inside that he wanted to kill himself and hurt himself by punching his forehead and banging his head against a wall. He couldn't understand why the other kids at school were scared of him or why the teachers called him naughty – couldn't they see it was an accident when he knocked over his friend he was trying to hug?

He was only four and he didn't understand why he was terrified that this new mum would not want him anymore. So please don't ask him why.

A lot of what he does and feels come from feelings held deep inside. Ask yourself why does the smell of chips on the seafront make you think of certain things or the feel of Fuzzy Felt take you instantly back to your childhood? These are feelings held in your body that you have no control over. Feelings are evoked for all of us by certain smells, sounds, textures. For most of us they are nice, comforting feelings of childhood or happy holidays. But not for everyone.

If most of those feelings were of being terrified, out of control, scared, hungry, lonely, wouldn't we be overreacting and appear to others to be acting irrationally? If all we can do as parents and teachers is to demand that this girl or boy must do their homework, must clean up their room, must go and sit on the naughty step, then we are missing the point. If a child has suffered months or years of abuse and neglect, we must all try to get them to really feel and believe that life is now safe, to know that when you are out of sight you are not gone forever. To know that you won't shout at them because you know that for them it feels like the end of the world and to know that you are not going to turn out to be as abusive as the last mummy.

Over the years Caydon has had a lot to learn and a lot to try to understand. He has done brilliantly. For him to be able to read and write as well as he does when he couldn't speak at the age of four because of neglect shows he is bright. The holes in his brain which formed because of neglect he suffered as a baby – the time when your brain grows at its fastest – are slowly repairing though some will always remain. He has begun to develop a conscience and empathy and will try and help others less able than him – such as older people and small children.

I've managed to stand by him through all his ups and downs, his achievements and his falls. I love my son Caydon and he loves me and he is finally now able to show me this in so many ways. It has taken many years to get here, but for anyone who feels there is no light at the end of the tunnel, then at least know in my house there is now a light which is shining brightly. He has grown to be so caring, patient, insightful and loving that I have to keep pinching myself or touching wood. He has moved on from a life where he only felt safe if he lashed out at everyone or ran away, where he destroyed his things and threatened to hurt himself, to a completely new way of being, feeling, behaving.

Today he comes home from school, goes off to do his newspaper round, asks Mum for a hug and agrees to come home at a certain time – and then does! No doubt there are more trials and tribulations to come in the future – not the least of which may crop up when contact and searching start to take up his thoughts. But for now he is doing what I always dreamed and that is being an ordinary teenager who is going out and enjoying his life.

Chapter 8

GOING IT ALONE

Most agencies now realize that single adopters are a very important and special resource with a lot to offer children who are often described as hard to place – but, as one adopter has said, 'hard to place' doesn't always mean hard to parent.

It is still the case that single adopters can find it takes longer to be taken on by a local authority or adoption charity and can even then find they are quietly discriminated against in favour of a couple. And it is still true that most single adopters will be encouraged to adopt children who have a physical or mental disability, a child with a particularly traumatic past who needs to be in a one-to-one family or an older child – but not always. It is also true that single adopters have amazing success stories to tell.

It is no more likely that a single adopter will crack under the unforeseen challenges that adoption throws up than any other adopter.

One single adopter highlights the special qualities a single adopter offers:

- self-reliance – decisions are more easily made because they are yours and your alone

- time – to focus on the demands of a child and give them the one-to-one care they will crave.

Single adopters are often more likely to put into place a strong support network of friends and family to help out and will not be tempted to rely solely on a partner. They have the advantage of making all the final decisions, whether on finance, schooling or indulging their adoptive child in whatever they feel is necessary – whether that is extra therapy, dance classes or commitment to a football team.

The downside as a single adopter is that you are on your own juggling time and money and dealing with the almost inevitable emotional traumas thrown up by your adoptee. You need a sounding board, not just from another adopter but someone in the same position as you. Adoption UK has set up a special discussion forum for single adopters and other networking sites have been set up such as www.singleadoptersnetwork.com.

If the decision to adopt is a breathtaking one for couples, the decision for single adopters is even more so, says another adopter. 'You are bound to have the feeling of jumping into the unknown and wonder if it is the right thing to do. You need to ask yourself the following questions – and you need to be able to give a definite "yes" to all of them:

- Do I have space in life right now?

- Do I cope well with lifestyle changes and increased responsibility?

- Am I a calm sort of person?

- Have I got a strong support network?

- Imagine life in ten years' time. Will you feel better having been through this life-changing journey with all the good and bad experiences it might bring?'

There's no good cop, bad cop – just tired cop

Elizabeth was 37 when she adopted her four-year-old son, Tim. Here she describes the ups and downs of becoming a single adopter.

Being a single parent has its pluses and minuses. After ten years, I have probably gone through most of them. However, the first big plus is that the decision to adopt is yours and yours alone. You don't have to get a partner to agree to commit to such a life-changing decision, which, after all, is not for everyone. You just have to convince yourself that it is the right way forward for you and that you are committed to becoming a lone parent.

I'm not sure when I embarked on the path to adoption that I realized just what an exhausting job being a single parent is. When you adopt alone, the day-to-day, hour-by-hour, minute-by-minute decisions are down to you. The juggling of work, play, housework and discipline is yours to keep up in the air. There's no good cop, bad cop…in my case, it was just tired cop!

Don't underestimate the tiredness when you go from looking after yourself and maybe a pet or two, to caring for a full-on toddler. After two weeks of introductions more than 100 miles from home, my four-year-old live-wire son came home permanently.

He was always on the go. Dancing, singing from early morning until his one last 'Watch me, Mum' as he got out of bed and spun around in a circle before finally collapsing into sleep. His initial shy attempts to wake me in the morning soon gave way to full-on assaults on my bed and my sleeping form as he gained confidence. Our days and evenings became filled with walks, days out, sports activities and clubs as I tried to soak up his endless energy. It was everything I had hoped it would be. My son skipping alongside me, holding my hand as we became a tightly knit unit of two.

My respite came in the form of a couple of hours at a nursery three mornings per week, and catching 40 winks during a Disney film, which had captured his attention. Then my brother stepped in and once a week he started taking my son on long bike rides and walks with his dogs. It was bliss knowing he was having a lovely time and I didn't need to feel guilty as I stretched out on the sofa!

With children, you are not allowed personal space, especially when the child is sensitive to any sign that might be taken as a rejection or abandonment. Having someone watching as you go to the loo, panicking if you've stepped outside to hang some washing up and talking very loudly when you try to make a phone call can be difficult to adapt to. However, it is something you have to do. This needy young person needs to know where you are, what you are doing and why you are not watching what they are doing and responding with huge enthusiasm.

I found it very sad during swimming lessons that as all the children practised swimming a width of the pool, only one little boy had his face turned to the parents' area, desperate to check that I was still there encouraging him on.

As the months and years passed, I found I had to represent my son and his interests in front of social workers, school staff and other professionals as his additional needs became more apparent.

Thankfully, I've never had a problem talking to a room full of people, and it became easier when it was on behalf of my precious boy.

My work had to become part-time, but Disability Living Allowance helped to stop the gap. My career took a back seat as evenings were spent researching for places and people who may be able to offer therapeutic support, and in the day times I invariably had meetings with professionals, support groups or had an urgent call to get to school to help my 'unregulated' son to calm down again after yet another 'incident'.

It was a case of needs must as I found my son's needs went far beyond the usual parenting ones. If I'd known this at the outset, I may have changed my mind all those years previously, but once you fall in love with a child, there is no turning back.

Sadly, many of my friends had left the area where we live for one reason or another. Fortunately, only a year after my son arrived, the head teacher at his school told me of a couple who had adopted and would be in the playground that afternoon. I looked round for some new faces and soon worked out which among them looked most tired and bewildered! And that day I found a friend who has been such a rock and someone to sound off to without having to go through all the explanations that 'no, not all children do that!' I would look eagerly out for her each day in the playground and, with a sigh or a roll of the eyes, we both knew instantly what the other was feeling.

We've been friends for more than ten years and can share just about anything. We've had many escapades involving our sons and also empathized during really tough periods. We've tried to make sense of certain behaviours over coffee and admitted our darkest thoughts to each other over a glass of wine. The relief of having someone to confide in was and still is immense.

Being a single adopter is not for the faint-hearted. You need support from family and friends. Thankfully, while some people do fall by the wayside or move away, others come and move into their place as long as you remain open, honest and willing to accept them into your new and chaotic life.

Adopting is one of the most amazing things you can do with your life. I wanted to be that special someone to a child who didn't have anyone. I have achieved that, and despite rejections and a bumpy ride along the way, I'm still there and he knows that whatever has happened he has me, his mum.

From heartbreak to joy

About three years into the adoption process I started asking awkward questions. I had been told long ago that I was the top of the list in the authority I was adopting from, so how come there was no family for me?

During the initial stages of my adoption journey I had been introduced to the idea of a family; specifically, two little girls were mentioned time and again. I was drip-fed information and led to believe they would be my family soon. I wanted two children but I didn't care if they were black, white or green and I didn't have a preference for boys or girls. I just badly wanted to be a mummy.

After I was finally approved – and that is a whole other story – I had a visit from their social worker. She spent around two hours in my home and shared life story work of these girls and showed me their photograph. She let me fall in love with them – something I had tried very hard not to do. She looked around my home, talked to me endlessly about pets, which I cannot have because I own a flat that doesn't permit pets and also because I am allergic to most animals. And she left.

I waited. There were no other families being considered for these children. They just had to decide about me. Did I have the skills? Could I be their mummy? Two days later, two whole days…and you can guess how long those days were…she got in touch with my social worker. It was a no.

One of the reasons implied was that one of the little girls was a 'runner' and it wasn't felt that my first-storey flat was safe. There was a four-foot wall around my first-floor patio and my own garden space is securely fenced in. Family and friends had allowed their children to play there over the previous decade. My heart broke. My journey for now was over.

After a period of grief I got angry. What was wrong with my flat? Why wasn't I advised to move to a house? How did people in central London or other large cities adopt if flats aren't safe?

So three years in. No other signs of a family. Losing out repeatedly to other families where there was a daddy and a dog. Why approve me at all if I had no chance? Why bother including us single bods if the chance of a family is so slim?

So I started to get stroppy as I felt there was nothing left to lose. I had been passed from pillar to post and had had such a variety of social workers I probably couldn't recall them all. I complained and made weekly calls to managers and finally threw in the Ofsted word! I implied I must be being discriminated against and that I wanted something done about it *now*, not when they would tell me I had waited too long and was too old.

Things started to move. I was allocated a social worker who was a rock and stayed with me until I finally became a parent and my little one was finally legally mine. This social worker not only got my personality, but she knew my child and accepted that I would be a good parent for her. She's sleeping peacefully right now – my girl, not the social worker!

I wasn't meant to have those two girls. I know because my daughter is so right. There are so many tiny ways in which she is like me and we are very alike physically. I loved her from the first footage on film I saw of her – I imagine like a mother feeling the first flutter of a heartbeat. It has not been an easy ride; it will probably always be a journey with huge mountains in our way. But I do believe our bond will see us through.

I still seethe at the pain I was put through, but without it would I know this joy?

Finding Nemo

Whenever I am asked, 'Why did you want to adopt?' I honestly struggle for an answer: the reason is not always just black and white.

My name is Marlin. I am a single black female in my thirties, very settled in my career as a teacher, and I have loved having kids around for as long as I can remember. As a child, our family home was always filled with someone's kids whether they were relatives or not, so it really came as no surprise to anyone when I finally told them that I was going to adopt.

The process for me (like so many of us) was long and arduous – leaving me at times feeling frustrated for being too honest in my answers or completely elated that I had successfully jumped through another hoop. It took two years, 24 home studies and three cancelled panel dates before I was finally approved as an adopter. By this point, my hope of becoming a mummy was at an all-time low and I actually contemplated whether to put a halt to the proceedings.

Whilst at a friend's house for dinner, her husband turned to me and said, 'Marlin, you can't give up now! For you know the delay is because your little one just hasn't been born yet.' So I got back up, dusted myself off and got back in the driver's seat so to speak.

Over the next few months I busied myself with reading any profiles that came my way and sending out flyers to agencies. Then one day in October I got the Call. 'Hi, Marlin. Now I don't want you to get too excited, but Gill (head of the agency) has told me to contact you with regards to a little boy who she thinks is the perfect match for you.'

How can you not get excited on hearing something like that? Isn't this what I've been waiting for? So I tried to pay attention and stay in the real world as she told me a little about him before sending me his profile to read through.

I asked her not to send any photographs at this stage (I did not want my heart to rule my head). As I read the profile, I was drawn to a hand-written sheet put in by his foster carer. She gave a very intimate description of him, his little quirks and likes, and as I read it I just knew he was the one for me. When his social worker came to visit me, she brought photos of him. This was now three months after I was linked to him. I turned over the photos and a bolt of energy surged through my veins as I stared into the most gorgeous milky-drool face I had ever seen. He completely took my breath away.

Fast forward two months to the morning of introductions. Until this moment I'd been in a kind of drunken haze of emotions ranging from borderline hysteria to the quietness of an almost comatose state. Here I was outside the living-room door at his foster home, heart beating so loud I figured people could hear it, and on the other side was my boy, my son, practising his new-found art of crawling.

I spent the day in awe of him, yearning to cradle him, kiss him and hold him tight. By day three I was smitten. He came home a week later. That was almost three years ago and last month I took some time to just reflect on how much I absolutely adore and love him.

As I prepared to celebrate his third birthday, I was grinning and beaming with pride at my beautiful son because I know him. Do you understand that? I know him...his fears, his insecurities, the things that make him laugh and cry, and more importantly I knew exactly what he wanted for his birthday.

It hurts my heart that he will one day come to know of his difficult beginnings and learn of another family somewhere who he was once a part of – yet at the same time I am so excited to be able to recall memories for him that we have created together. Like when he completely covered himself in yoghurt or was admitted to hospital in the middle of the night or when he decided to lick his uncle's hairy chin out of curiosity or the time he brought his little guitar to church and proceeded to heckle the praise and worship team.

At the end of the day, being a parent, however you come by it, is no easy feat. There have been times when I've just wanted to stay under the covers and hide away, when I've worked myself crazy over the what ifs, when he has pressed all my buttons and I feel so angry I could burst.

Then this little bundle of joy, completely oblivious of the way he has filled up every corner of my heart, would hop into my lap and give me his 'bestest huggle' and the cutest grin ever, and the rest just falls away as I remember how much I love him and how richer my life is for having him in it.

There's nothing else like it and I wouldn't swap those moments for the world. I just simply smile back and say, 'Come on, Nemo, let's go find an adventure.'

Look after yourself

You will often hear adopters telling others to look after themselves. It's even more important for singlys, because, at the end of the day, no matter how good your support network is, ultimately it's down to you. I think it's really important that you have time for yourself and you can't count on getting that in the evenings.

I work three days a week. I'm writing this in between chivvying my son off to school. Now he's gone, I don't mind admitting I'm off back to bed for a couple of hours, then I'm off to the allotment, gym and lunch with the newspaper. All by myself. Quietly. No interruptions. Bliss. Sanity saving. I will then run round the supermarket and do the housework before he gets home from school so that I can spend the weekend focusing on him.

Bringing Starlet home

I was approved as an adopter for one child aged 3–7 and I brought six-year-old Starlet home over two years ago.

For me as a single adopter, practical issues were a big part of the adoption decision – I needed to ensure my child would be in school relatively quickly as I wouldn't have been able to afford full-time childcare. However, I have also never been bothered about the 'baby' stage and have never bought into the theory that getting them younger makes it easier or makes them more 'yours'. I know of adopters who have brought babies home almost from the hospital and still experienced the same issues faced by adopters taking on older children.

There are many advantages to an older child adoption. Starlet was very much able to verbalize how she was feeling and what she wanted; this helped with practical things such as eating, sleeping, illness, etc. in the early days when we were getting to know each other. We are also able to talk about her past and her emotions/life story which I think has helped with the bonding process. I knew so much about her before she arrived because social services had been involved since birth. So far there have been no nasty surprises. I knew she was relatively well adjusted at school, had friends, was popular with other children, was sociable and enjoyed adult company, could cope with holidays. All a huge advantage to me and my lifestyle, and all have proved to be true.

It's a brilliant match and I couldn't imagine a better one. She is a joy to care for about 80 per cent of the time and we have a lovely life. She can be extremely challenging; we have major meltdowns where she goes into free fall and can't control her emotional state – the flip side of being very able is being able to remember very much what it was like living with her birth family, but only with the benefit of rose-tinted glasses, so she sometimes struggles to see why she had to leave.

As a single adopter, don't be put off adopting an older child. It is a different but not less meaningful or less rewarding a decision to make.

I will always love you

It was a beautiful, sunny Saturday in late Spring: six weeks earlier, I had had Hannah, a one-year-old baby, placed with me for adoption (and me a lone parent!).

She came fully equipped with a range of problems. She was underweight, having developed feeding problems in foster care. She had fine motor skills difficulties, couldn't feed herself and had only just learned to sit up. She had a whole pod of siblings we had to meet regularly, living with different families. She also cried when I left the room for a single second but, in truth, I had really enjoyed the first few weeks of getting to know her.

However, that morning, something changed. Hannah was asleep when I woke up, so I popped to the loo. Her cot was by my bed, and coming back I looked at her as she started to wake. Something happened. Don't ask me why or how it happened but it did. I looked at her and became completely overwhelmed with the deepest feelings I had ever had about anybody or anything. I picked her up and for the next two days couldn't put her down.

To me she was perfect, everything about her was perfect. Her face, her eyes, her hair, her skin, her laugh, her clinginess, her secret little smile that only I could see. I'm sure she must have got a bit fed up with being held, stroked, stared at and cooed at by me for two days, but she didn't seem to object! I had fallen for my child. I thought I had loved her before then, and I did, but this was real, intense and unconditional love.

The funny thing is that this has not gone away. I still feel the same. She is four and a half now, can be a little so-and-so sometimes, and tries to boss me about, as do most four-year-olds, but is she gorgeous or what! Funny, exasperating, annoying, beautiful and wonderful.

The moral of the story is, if you expect to feel instant love for your child when you first see them, you may be disappointed. Birth mothers often take weeks to feel love for their child after a traumatic birth experience but some feel it straight away. There are no rules. It can happen at any time, and for some parents the moment never comes. But if it does, boy, you are in for a treat!

Keep an open mind

Like most of the adopters I've spoken to, I didn't set out to adopt an older child. I think it's because I had preconceptions about what older children might have been through and if I would be able to help them overcome those issues. I thought that the younger the child, the less trauma they'd have been through. I also thought the younger they were, the more he or she would seem like my own child.

But I also knew that babies would not be available so I set out for a child aged 18 months to about three or four years old. I thought I'd like at least a year with them before they went to school.

The adoption process could not have been simpler for me. In the second week of the prep group they showed us profiles of children in our area who were looking for families. I didn't know but they were the more 'difficult to place' children. I looked at about a dozen profiles and saw a picture of Daniel and knew instantly he was my son. I felt like there was a voice in my head saying, 'I'm your mum' – not in a mad way – that's just what I thought when I saw his picture. It was the strangest thing.

The interesting thing was that initially I thought I wanted a girl. I went on to look at lots of profiles of girls, just in the age range and certainly younger than Daniel, but I just didn't get the same reaction.

There was something about his face...his smile spoke to me. Then I read the profile and I had an overwhelming feeling I could give him what he needed. I spent a bit of time struggling as it was so different to the idea I had in my head. But once the feeling of becoming a parent was linked with a particular child, I couldn't move away from it. Daniel was a child that deserved to be loved.

Two weeks after I was approved as an adopter I was matched with Daniel. I became aware that there were a lot of advantages because Daniel had had contact with the professionals who understood his attachment and his needs. He'd had a long and good relationship with his social worker and had undergone play therapy, so everyone was able to give me lots of examples of how he would need to be parented and to assure me that he was looking to attach to a parent and was able to attach.

I know a lot of people in the same adoption preparation group as me, looking for younger children, had a much rockier ride because their children hadn't developed emotionally as much and there were a lot more unknowns about how they would attach.

Daniel had a lot of emotional issues which needed to be resolved, but it was very clear what they were. He was seven when he came to me in mid-2013. I'd no idea at the time how unusual it was for boys of his age to be adopted.

My advice to other prospective adopters would be: don't rule anything out. If I had remained too restricted in my search, I would never have seen the profile of my son and I would never have had such a reaction when I saw him.

There's a lot of emphasis on thinking things through and evaluating, but it's also important to have that emotional reaction to a child. We have an amazing relationship. Daniel's chatty, loving, funny, creative and great company.

The other thing that puts some prospective adopters off older children is that they want to experience parenting a baby and a toddler and a pre-school child. I believe I have experienced that with Daniel as he missed out on being parented at all those ages and was, emotionally, a lot younger than seven when he came to me. So just as I need to parent the nine-year-old he now is, he still also needs lots of soothing and cuddles, just like he would have done as a baby. We've also read some of the same books I'd have read a toddler, because they've been good for his emotional and social development, and we've played lots of games like hide and seek which have helped build the trust and attachment between us. So I don't feel like I've missed out at all.

One thing that stays with me about Daniel is that if I'd not picked him, his chances of being adopted were next to nothing. All of his other siblings had been adopted so he would have been the only one who wasn't adopted. There are children like Daniel all over the country where the eldest one is left on their own because of their age.

Chapter 9

SAME-SEX COUPLES

There has been a sea change in attitude towards lesbian and gay adopters in the adoption world in the last decade.

Fifteen years ago, lesbian and gay couples struggled to find an adoption agency that would assess them and then had to struggle again for selection. The 2005 Adoption and Children Act changed all that when it gave lesbian and gay couples the same rights as straight couples.

As a result, in the past ten years the number of children adopted annually by lesbian and gay couples has dramatically risen; there are now three times as many children being adopted by the lesbian and gay community. Social attitudes have also changed and social workers now generally recognize the special value of lesbian and gay adopters, significantly their 'openness to difference' which equips them for supporting a child with a sense of difference – something common to all adoptees.

One of the other major pluses is their empathy with anyone who has suffered wrongful rejection and their understanding of the social challenges faced by a member of any minority group. They also decide to adopt for very different reasons. For many gay and lesbian couples, adoption is a first choice as it enables couples to be equal partners in terms of their relationship to the child or children who become their forever family.

This is completely different to the majority of heterosexual couples who turn to adoption as a second choice after years of infertility treatment and who first need to come to terms with a personal sense of loss, a problem few lesbian and gay couples face.

A recent Cambridge University study looking at the effectiveness of parenting by different types of adopters studied 41 gay father families, 40 lesbian mother families and 49 heterosexual parent families with an adopted child aged 3–9 years. The children's teachers as well as the parents and the adoptee were interviewed. One of the most interesting findings was that the survey indicated more positive parental well-being and parenting in gay father families compared with heterosexual parent families. Gay couples generally were found to face fewer problems with their adopted children. 'Parenting stress, rather than family type were found to be predictive of child externalizing problems,' said the report, which was compiled under Professor Susan Golombok, director of the Family Research Centre at Cambridge University.[1]

But despite this positive research, lesbian and gay adopters do still face criticism by society at large. 'I know some people think we should not adopt,' said one gay father. 'Many also think that single people shouldn't be allowed to adopt either. In a perfect world I might agree with those who claim that a child would be best placed with a mum and a dad. But many birth children nowadays live with a single parent, or with permutations of mummies and daddies from relationship break-ups. The concept of family has evolved. Most importantly, in an ideal world there wouldn't be any children in care.'

Another adopter says that it is time for more effort to be put into countering homophobia in society. 'To give us the same rights and then not back that up with both literature and training, particularly in schools, is wrong,' said writer and adopter Carolyn Robertson, who has written two children's books for children of lesbian and gay families, *Two Dads* and *Two Mums and a Menagerie*.

Interestingly, she says that it is adoption that now defines her as a parent rather than being a lesbian:

> Adopters today of all types and genders face many problems that other parents cannot even begin to really understand. We are all caring for a child that has been rejected and often a child that has been deeply traumatized by his or her early life. There is little understanding in schools or the wider world of how emotionally complex these children are.
>
> Adoptees are already a misunderstood minority, my biggest concern is that by being the children of lesbian or gay parents,

---

1   S. Golombok (2015) *Modern Families: Parents and Children in New Family Forms.* Cambridge: Cambridge University Press.

they are further misunderstood, isolated and ostracized because of ongoing homophobia within society.

The government has legislated in favour of giving LGBT parents the same rights in adoption as heterosexual adopters. It does not make sense to do that and not to back it up with legislation against homophobia in schools and within society generally.

Lesbian and gay adopters have set up their own self-help membership organization, New Family Social, which hosts an annual Adoption and Fostering Week to encourage more LGBT couples to consider adoption. It involves more than 60 adoption agencies with events held all over the UK. Their online forum discusses everything from being taken on as an adopter to the challenges of adoption itself. But the discussions ultimately resolve around the same problems that all adopters face. 'Our children are all hurt and require the same therapeutic parenting to help them understand their feelings and behaviour,' said Carolyn.

We both love motherhood

My wife and I got together 11 years ago and entered into a civil partnership four years ago. We always wanted to have children. We came to the decision that adoption was the best option. We approached a local authority in the North East and New Family Social (an LGBT adoption and fostering support charity). We've had friends who've approached local authorities and not had a good response, but our local authority was great.

We both love motherhood, it's fantastic. Our son will make a wonderful big brother so we want to adopt again.

There are a lot of misconceptions. Some people think, 'Because you're gay you'll only be able to adopt someone who's disabled', which is rubbish.

We knew when we were going into adoption that some people might have preconceived ideas. We knew we would have to break down some barriers – some with social workers – but we found the whole thing was fine. At panel we felt discrimination but not because we were a lesbian couple – it was against my wife's disability.

We found that difficult as we were fielding some questions that we thought were offensive.

Making the right match? – trust your instincts

My partner and I embarked on our adoption journey nine years ago. We had never wanted a baby as, quite honestly, nappies and sleepless nights are not something that I cared to even think about.

We went through our preparation course and assessment continually referring to our daughter, and in our heads we had a vision of a blonde-haired, petite mouse coming to live with us. If you asked me her age, I would have told you that she was between three and six years old.

After panel the hunt for our family began. Our local authority did not have anyone they considered a match so, unusually for 2006, we were immediately placed on the adoption register and advised to register for *Children Who Wait* – which of course we did.

The first edition of *Children Who Wait* arrived, and the strangest thing happened. We did not find ourselves drawn to any child that could resemble our daughter. It was a worry, as there were a number of girls we thought fitted the bill. We made no enquiries from the first edition, or the second. We found ourselves drawn to sibling groups, and we had never considered siblings before.

When we received profiles of children or *Children Who Wait*, we read them separately, so that we didn't influence each other and could give each child our own amount of time. Writing it now, it sounds clinical; however, given that we were trying to make a decision that would affect us for the rest of our lives, we wanted to ensure we had a connection as individuals before discussing it as a couple.

After reading our third copy of *Children Who Wait*, when we got together there were three profiles we were interested in finding out more about. Top was a pair of brothers, who were seven and eight years old. Our social worker was due the same day, so we thought we would ask her for her opinion. We were in shock when she arrived with exactly the same list. None of the profiles we had chosen matched our original plan of having that little girl.

Gut instinct is a wonderful thing sometimes; there was something about the two older brothers that we fell in love with straight away.

We all decided that we should find out more. Our social worker was more hesitant, but eight weeks later those two boys were about to meet their new parents: us!

Looking back, I believe that our need to have a little girl was as a result of our experience with our niece and god-daughter, who we had cared for over certain periods of time, and it just seemed natural that we should continue in our own family with girls.

I honestly cannot answer what life would have been like if we had had a girl. What I do know, though, is that I am happy that we made the right decision. My boys were chronologically older when they came home to us; however, I was surprised by just how many kisses and cuddles we received, how much love they gave us, almost instantly. I never once thought that an older child would need or want that. I am so glad to have been proved wrong. Gut instinct is key...some adopters will end up with the families that they wanted from the beginning; however, it always surprises me how many people may not consider a child because of age, behaviours or even some disabilities. Every child deserves a secure future, and by enquiring it does not mean that child will become yours.

Nine years on, the profiles we read with anticipation and elements of fear around behaviours, special schools and age have vanished. We have coped better than we gave ourselves credit for, and we have two fantastic teenagers who are almost (but not quite) ready for elements of independence. We have had more good times than bad, and don't get me wrong, the bad has been bad, but we love those boys more now than ever, and I would not be the person I have become without them.

Happy Fathers' Day

Pablo and Mike found their children through Adoption UK's *Children Who Wait*. Author Pablo chronicled their experiences in his book *Becoming Dads*. After approval they were eventually matched with a six-year-old little boy, Charlie. One year into the adoption he writes:

It feels like Charlie has been with us forever, and sometimes it's hard to remember our lives without him. During the first few weeks Charlie tested a lot of boundaries as he learned to trust us. He came from a very violent background, and as he regressed, as most adopted children do, there were a lot of behaviours to 'unlearn'.

However, we are a family – it doesn't matter to us that we missed out on the first six years of his life. In fact, most days we almost 'forget' about it. It's not about the past, but about the present and the future. We need to be aware of his past to be able to accept and understand some of his behaviours, but on a day-to-day basis he is just Charlie our son.

Facing the critics

My name is Fernando and I'm a gay man. My partner and I were approved as adopters last April, 18 months after we first made inquiries with our local authority, and we are now waiting to find a suitable match.

I know some people think we should not adopt. Many also think that single people shouldn't be allowed to adopt either. In a perfect world I might agree with those who claim that a child would be best placed with a mum and a dad. But many birth children nowadays live with a single parent, or with permutations of mummies and daddies from relationship break-ups. The concept of family has evolved. Most importantly, in an ideal world there wouldn't be any children in care.

My partner and I knew we wanted to adopt a long time ago. One of the things we considered was that we weren't sure if it would be fair on the child. Should we bring them into an environment where they may get bullied because of having gay dads when they have had enough upset in their lives? To a certain extent we also wondered if we were the only gays in the village who wanted to adopt.

We made enquiries with our local authority and got into their preparation groups. We engaged with discussions in the Adoption UK online forums and started volunteering at a local school and Beavers group. Then we got in touch with New Family Social, a charity that organized social events for children adopted by same-sex couples and provides support for prospective same-sex adopters. We also read lots of publications on adoption in general and gay and lesbian adoption in particular.

One thing that became clear is that even if we are not the mum and dad some social workers would like, we are a better option than staying in the care system. Another is that there are many successful placements with same-sex couples and gay and lesbian individuals where children thrive at least as well as with other adopters.

Our social worker has been great. We believe she has always treated us as any couple who wants to adopt. Obviously, our being gay has been the subject of discussions to find out how we coped with homophobia and how we'd explain to a child about our circumstances and help them to cope with any abuse they may suffer because of it…

How would we teach our child to cope? Well, at the end of the day a child will be bullied because they have big ears, red hair or wear the wrong clothes. We think the best response will be honesty. We plan to be involved in our children's schools. There will be no secrecy or element of surprise to the children having gay fathers. At the end of the day, being matched with a child is only the beginning of the adoption process. We will need to cope with all the issues that adoption brings (attachment, school support, contact, dealing with trauma) as they arise and we've received a lot of preparation for it.

No one thinks you are a lesbian any more!

We are lesbians. Two years ago we adopted two children and have a two-mummy family! We are an all-female household, with the only bit of testosterone coming from our male cat and considering his 'little operation' in his early years that is not much to boast about.

So is it any different being lesbian adoptive parents? In some ways, no, not at all. The cross-over of discussion topics between the lesbian, gay and bisexual boards and the other online discussion boards is testimony to that. Our children are all hurt and require the same therapeutic parenting to help them understand their feelings and behaviour.

Most of the time we are confident and happy in our role as mummies and lesbian parents, and this is important for the children to know and see. We see it as vital that we answer all questions about our relationship honestly to demonstrate clearly to the children that we have nothing to be ashamed of or to hide; again, though, you need to be aware that some people do not find the idea of two lesbians being parents acceptable and don't want their children in our company.

As lesbian parents, the way that we parent our children and divide up the roles in the family are sometimes quite different from other couples. For example, we are both completely involved in the children's care. We are both lucky enough to work part-time and to divide this so that we are both at home an equal amount of time.

Both being at home equally has been the single most important factor in keeping our relationship and family going. Both knowing what it feels like to be at home with the children and deal with their needs, behaviours and hurts has been invaluable in allowing us to support and help each other. Both going out to work has given each of us a much-needed break, contact with other adults and an outlet outside of being a parent. Sometimes it's very affirming to realize that you do have talents and can do something right when your role as a mother and carer has been rejected so often at home.

We have only had two years in our new roles and have only just started out on this journey as a family. So far we have received nothing but support for our family and are confident that this will continue. It won't be easy, though, and we are prepared for those times when the children and our family will be ridiculed and the brunt of cruel taunts. For now, though, we will continue like all adoptive parents, loving our children and trying to help them make sense of their hurts.

But it's a sin, Miss

The biggest difference about being a same-sex adopter lies in the way society treats our types of families. Many of the children adopted by same-sex couples have been removed from unsafe (heterosexual) families where their physical and/or emotional welfare has been severely compromised. Many of our children have ongoing difficulties coping with the stresses these early relationships brought upon them; they have emotional and physical scars and some suffer from attachment disorder. In short, our children are vulnerable.

However, news channels, radio broadcasts, newspapers and magazines often show stories that reflect bigotry and hatred towards the LGBT community; this is deeply unsettling for our children. Stories pervade about queer-bashing and various religious groups are given air time to discuss their bigoted beliefs on how unsavoury same-sex couples are to them. Seeing images of 'Islamic State' throwing gay people from parapets sends our children into obvious panic.

Same-sex couples being able to adopt was an important piece of legislation that has begun to tackle the travesty of children being placed in and ultimately left in the care system. Studies are already showing that children of same-sex parents do not suffer as a result of being brought up by parents of the same-sex. In fact, early results seem to prove that children fare extremely well if not better than within heterosexual families. However, what they do suffer from is homophobic bullying, taunts and unchallenged asides that undermine the families they are in. The education system is already failing the children of LGBT adopters through its ineffectual treatment of endemic homophobia and failure to provide resources reflecting our types of families. This is especially true of faith schools.

So how has legislation protected these children within schools and colleges? What further acts of parliament have been introduced in order to help our children feel included, secure and supported? How have schools been encouraged to tackle the homophobic language that pervades in the playgrounds, classrooms and corridors? What resources do schools offer in order to reflect our types of families? The answer is pitifully little. Education is at the grass roots of homophobic bullying; it's where the majority of our children learn that their new families are part of a minority that is an easy, unchallenged target of ridicule.

Schools have been encouraged to implement successive anti-racist and multicultural policies which have done a great deal to lessen racism in society. Classroom resources such as early years picture books, fiction and non-fiction books, textbooks, posters, audio/video resources, etc. now reflect the diversity of cultures within our society. We celebrate black history month every October; our children share foods and customs; they visit mosques and temples and churches. Our children are encouraged to celebrate and accept difference. Such resources, no longer so white and Eurocentric, such experiences, have enabled the children of ethnic minorities to feel included, to feel valued and to feel respected.

When my adopted son first started school, I told the teachers that he was adopted and had two mums. That should have been enough really, enough for the school to be sourcing some books perhaps that would reflect our family background in some way or to lead circle time discussions on different types of families. It didn't. My son is beginning to realize that his family is very different from all the rest in his class because his is the only type of family that isn't being validated or reflected back at him.

I taught in a church school for 11 years. Was I able to teach about gay relationships? About marriage? Nope. The 'you're so gay' comments aimed at anyone in school who was deemed weak or ineffectual pervaded. I remember challenging such a comment made by a Year 5 child who made such a comment in order to insult a peer. When I reminded him about being tolerant and that there was nothing wrong with being gay and to stop using it as an insult, he responded, 'But it's a sin, Miss.'

Chapter 10

ADOPTING SIBLINGS

It might be daunting but it can sound like magic, an instant family: not one but two or three brothers and sisters looking for a forever family – together.

But these are the children that languish on adoption registers for the longest time and are thought of as particularly 'hard to place'. There is a mismatch of resources: just not enough families willing to take on a sibling group. The majority of prospective adoptive parents are childless families who, for very good reasons, opt to adopt just one child with the thought at the back of their minds that perhaps they might adopt a second if all goes well. It makes sense.

Social workers face a balancing act; they must make the difficult decision of whether to wait to find a family who will take a sibling group or split brothers and sisters up with the hope of finding them families faster. Beyond this they need to decide which option would most benefit each child. Views on the best practice fluctuate. The Adoption and Children Act 2002 refers to the desirability of placing siblings together. Indeed, not that long ago an adoption agency's success was often measured by its ability to find families for sibling groups. The benefits for all concerned were thought to be clear: the genetic link with a brother or sister would allow adoptees to feel better connected with a clear link to both their past and their future.

But today social workers are increasingly and more frequently asking themselves whether placing brothers and sisters in the same family is always the right answer. Opinions differ depending on the agency, the adoption panel, the family in question and the individual social worker.

One family will report the extraordinary and important bond that exists between brothers (see *Celebrating siblings* below); another will tell you of the destructive – indeed toxic – relationship that exists between competing siblings (see *Lunch time* and *They are still our children*). There is no absolute right or wrong, as in all families each child is different and many will fight to assert their individuality and for the attention they perceive they need and indeed deserve.

Appearances can be deceptive. Some brothers and sisters may look as alike as peas in a pod but be temperamentally as different as night and day, despite having had the same start in life. Our uniqueness as individuals means that each child's long-term reaction to being taken into care and his or her ability to deal with early trauma of neglect and abuse are entirely different and not solely reliant on age or circumstance.

However, it is generally believed that siblings placed together have a stronger sense of who they are; they will feel less cut adrift by having a brother or sister with them with whom they have a shared history. 'Having each other made a big difference to the children,' said one adoptive father of four. Sometimes the bond with a birth sibling is vital. One mother of two brothers said:

> I was not prepared for how protective one sibling becomes of the other when there is a threat and this occurs even when it appears they do not have a strong relationship. It is almost innate, one minute they are cursing the day the other was born and yet as soon as there is a threat that all seems to diminish and this strong need to protect takes over.

But sometimes traumatized siblings are locked into a relationship with each other that is more likely to be destructive than supportive. 'They carry a collective memory of their past trauma. Through their ongoing interactions with each other they help to keep the ugly past alive,' said one seasoned foster parent and adopter. 'Primarily children need to bond to a loving adult in order to ever be able to deal with issues of trust, authority or real intimacy. A bond with an unhealthy sibling often stands in the way of the parent–child bond.'

'My view, taken from the relationships within our family, is that placing traumatized siblings is actually a very complex area... handling their interactions is, and always has been, incredibly complicated,' says another adoptive father of three siblings.

If the relationship is destructive, the angry behaviour of one child can pick away at and destroy the carefully built links an adopter is making with the other siblings in the group – as well as challenging their patience to the limit.

Another adopter advised, 'When choosing a group of siblings – be realistic. It is realistic to adopt one child with major difficulties but it is not realistic to meet the needs of four children with major difficulties. Your time has to be split with four children.'

The message is to read all information about each child within the group carefully and to ask questions forensically about their past and about their current behaviour. It's well worth doing because when it works it can be magic. As one mother said of her sons, 'These two little characters have transformed and enriched our lives beyond measure.'

Lunch time

Relationships within our family are a very complex area. Handling their interactions is, and always has been, incredibly complicated, not least because Jamie has a problem with regulating his emotions. He gets angry or excited and he can't bring himself down again. Take this as just one of numerous examples.

So, there I am in the kitchen, trying to be a good parent and rustle up something nutritious and delicious. This means leaving the kids in another room. All goes fine until I've reached a critical stage with the sauce and then I hear it: the tone is escalating. I whip the pan off the heat and rush through to the living room, but it's too late. Connor is crying on the sofa, Jamie is storming around the room and Gemma is shouting at them both because she's trying to watch a DVD.

I find that Jamie and Connor were horsing around together and Jamie couldn't keep it at a fun level. He got overexcited, did something daft and now Connor is injured. This is an oft-repeated scenario and I'm still at a loss as to how the experts would handle it. The advice for Jamie is, of course, time in. He's become dysregulated and needs an adult to help him to get his emotions back in check. In short, he needs a cuddle.

Unfortunately, Connor doesn't see it like that. His view is that Jamie jumped on him and hurt him, and there should be some sort of punishment: like most kids, he has a very highly developed sense of justice. To him, seeing his brother, who has just hurt him, getting a cuddle just isn't fair. And I can quite see his point.

There are, of course, a number of potential solutions. We could move house. If we picked one with an open-plan kitchen/living room, then I'd be able to keep an eye on things better and stop things escalating. Unfortunately, that's not practical for us. I could keep Jamie in the kitchen with me as I cook. Again, a great idea, but he objects vociferously. He wants to be with his siblings, and trying to cook with a stressed and angry young lad could be dangerous.

I could try to send them all to their rooms every time I cook a meal. That has certain attractions to me, but not to them. They find isolation very difficult to handle and so it would result in huge levels of stress for everyone.

Or we could stop cooking. We could live on sandwiches, salad and cereal for the rest of our lives. Gemma, who turns her nose up at almost all cooked food apart from fried eggs, would love the sandwiches and cereals, but somehow I think I would have trouble explaining it to the social workers.

Yoghurt, milk and a seven-seater car

We saw our kids in *Be My Parent*. The day before the profile arrived I had been thinking if there is one phrase I would use to describe the children we were looking for, it would be that I just would love kids who are interested in the world around them. That exact phrase was used to describe Sophie in the documents that arrived the next day! The more we read, the more we were sure they were right for us – all four of them!

At the time, our children were aged two, four, six and seven. The first day we met them for just an hour in a play centre. That was when it really struck me that four little people I didn't know were going to be coming into our lives. Before you meet the children, you read about them and see pictures and have an idea in your head of what they will be like, but really you don't know at all.

Visits built up over a week and then my husband drove home with all their things and I came up on the train with the kids, the foster carer and her daughter. The children had lived with her for 18 months so she was a significant part of their lives. She came to the house and settled them into their rooms and then we took her to a hotel. It was lovely to see them run into the rooms and say this is our room, this is our playroom – they had seen the photographs and it had helped them to picture everything. We had already been given lots of toys and clothes, and they brought some with them so their playroom was full.

In those early days we got amazing support from family and friends who gave us beds, toys, etc. People apologized for offering us second-hand things but with a large sibling group it is great. It is like a birthday for the children when we get a bag of clothes or toys. The local authority were also amazing and gave us substantial financial support, including an upfront grant for a seven-seater car and things we would need for the kids. We felt uncomfortable asking for financial help because it wasn't why we were adopting, but our social worker reminded us that it was going to be a big change and the support would be of benefit to the children.

Having each other made a big difference to the children; the boys share a room and the girls do too, so they had that security to start with. There was a lot of changing of sheets in the night because two of them still wet the bed and the little one was still in nappies. I think everyone thought we were a bit mad but knew we were both very active and had done a lot of work with kids so they thought we would get through.

I always joke that the hardest thing about adopting at first was keeping enough milk and yoghurt in the fridge. Our social worker asked for help for us with cleaning and babysitting. The washing, cooking, cleaning, shopping takes longer to start with as you get into a routine and the kids explore boundaries in terms of how much mess they are allowed to make throughout the entire house. This all comes at the time when you need to be building the relationship with the kids. It was really helpful to be able to go for a walk in the woods with the kids rather than trying to keep on top of the housework. Eventually, it all becomes normal and you can fit in both.

They settled in quickly and there was a honeymoon period where they were on their best behaviour. Then they started challenging boundaries in different ways to see what was and wasn't allowed. We had read in books that it was important to be strict from the start as it actually helped them feel more secure. I would say this is definitely true. It is hard because you think they are so small and have been through so much. We knew one of the boys was likely to have emotional issues and these do come out in cycles – life can be quite settled and then we can have periods when things are quite difficult.

The main thing I would say when choosing a group of siblings is: be realistic. It is realistic to adopt one child with major difficulties, but it is not realistic to meet the needs of four children with major difficulties. Your time has to be split with four children. Having one with greater emotional difficulties and a couple with minor issues is probably about all that is realistic if you are going to remain sane.

What you also need to remember is one child with emotional difficulties does impact on the other children, so you may end up with more than one tantrum on your hands at once.

We met the birth parents during contact and we were glad we did so we had a realistic picture of what they were like – not just what we thought from the reports. The children get letters every six months from mum, dad and grandparents and they respond. They settled into school quickly – I think because they are all bright kids and school was a safe place for them where they got a lot of praise and encouragement.

So what is the best bit of having four children? You always have a full team for a game and your house will be full of laughter and fun. We would highly recommend it, but make sure you are realistic about the individual difficulties within the group and make sure you have friends or family around to keep you sane.

Celebrating siblings

Our three siblings, Aiden, Ella and Zoey, were adopted 14 years ago and are now 'adults' in the eyes of the law. However, two of them function in most areas at around age 12. Developmental delay is something that is not readily acknowledged and the gap doesn't close as the children grow older. Once they are past the magical age of 18, the world expects them to be grown-up. If they aren't – and it is only you that are aware of the 'problems' – you have to fight for a place in the unsophisticated Adult Learning Disabilities team.

Our eldest is doing quite well, finishing college this year with an NVQ3 which is already drawing job offers. However, school did none of the children any favours. The first fight for the two younger ones was for statements, initially 15 hours each then rising to

30 when they reached secondary. It didn't help their education. They were 'contained' and 'entertained'. Teachers didn't understand what 'differentiation' meant, even less the teaching assistants, who held their hands, told them off or compared them unfavourably with their own little dears who went to grammar school. SENCOs sucked their teeth and searched for 'labels' and, not finding any, stamped them 'EBD' (emotional and behavioural disordered) and shoved their files in the 'too difficult' tray. Head teachers put our names in their private 'Parents from Hell' register and the disinterested representatives from the local authority's special educational needs section grudgingly attended the Annual Review meetings.

Our choices of college were plainly limited. Their reading ages at the time were about nine. We found places eventually, almost 20 miles from home and that, of course, required transport to get them there. They still can't 'do' money, time, distance, and they are far from ready to travel independently. It was a shock that full-time education in the further education (FE) world is only two and a half days per week. This means we suddenly had two ebullient teenagers at home, both requiring supervision and stimulation. Thankfully, one of us is semi-retired and able to arrange safe work experience and other activities during what's left of each week.

But a parent pushing 70 is not who most teenagers want lurking around the swimming pool or where they're doing work experience, and it's impossible for one of us to give them the individual support they need to follow their individual interests. So we needed an assessment by the 'Adult Learning Disabilities Team' (ALDT), a shadowy branch of social services who I had never heard of. They trundled into our lives cautiously. Needless to say, nothing is easy and nothing happens quickly. The bureaucracy is mind-blowing, especially when you move on to applying for benefits. We are leading, we hope, to the time when with the ALDT's support (and funding) we can directly employ Personal Assistants (PA), someone to take them to activities and to ensure their safety and well-being. In the meantime, I have become their Registered Carer, along with being their dad, and a nice lady from Carers' Support phones once a month to see how I'm feeling.

Another concern was the third-party approaches we expected from the birth parents asking to re-establish contact. When the contact letter arrived shortly before their 18th birthdays, our eldest wanted nothing whatsoever to do with them and probably has the mental capacity to say that. Not so the younger ones. However, having explained their degree of delay to the charity that handles requests, the letter came to us instead and it leaves the responsibility to us to decide when to broach the subject. The papers remain under the bed.

So, is this a 'Celebrating Sibling Success Story'? It is as far as we're concerned. The three children were abused for four years; they had countless foster placements and were about to be split up when we adopted them. They are still together, they still love each other and they will be there for each other long after we turn up our toes. Do they love us? There is nothing to show that they don't love us. Do we love them? We do, unconditionally.

When being together isn't such a good idea

An adoptive mother of two describes how they have maintained contact with her children's three other siblings.

During the time of matching introductions I did believe the children could have been placed together, and as happy as I was to have my children, I also felt sad that they were being separated.

However, over the years, most of the children have had various problems surface (attachment, trauma, learning, etc.). When I look at the children now, I absolutely know they needed to be split up. No parents, even the best of the best, would be able to give each child all the love and attention they needed.

At the time of placement, the children were aged 12 months, two, three, four and five years old. The youngest was placed with a couple who already had one adopted daughter. The two- and three-year-olds were placed with us and the four- and five-year-olds were placed with another family, who had no other children. That was six years ago.

All this took place between the months of August and October; in December the families and children met for their first contact supported by social services.

The plan was to then have contact every February, June and October. However, during 2006 all children were invited to each other's birthday parties, meaning an additional four contacts. The following year followed the same pattern, and increased to include extra activities like swimming, general day trips, visits to each other's houses, etc. However, we always stick to our three 'official' contacts in February, June and October, and always do something extra special on those dates.

I feel all of the children benefit greatly from this contact. They know they are brothers and sisters, they know they 'came out of the same lady's tummy' and lived with their birth parents when they were younger. The biological link is one which is explained, re-explained and explained again – but I am sure that as they get older this will mean much more to them.

I feel that because they see each other so much there is no big build-up or emotional ending; they all feel very confident and secure in their relationships and the fact that they will see each other again – soon!

Myself and one of the other mums had a meeting with the social worker before we had even met our children (the third set of parents were only just in linking stages, so not able to come). During this meeting we decided on which months were best for contact and for how long this contact should be. We also discussed things like birthday and Christmas cards and presents – for example, were we comfortable to receive cards with 'brother' or 'sister' on? It was also a chance to meet the people who would be parents to our children's siblings, suss them out and try to get a picture of how things might be. It helped to be able to sit down in this quiet room and really have some thinking space to discuss how things would work after placement.

I do feel very proud of what we have achieved over the years, and we all feel very positive about it. I do feel this is something that could work for other families too, if the right training and ongoing support is provided. All too often we hear of children being separated from their siblings and being offered only letterbox contact, or once-a-year direct contact. I know our situation is fairly unique in the fact that our children had always lived together, that they were placed with three sets of parents who were very committed to contact, and that all families live within 20 miles of each other.

However, all sets of parents have said we would have fought to keep the contact going even if these circumstances had been different. I do feel that social services will spend months, if not years, searching for a family for large sibling groups, wasting precious time in the lives of these children. I believe a practical solution would be to separate the siblings earlier, depending on the families available, but with a plan for increased contact.

It's all about survival

We adopted three children, Sally, Sam and Grace, now aged 12, ten and eight, four years ago. The first year with three was incredibly hard – it was mostly about survival and trying to establish positive patterns. We did survive, just, but had I known just how hard it would be, I wouldn't have done it. If anyone asks, I wouldn't recommend taking three at once, but neither would I give them back now.

Things that have worked for us include making time for them as individuals. This has been one of the most worthwhile things, but it does require some imagination to make it work. We stagger bedtimes, let them come home from school for lunch individually; each of us takes one off to do something at a weekend.

We try to parent therapeutically; we use Theraplay techniques, listen to them and give them space to express themselves. We have also had to learn to stay calm, no matter what they throw at us (but we are human and some days it just doesn't work).

We try to ensure we have a lot of stability – routines and traditions are important – mornings, bedtimes, weekends, holidays, festivals, etc. In the early days bedtime routines were fixed to the minute and never varied (which did somewhat limit, as do chocolate cookies for Saturday lunch, church on Sunday morning, Easter egg hunts and chocolate crispy birthday cakes – seems to be a chocolate theme there!).

We encourage them to talk about their early lives/birth family and have a memory box for each which includes their life story books, photos, cards and certificates from both then and more recently. We use films and books to bring the topic up if we feel there is something bothering them. They have a huge amount of security from staying together. Our Christian faith has also helped us through.

There are times when it can be difficult. All three can be very demanding and have different needs, so trying to be consistent but also meeting their needs as individuals can be hard. For example, ignoring something might be best for one, but a consequence may be more appropriate for another for the same thing. They really struggle with any inconsistency, perceived or real. They are still unpredictable and don't cope well with disappointment, so sometimes we can't do planned things.

There is intense sibling rivalry, with far more physical and verbal abuse than I am entirely happy with – but for the most part, ignoring it seems to be the most effective way to deal with it, with chats at calmer times about respect and better ways to interact. On the other hand, they will defend each other against any 'outsider', which can also at times include us as parents!

They need one another

For me, being a mother of siblings was never a question. I was one of three children growing up and the lessons my sister and brother taught me about relationships were invaluable. They were my best friends, confidants and even though we did not always see eye to eye, they taught me about forgiveness, sharing, being responsible for my actions, unconditional love, how to resolve conflict amicably, the importance of family and how to appreciate the bond that makes that possible. They also taught me the art of laughter and the joy that results.

When planning our family, I wanted my children to have the same experience that I had with my siblings growing up. So, when we heard that our first son was soon to be having a sibling who needed placing and were asked if we would be interested, I immediately said, 'Yes.' My husband did not share my enthusiasm, and as he sat deliberating how he was going to break this uncomfortable news to me, I looked up and said, 'This is non-negotiable!'

On reflection, I would not recommend this manner of decision-making when it comes to having one child or more but, as my relationship with my siblings was on the whole very positive and my husband was an only child, I felt I was in a better position to take responsibility for that part of our life. So, siblings it was, and even though it has at times been a hard and long road, I would not change my decision for a minute.

It took me a long time to understand that my children had to work out their relationship for themselves – it was not immediate.

Being two boys, it was difficult to comprehend how they interacted with one another. One punch usually means hello, but two might mean it is time to intervene and discuss the benefits of boundaries. One likes to be read to before bed and one likes to be tickled with the light off until he falls asleep, so multitasking has become an essential requirement. What I was not prepared for was how protective one sibling becomes of the other when there is a threat, and this occurs even when it appears they do not have a strong relationship. It is almost innate: one minute they are cursing the day the other was born and yet as soon as there is a threat that all seems to diminish and this strong need to protect takes over. It has been fascinating to watch my two boys grow independently of one another yet by one another's side.

One likes trains, the other likes horses, one likes to read, the other likes outdoor sports, one likes to be on his own, the other needs people around all the time, one is a good sleeper, the other wakes several times a night. They are as different as night and day, but that does not have an impact on how much they need one another and how much that relationship helps them to face some of life's biggest challenges.

As adults, we often think it is our responsibility to teach and guide our children, but it appears that through our children's relationship with one another we learn so much more than we could ever offer them. They so naturally move through feelings that are pure and fundamentally essential for a healthy life. I watch in bewilderment as my boys rough and tumble, giggling, cavort and, what appears to me, generally hurt one another, only to find this is their way of working out their relationship, their boundaries and formulating their bond.

I didn't need to teach them how to interact with one another or tell them how important it is that they have one another. They are working it out themselves, and while they are doing this it is me who is doing the learning.

My younger son has a diagnosis of autism and, as a result, his ability to socialize has been impaired; it has been his older brother who has taught him how to play and the benefits of relationships. He encourages him to come out of himself so that he can be a part of a social group and this has allowed him to develop friendships in and out of school.

As I watch my sons trundling through the developmental stages of their life with one another, I have come to appreciate the true value that my siblings have made in my life. My sons' relationship with one another has forced me to ask, 'When did I stop watching the flowers grow?'

As they jump on the trampoline, not recognizing that I am much older and larger than they are, their invitation to join in becomes too enticing to reject. They jump on me, tickle me and laugh hysterically as if I was one of them, yelling in their height of hysteria, 'Higher, Mommy, higher', 'More, Mommy, more'. I have just been accepted into their sibling group and it dawns on me what a privilege that is and just how blessed I am to be a part of their lives.

It felt like it was the right thing to do even if it was not the easiest option!

My children Molly and Paul, brother and sister, were placed with me 12 years ago.

I knew most people wanted to adopt babies and there were a lot of older children who desperately needed a family. I'm a teacher so I knew just how young, underdeveloped and vulnerable children, especially those aged between four and seven, could be. I also knew how even traumatized children could respond to care and attention.

When I saw the profile of these siblings, I had a connection straight away. It was one of those moments that you hear about – we thought they'd fit into our family. When the children came, we looked and felt like a family. But we knew relationships, love and trust could be built using language and thinking as well as the nurturing you offer to a young child.

The first six months were absolutely wonderful. It was the loveliest experience of my life. There were some struggles, but both children fitted in quite well to school, extended family and community. My fondest memories are being physically close to the children, feeling their affections, holding them and being able to talk to them.

They'd never been taught to play in water as they'd never been to a swimming pool, or in the sea, so we were able to re-parent them and enjoy activities with them for the first time.

Adopting older children does not always appear to be the easiest route, but the best thing to do is to find the best match for you.

They are still our children

Brief outline of our family: Mr Grumps and I adopted a sibling group of three. They were then adopted son eight, middly daughter six and littly daughter five years old.

We jogged along nicely with the normal problems: education, one child friendless and aggressive, lying, stealing and just odd behaviour, all of which we lived with and dealt with. We understood their issues, we went on courses, we sought and accepted the limited resources on offer to help our children to move on in life; some times were good, some times were even normal, but their underlying issues always made our lives different from the norm.

Sadly, none of my children are living with us. They are now 19, 17 and 16. Our adopted son just never came home after we had taken him out for lunch with one of his sisters, and both girls had to be accommodated after being charged by police and the Crown Prosecution Service (CPS) for domestic violence and criminal damage to us. But they are still our children and will always be our children; nothing stops me from worrying about them, or from still trying to support them. As I type this, Mr Grumps is out meeting Middly for lunch. He has taken down some money for her and our adopted son who will not be attending the lunch, but Middly will be seeing him later; he too will be given a note from me and a small amount of money to get food. Neither of them want to see me or even ask after me, but that is how it is.

Littly and I have a much better relationship. She has chosen not to see or speak with her sibs, and even though she is living some distance from us we meet regularly. She and I had a week away recently as her foster carer needed a break. We took her for her college interview and she has been accepted. They know about her past and recent criminal stuff and are willing to give her a chance…we are so proud of her.

The sad, annoying, frustrating thing is that these children should never have been placed together. After yet another exhausting assessment four years ago it came to light that their relationship is toxic and they have a serious sibling trauma bond that won't let them move on and be themselves without many years of extensive therapeutic work. It was never offered and now they have the right to refuse help even if I could get someone to fund it, but hey ho that is a tale many of us could tell. Times for us have been exciting, loving, desperate, but we have had so many firsts with our lot, some of which weren't wanted but we are still here to tell the tale.

Update 2016: Our Middly gave birth to a lovely baby boy recently and we have been a bit busy. Our adopted son is in a stable relationship and has a nine-month-old son whom we see regularly, and Middly will be coming to stay with us for a week soon. Sadly, Littly has not spoken properly to us since Christmas of 2014 and is now herself pregnant, but we keep trying with her. I do think it's important that the message gets across that things do and will change, just from our own experiences. Although our children think they can manage on their own, they do know that I am always there in the background and that they can come to me…they also know that I will say it as it is and they accept that.

Chapter 11

ONE PLUS ONE – ADOPTING A SECOND CHILD

The relationship between brothers and sisters is, at its best, a very special one. You might fight over the little things in life like whose turn it is to clean out the hamster's cage, set the table or take the dog for the walk; you might look murder at your little sister when she borrows your favourite T-shirt without asking or spends an hour in the bath when you are waiting for a shower; you might tease your brother mercilessly when you know he has a crush on a girl in Year 8. But even if you don't always see eye to eye, they are, when the chips are down, your closest allies and confidants.

It's with them you learn about forgiveness – because you have to; it's with them you learn to share – because you have to; and it's with them that you share a life history that no one else can fully appreciate, laugh or cry over in the same way.

It's because of this that many adopters or parents of one birth child decide that it is important to complete their family by adopting a second child.

For adopters this holds all sorts of new challenges and changes. Few birth parents would consult their child about their plans to have a second and even a third or fourth birth child. But adoption is different: an adopted child comes with a history, and if your first child is a birth child, they need to be very much part of the plan.

'The birth child has to deal with sharing their life with a full-fledged little person where, before that, they had their own space and limitless time with Mum and Dad. Unlike a new baby joining the family, this sibling comes walking, talking, arguing, playing with their toys and generally being right in their face,' explained one adoptive mother.

Adoption agencies suggest that one of the first things to consider is the security of your first child – this is particularly important if they are also adopted. It takes time for a child to learn to trust new parents if they have experienced worrying and unsettling times in the past. The length of time is variable and is dependent on the age of the first child joining the family and the experiences they have been through.

Most agencies would suggest a gap of at least two years – whether the first child was adopted or a birth child – and that the second child is always younger than the first. Conflict between siblings can be reduced even further by a larger gap of 3–4 years.

And once your second child arrives, be prepared for some pretty strong reactions from the first child who is suddenly not always the centre of attention.

Is she my sister?

Eli, our birth son, was eight and a half when Anna arrived, and he wasn't very interested. She took a lot of our time and she was taking the place of our previous foster child, Macaulay, who we had thought was going to stay permanently but at the last moment was taken on by an aunt and uncle. I knew that Eli was upset about this, but it was only over time that it came out just how upset.

When it came to Eli being interviewed by the social worker about Anna staying, he did not want to talk to her. His trust in social workers had been completely lost over the situation with our last little boy who Eli believed had been unfairly taken from us. No amount of explaining seemed to help. On the fateful day of the interview the social worker came to the house and Eli sat silently in the corner of the room and refused to answer any of her questions. She persisted, really trying to get out of him if he was happy for Anna to stay. He kept saying, 'My mum will tell you, she knows,' which was true as we had had the conversation several times ourselves, but that wasn't good enough for the social worker. In the end he threw himself on the floor and started shouting and crying! I was mortified and also cross that the social worker had kept pushing until this happened and that I hadn't stepped earlier to stop her questioning.

She left and I felt like everything hung in the balance. Thankfully, she did later accept a short letter from Eli explaining his feelings although she did also insist on returning one more time to talk to him. This time I was ready! I made it very clear to him and to her that he did not 'have to' talk to her. I plied them with hot chocolate and cake and got Eli to sit on a big armchair and positioned myself between him and the social worker. He was still fairly monosyllabic but he managed to answer her questions and not get too stressed.

We realized over this period that Eli was still hoping that Macaulay would come back. We made an appointment to go and see Macaulay and his new family so that Eli could see that he was happy and that he wasn't the little 16-month-old that Eli had in his head any more. Macaulay had moved on and I think that helped Eli to do the same. But still because of that previous experience it was hard for Eli to allow himself to bond with Anna. He knew that you can be told one thing and the next day it can all change. He couldn't let himself love Anna as his sister if she was just going to be taken away from him. So for him the process has been very gradual. I believe he does love her now, especially now that she is older and so obviously loves him, but I think that the celebration hearing will be really significant for him.

Anna already calls Eli 'brother', but he needs to know that she is 100 per cent ours and there is no risk that she can be taken from us before he can call her 'sister'.

There were times when Sam wanted to send his sister back

As I look around the dinner table, I am once again struck by the difference in my two children. My son Sam, now in his mid-20s and living away from home, is tall, blonde-haired, well grounded, mature and always has plans for life; my daughter Libby, in her mid-teens, is petite, brown-haired, volatile and doesn't seem to know from one second to the next what is happening. Both are special and unique individuals, both are loved for being themselves, but there is one major difference between them: one is a birth child and one adopted.

My pregnancy with Sam was normal, straightforward and uncomplicated. We saw no reason why we could not repeat the process but it was not to be. We decided that in order to complete our family we would find out about adoption. Not as a second best option but as an alternative way to have the family we wanted.

Like most people who have birth children, we spent a great deal of time agonizing over how adoption would affect Sam. We were fortunate to have a very good social worker who allowed us to explore all of the issues that we needed to and some we hadn't even thought about.

We had been open with Sam from the time of preparation groups. At this point he was aged about six and we had explained to him that this was another way of him getting a brother or sister. He seemed to accept and understand this, his only stipulation being that he did not have an older bossy sister.

Sam was involved throughout our home study, our social worker lending him books, discussing things with him and allowing him to ask questions. As the home study progressed, we returned regularly to the question 'Are we making the right decision for Sam?' and spent hours talking about it.

Our social worker was always very firm that although our son's feelings were important, it was us, as adults, who were making the decision to adopt and asked the question 'If we decided to have another baby, would we consult him?'

We were approached about two-year-old Libby about a year later because we had always been open to the idea of direct contact, at that time not usual, and there was a very complicated contact arrangement. Libby was placed with us, aged two, one month after Sam's tenth birthday.

It wasn't easy for Sam to explain to his friends that he suddenly had a two-year-old sister. Inevitably, there were times when Sam wanted us to send Libby back because we couldn't do the things we had done before with a toddler in tow. There were times when he struggled to understand her behaviour. He also struggled with the direct contact we have with her birth family, with birth siblings almost competing for who is the rightful brother. As Sam became older, he chose to opt out of our meetings and we decided to respect his decision.

If I could turn back the clock, I would have considered how Libby's history of developmental trauma would impact upon her as she grew and therefore on us as a family. I would have asked for help and support for us and for Sam earlier on to help him understand this small sister who created havoc wherever she went but who at the same time was loveable, adoring and worshipped him.

On a positive note, Sam is very tolerant; he tries to understand what is going on for Libby, even offering to go to her school to explain her behaviour when she has been excluded.

From early on, in many respects, they have had a normal sibling relationship. They get on each other's nerves one minute and are the best of friends the next. He is very protective of her and she adores him. Looking back, we did the best that we could with the knowledge and information we had at the time, and on the whole things seem to have worked out as well as they could have.

One plus one

We always enjoyed fostering but, like all foster carers, found it very hard each time we moved children on and we always knew we wanted to adopt at some point.

We fostered our daughter from when she was five months old, so when she was freed for adoption at two and a half years old, we asked to be considered and were matched just over two months later.

It took three years from start to finish, but it was worth every moment's wait to be able to know she was now with us forever. We always knew we'd adopt again at some point but weren't in any hurry as we wanted to take some time to enjoy our daughter and felt we'd know when the time was right. Well, two years later that time came when, after months and months of discussing it both together and with our daughter, we decided the time was right and asked to start the adoption process again.

We took our time to prepare our daughter for having a new addition to our family. We wanted to give a clear message to her that this child would be permanent and that we wouldn't have to do another goodbye.

I'd previously written our daughter's life story book, so I now wrote her a story to help prepare her for a sibling and some of the changes and struggles this might bring. During discussions with our social worker we let her know we wanted to be proactive in the search for our new addition and she agreed this was no problem. We enquired about three different children over the next few months on *Children Who Wait* but, when we had their permanence reports, we didn't feel they were the right match for our daughter or that we would be the right family for them, so did not pursue these.

Then one winter's day we logged on and were met by a little face with the most amazing smile that lit up his face – we knew we'd found our son. We sent off an enquiry and let our social worker know.

We were approved again three months later and matched in June, with introductions starting a week after matching. I'll never forget the excitement of being able to tell our daughter she was going to have a little brother – she was bouncing up and down! She had her own calendar with the dates on it for meeting her brother and him moving in so that she could count down as well.

We were incredibly lucky as they really hit it off straight away and get along very well. The introductions were exhausting, especially with all the travelling, but we have an amazing support network, which was absolutely fantastic and helped our daughter keep to some of her routines. Our son moved in a few days ago and the four of us are enjoying getting to know each other properly as we settle down into family life.

The approval process felt like it dragged whilst we were going through it but, looking back now, the last year seems to have gone quickly. We're very aware of how lucky we are as we know of people who have been approved for over a year and are still waiting to be matched.

Our fostering experience was great for knowing some of the potential issues that could arise for children and giving us experience in creating strategies to help with some of these. It also means we have a good support network that has more of an idea of some of the difficulties we may face. We know there are going to be some tough times ahead, but we believe in taking each day as it comes and making lots of happy memories to store away that help get us through the tough times.

Now we are six (if you count the dog and the hamster)

When our beautiful daughter, Tigger, was born, we planned to have another child fairly soon afterward. Naively, we believed that this would be easily achievable. Unfortunately, fate had a different plan, and several years, endless investigations and many miscarriages later, we decided enough was enough.

We settled into life as a family of three, deciding to give up our hopes for another child and focus all of our attention on enjoying our miraculous, bouncy little girl. As a compromise, we added an amiable Bernese mountain dog to the family. Around the same time, my sister-in-law permanently fostered an adorable six-year-old boy. The ease with which he became part of our wider family made us believe that we could love and care for a child who wasn't our biological offspring and so we embarked on the arduous adoption process. After two long years of talking and planning, we became parents to a gorgeous four-year-old boy.

The first few days after Piglet moved in went past in a whirl. Tigger was now six and at school most of the day, giving us time to dedicate to Piglet. It was utterly exhausting as he needed constant attention and he could only focus for a few minutes. An hour felt like a day and the pressure was hard to take. We had to operate as a tag team just to be able to cope. We tried to give Tigger as much attention as possible when she wasn't at school, but it felt exhausting, physically and emotionally.

Piglet seemed to be much more attached to his dad than he was to me and I descended into periods of tearful despair. I felt like a failure as an adoptive mother and attached myself more closely to my daughter. Our household seemed to split along gender lines. This schism was enlarged when Tigger caught scarlet fever and was bedridden for a week with a high temperature. She became distressed when I wasn't with her, so my days and nights were spent lying beside her watching endless Bugs Bunny cartoons and barely interacting with my new son at all.

Over the coming weeks things settled into a more even routine. Tigger was absolutely fantastic about sharing her life, and although Piglet still required constant entertainment, he seemed to be settling in well. Things were very full on, overwhelming even, but our expectations of the early days hadn't been high, and we looked forward to reaching some kind of normality in the coming months.

However, things actually got much harder. For both children the reality was sinking in that Piglet was here to stay. Now that Piglet realized that he was home and safe, his range of emotions broadened and he would scream and rant at us. In addition, when frustrated with us or other children, he would hit out or break things. This was, and still is, incredibly difficult to deal with as he doesn't remember and so can't take responsibility for his actions and learn from them. He sought security in copying Tigger – in his mind, she is a child whose parents chose to keep her, and so if he could be like her, he would be kept too. The copying was a constant source of friction. He copied what she ate, what she said, anything she did (including every line of a drawing) and followed her everywhere.

At the same time Tigger was struggling really badly with the reality of having to share her life with a little brother. She would often curl up in a ball and scream. In a fury she would tell us how much she hated us because we had brought him into our family. She yelled at him that she wished he had never come and that he had stolen her life. In tearful breakdowns she would share how she regretted ever wishing for a little brother because it was awful, or that maybe it would have been OK to have another younger sibling but just not him.

We started to separate them, building a schedule where they only had limited time together because anything else was too hard to deal with. Emotionally, it was also very difficult for us to deal with. For any parent when their children are fighting it is hard, but there is so much more complexity where one child is a birth child and the other adopted. The birth child has to deal with sharing their life with a full-fledged little person where, before that, they had their own space and limitless time with Mum and Dad. Unlike a new baby joining the family, this sibling comes walking, talking, arguing, playing with their toys and generally being right in their face. The adopted child has all their own history to deal with, along with a massive change in their life. There must also be a sense that the birth child is somehow better than them, more loved because that child hasn't been rejected in the way the adopted child may feel that they have. In addition, for the parents there is a lot of guilt. Unlike giving birth where the only real choice is whether or not to have a child, in adoption you have also made choices about the age and the sex of the child.

On the bad days those choices come back to haunt you. Especially early on, it was really hard to come to terms with the anger I felt towards my adopted child when he did something to hurt my birth child. This resulted in flashes of rage and vindictiveness at Piglet followed by guilt and contrition.

As the months went on, things steadily improved. Harry (Houdini) the Hamster has joined us, Tigger and Piglet have negotiated a shaky truce, although at times our house can resemble more of a war zone than a home. Dealing with either child on their own is easy, but when they are together things can still get tricky. We are coming to terms with parenting in this challenging environment, and have had invaluable support from a parent-mentoring programme, which has opened our eyes to a world of different ways to approach parenting, especially where dealing with a child with a traumatic past.

Two years on, I can't imagine a time when Piglet wasn't with us. When I remember events before he came, my memory fills him in because I can't believe he wasn't there. Our life will follow a rockier road than that experienced by many parents, but it will be all the more rewarding for that and I wouldn't change anything.

He is our beloved son, our gorgeous boy, and always will be.

SURVIVAL

Do you compare her to your birth child?
You feel perhaps she will not do.
She is more hurt, stubborn and wild,
Than any daughter born to you.
Sometimes from afar your scathing eye does look
And often is her goodness overshadowed
Her qualities ignored by your parent book
Which boasts your child's every virtue out loud.
But she will thrive, my lively loving girl
And when from that skin for which I grieve
Her slumbering snake does steadily unfurl
Here potent strength you will perceive.

He just didn't feel like mine

We had the call in December. A little boy, Bean, had been born, a brother to our daughter Lola. Would we be interested in becoming second-time adopters? When I put the phone down, I howled. It felt as though a bombshell had been dropped on our content and happy lives and I knew life was about to change. I was terrified.

Lola had been with us for two years and it had been a very successful placement. We adored her. My husband and I had always agreed that if a sibling arrived on the scene, we would be very happy to adopt again. We knew that a sibling for Lola was the greatest gift we could ever give her, and ideally always envisaged a family unit of four. So we should have been thrilled at the possibility of another child, particularly a boy so young and related to Lola. The reality was we were anxious and had doubts.

Could we be so lucky second time around? I dreaded the idea of having less one-to-one time with Lola and didn't relish the prospect of going back to babyhood with sleepless nights and nappies! But these were all normal feelings for second-time parents.

After an arduous year of uncertainty, a placement order was finally granted and plans were made to meet the foster carer and start introductions the following September. We spent lots of time preparing Lola for the arrival of her baby brother, talking with her, going through her own life story book and reading to her. Baby Bean was approaching 12 months old and we felt the three-year age gap between siblings was perfect. We were nervously excited at the imminent arrival of our son.

Baby Bean was a big, healthy, beautiful boy and we started the exhausting week of introductions. He seemed to be content and happy, and we were told that he wasn't a cuddly baby, being happiest on the floor playing with his toys alone, with the occasional check-in with his carer. He had formed a healthy attachment and we had no major developmental or health concerns.

The first weeks of placement were horrendous. On top of the exhausting adjustment and settling into life with a second child came the added difficulties of trying to form attachments. Baby Bean gave very little eye contact, appeared to be grouchy and grumpy, and cried constantly, particularly through the night. He would cry inconsolably when he saw me in the morning and cry when I put him to bed. He hated to be picked up and squirmed when held, often lashing out. We rarely saw a smile and never heard a laugh. We knew that it was actually healthy to see that a child is distressed by such a massive change in their lives and to grieve the loss of a loved one, and, as hard as it was not to feel rejected, we understood how hard things were for him What was very difficult to watch, however, was the interaction between Baby Bean and Lola.

She adored and accepted him from the start but did have a tendency to treat him like a doll and we found ourselves saying constantly, 'Put him down, give him some space!' He was just not used to an excited four-year-old constantly trying to cuddle him and he hated it! As a result he cried whenever he saw Lola and would lash out, biting and scratching her in the only way a one-year-old knows how to say, 'No thank you, I don't like that!'

My biggest and growing concern started to become clear very soon. I just didn't feel anything for this little boy who was now living with us and we called our son. I went through the motions of being a mother to him but felt no love for him, and at times I am ashamed to admit I didn't even like him very much. He just didn't feel like mine. I consider myself a warm and loving person, and we are a cuddly and fun-loving family. How could I not love him?

I did touch on some of my worries when the social workers came for their visits, and although they were reassuring, telling me it was all going well, and not to beat myself up, they were so under-resourced that I got the impression they felt that as previous adopters with a good support network we just weren't a priority in their heavy caseloads.

Our families were great and bonded with Baby Bean very quickly. My parents offered lots of practical help, particularly in giving us breaks to help with the lack of sleep. Although this is frowned upon in the newly adopted world, we were at times on our knees with exhaustion and those moments were invaluable to us. However, they just couldn't comprehend my lack of emotion for him; why would they? Who couldn't love this beautiful baby boy? The shame I felt was immense.

About two months after Baby Bean joined us, I met up with another adopted mother. She had had similar feelings when her second child arrived and was very candid in her experiences. It felt so good to talk to someone who understood and didn't judge me.

She now had a very healthy relationship with her children and the positive story gave me lots of encouragement.

A turning point was about three months after placement when, while tickling Bean's tummy, I had my first belly laugh from him. He was finally starting to settle and trust us. He gradually became happier, giving more smiles, sleeping through the night, becoming more affectionate and playful. A magic moment for us was when Baby Bean and Lola started to play together, chasing each other and laughing. He now adores his big sister as much as she does him, although he still dislikes it when she tries to pick him up!

We are now six months into the placement and things feel so much more natural; his quirks and qualities are no longer alien but endearing to me. Although there is still a way to go, every day my bond with him deepens. We are gelling together as a family and developing love and trust, and I no longer worry, as I'm sure all will be OK.

Patience has never been my virtue and I see now that the social workers were right: I was doing OK and just needed time. I am convinced that there are many others going through similar experiences, many, I'm sure, feeling too ashamed to admit them and suffering in silence. I also believe that in the vast majority of cases, like ours, in time the love will come.

Families come in all shapes and sizes

Our path into the world of adoption began with a botched vasectomy reversal and the agreement that IVF was not for us as a couple. We approached social services and were introduced to Eva who became known to us as the third person in our marriage.

Jay was 15 months old when we met him for the first time. Blonde curly ringlets covered his head and an active determination to discover and talk about his discoveries filled his life and ours. Then out of the blue I became pregnant and we had our birth son Flynn. Our continued involvement with Eva meant a visit when Flynn was six weeks old, which we thought was to congratulate us. But it wasn't; instead, she had come to tell us that Jay's birth mother was pregnant again. Will was born in early summer, meaning there was just seven months difference between him and our birth son.

The time from when Will was born and the subsequent assessment of his birth mother's abilities was utterly heart-wrenching. From the beginning, Will was our baby and he was growing up elsewhere; his first Christmas passed in a loving foster home, good, but not where we thought he should be.

Two weeks before panel and matching, we were sent a medical report which stated Will was suffering from developmental delay. Despite Eva urging caution, we had made our decision; Will was coming to be part of our family. I have never doubted this was the right choice, but sometimes my confidence is undermined by thoughts that I have not fulfilled Will's needs.

Life with two babies was mindblowing. I can only describe the first two years as being like a bad episode of *Super Nanny*. It was just amazing that the boys seemed to be surviving despite me feeling like the cartoon character that spins around in circles and disappears into the ground.

Raising Will is a challenge. You constantly have to be two steps ahead of his next thought, and invariably in this game I don't always win. This is why at the age of five Will goes virtually nowhere without a wrist strap – he just doesn't understand safety. Our experiences with Will disappearing in a flash and appearing in the oddest places have taught us that vigilance is not quite enough which has resulted in the family catchphrase: 'Has anyone here seen William?'

I do feel that Will has helped me appreciate all the boys and his fragility with understanding has helped me to celebrate the small steps that children make.

That is nearly the end of our story, but this is also where it begins again. A phone call from Eva came as a shock. Jay and Will's birth mother had given birth to another baby. I would like to say there was a huge period where reassessment was debated, but my gut reaction with Will had led us to a happy family and I was sure that this new baby would add to ours and the boys' happiness.

Our baby boy has been with us now for a year. It was never important that he may have extra needs. He was just a baby who deserved to be with his family. The rest would fall into place.

No mum could be prouder than me of her beautiful band of boys. When I listen to them playing, when I watch them hugging or helping each other, all indecision goes out of my mind and I know I am truly lucky.

Chapter 12

ADOPTION, RACE AND RELIGION

Race and religion are sensitive and emotive subjects in any context.

It is now well established that a same-race placement for a child should be a preference but should not ultimately hinder the adoption of a child in the long term. A religious preference for the upbringing of a child is one of the few choices that a birth parent can state when their child is taken into the care system.

In both instances there is constant debate and argument between potential adopters, adoptive families, the social work profession and the media. Some prospective adopters believe that having a strong faith of any kind can sway social workers against them, but in some instances families with no faith may also be discriminated against.

One committed Christian says of her experience of the assessment process:

> I totally understand the need to scrutinize people carefully – in fact, I welcomed the opportunity to think carefully about my faith and its role in my life. But I just felt there was an over-emphasis on it at the expense of other things – I was asked more about my Christianity than about how I would protect a child's physical safety!

Placement of children in the 'ideal' environment in terms of their race and their religion can be problematic; there is often a numbers imbalance in race and religion between the potential adopters and the children waiting in care for adoption.

Adoption UK believes that:

- When children are unable to remain with their families of birth, it is in their best interests that alternative families which reflect their original culture and background should be sought wherever possible.

- Strenuous efforts to achieve this aim should be positively and warmly supported.

- Time to achieve this aim must be limited. The needs of individual children must be borne in mind. If, at the end of an agreed period of energetic and well-documented effort, a suitable same-race family has not been found, the child should be placed with the best family available. This may mean placement across racial lines with families who have positive views about becoming a racially mixed unit and the ability to achieve it whatever the racial/cultural background of the parents.

- There should be full and ongoing support for established racially mixed adoptive families.

Adoption UK remains convinced that to remain parentless is an impediment few survive without deep scars and that perfect parents do not exist anyway.

Why black heritage needs to take priority

Transracial adoption is still controversial, and racial politics in this country is a very complex issue which I am not sure many white prospective adopters understand. I didn't set out to adopt a mixed-heritage child, but there are reasons why we have ended up together. Simba's birth father is Zimbabwean and his birth mum is white British. To that extent I reflect his ethnic/racial heritage. I was told that if I had been black and his birth mum white, this would not be the case, and I probably wouldn't have him.

Many white people question why black heritage takes priority. On one level I agree. Why should the white inheritance be discounted? But quite simply, my son is perceived as a black boy, and carries the baggage that goes with it. As a transracial adopter, you really do need to have an above-average understanding of race issues. I think there are factors in my personal experience that counted for a lot. I was in a mixed-race relationship in the 1980s and 1990s when it wasn't quite so common or acceptable. I experienced racial abuse from both the black and white communities. I had people make monkey noises behind my back at my brother's wedding. I've been called a black man's bitch and worse. Until it happened to me, I really had no idea what that prejudice felt like. Most white people don't, because we don't experience it.

I often see posts on various forums from white prospective adopters stating that they would adopt a child of any ethnicity. But Asian cultures are vastly different to black cultures and there is a huge difference between African and Caribbean cultures. 'African' itself represents thousands of different ethnic groups. Could you really adopt a child of *any* ethnicity?

In our case the social workers liked that I had personal knowledge and experience of Africa. For my part, I was confident that I could meet his needs with regard to the promotion of his ethnic heritage because of that knowledge and experience. I wouldn't have considered a child from an Asian or Caribbean heritage because I just don't have the personal knowledge and connection.

When talking about transracial adoption, everyone seems to default to talking about hair care, food and music. Whilst those things have their place, for me there are more important and complex issues about raising a black son and promoting his ethnic heritage.

Children in this country don't exist in some kind of ethnic bubble. Why would I go to the bother of African food when his birth dad fed him McDonalds and he prefers sausage and chips anyway? We do listen to African music but that's because we both love music. I wouldn't foist it on him if he wasn't interested. None of this should be tokenistic. Our home is full of things I have brought back from my travels, things he sees and uses every day – books, music, photographs, tablecloths, pots, my earrings and handbags. These things are just there, part of our everyday life, they are not things I have had to graft on.

What is more important, though, is that he has positive role models, that he sees himself reflected in the community in which he lives, that his self-esteem rides high, that he has pride and aspiration, that he has the self-confidence to rise above what may be thrown at him.

Obviously, I think that transracial adoption can work, but please don't underestimate the importance and complexity of race and ethnicity. I wish they didn't matter, but they do.

Finding a cultural hook

I am an adoptee and was always told my birth father was Jamaican. But since revisiting my adoption records, I have found that it doesn't state that anywhere – instead saying he is West Indian! I don't regret the misinformation, though, as it was helpful to have a cultural hook when growing up as part of my identity. I grew up in a predominantly white area and being mixed-race meant that I was frequently asked where I was 'from'.

This always led to me feeling I had to out myself as adopted due to growing up with parents of a different ethnicity. This was quite difficult during teenage years as I had a double difference of being of a different ethnicity to others and being an adoptee.

I now live in a much more multicultural area so hardly ever get asked where I 'come from'. I would therefore say that life would have been easier living in a more culturally diverse area growing up. Easier said than done, though!

Update 2016: I have now adopted my own child who is also dual heritage and so face the same dilemma that my parents did about whether to seek more space and a better quality of life in a less culturally diverse area or to remain in the city. My child's birth father is unknown, like for many modern adoptees, so he won't have the cultural hook that I had and I do worry about how this will impact his ethnic identity.

Our family is different but so are our friends

My husband and I have adopted Chloe, a little five-year-old girl with curly black hair, dark complexion and deep black eyes. My husband is very fair. I am French with brown hair and olive skin.

When you adopt mixed-race children, it's important to remember that in biologically mixed-race families everyone can have a different skin colour varying from light to dark. Mixed-race families do not expect homogenous children. Our child compares our skin colour and difference and we tell her where she gets her biological features from, but we still look like a family when we are together.

We spend our summers in France with family and friends where there are many mixed-race couples as well as mixed nationalities, so our daughter tends to understand that there are differences in appearance but also in culture and food and customs. She knows our family is different but so are our friends and she shares in a community built on differences and the richness of variety. She understands that we laugh at the same things and enjoy being different because of adoption not because of race. We try to teach her that even though adoption and race make her different from the majority, this does not mean she is alone or diminished in any way and ultimately it is a strength.

Inner worth is not based on appearance. This is the lesson I hope to share with my family. We do not have heavy conversations (she is only five after all), but when it is relevant we point out things about adoption, about tolerance and differences, and we acknowledge how everyone can have something that makes them feel lonely or different.

We tell her stories from the Bible and the Koran. Knowledge of religion and cultures will go a long way, and for now they sound like fairy tales, but later in life they will take on more meaning and give her familiarity with other beliefs and cultures.

We also rehearse what to say when someone says something unpleasant, thinking of bullying in general and not just facial bullying. We have not encountered difficulties so much on race as on appearance. She pointed out how some children made fun of her teeth, and I pointed out I love her teeth and that in France a gap in the teeth is a sign of good luck.

We practise what to answer when someone asks her questions about adoption or why I do not have the same accent as her or look like her. Role play gives her confidence and gives her a sense of self-worth.

Being politically correct at home with your children does not help them face the realities of the world. Being fair and accepting of differences does not mean glossing over them or ignoring them. You cannot live with your family this way, so when I describe a black man I say 'black'.

We want our child to understand where she comes from and be proud of who she is and who she becomes, but the transition is not only of race or ethnicity but also of social heritage. There seems to be a void around transracial adoption.

That's my boy

Caroline and Tony have a birth daughter aged eight and an adopted son Zak, three, who is of mixed heritage. Caroline describes the sense of responsibility she feels to ensure her son has a strong sense of his own identity.

I applied to adopt 12 years ago as a single adopter. I was about a year into the process and getting nowhere when I met my husband, got married and had a birth child, and then, when my daughter was two, we phoned our local social services to again enquire about adoption.

The reception we got was very negative. We are white and they felt we were not what they needed. They told us to wait a while and come back when our daughter was older. Over the next couple of years both myself and my daughter needed medical treatment. So it was a while until we were in a position to reapply. This time we decided to look at local agency Ofsted reports for our region. We made a short list and decided to ring round before deciding who to apply to. We got such a fabulous reception from the first agency we rang that we didn't even call anyone else.

It took two and a half months to get through the medical. We then did our training and were approved as adopters for a child under two and a half because of the needs of our birth daughter. At the time I thought it was unnecessary but now I think it was a wise decision as, knowing the needs of a newly placed child, I think a smaller age gap may have been hard on all of us.

We first heard about Zak two months later and were given some brief details. He was considered difficult to place as he is of mixed heritage and there was some uncertainty about his ethnicity. The area where we live is very ethnically mixed and our community and friendship groups include people from a variety of ethnic and religious groups.

We heard nothing so we assumed another family had been found for him as we could see that, both being of white British heritage, we were probably not the ideal family for Zak. But two months later another call came and we finally met his social worker and saw a picture of an amazingly beautiful little boy. A month later we were approved as Zak's adopters. We were so happy; we had hardly dared believe it was actually happening until then.

It was lovely preparing his bedroom and getting all the things we thought he would need. We had to wait nearly another two months to meet him. By then Zak was 14 months old. He had been removed from his birth mother as a baby due to the neglect suffered by his older sibling and was in foster care before he came to us. It was extremely emotional to meet him for the first time. He found the move traumatic but after a month became more settled. He still struggles with sleep now and we're pleased to be seeing a psychologist to hopefully get more advice on helping him with this. It feels like he has to hold on to us – he can't relax and go to sleep. It sometimes takes two or three hours even when we know he is tired. I guess his first family disappeared and, on some subconscious level, he fears that we will too.

Zak and our birth daughter are fabulous together. The first month he was with us, he couldn't walk and was a little behind developmentally. She would carry him here and there. She had to learn to respect he was a person and not a toy. Now their relationship is very strong. If he's distressed and can't see us, he looks to her for comfort. They have great fun together. She's now eight and he's three.

We met Zak's birth mother, which was a powerful experience, and I'm glad we did – I was very aware that she is very much a victim too. I can imagine I would have very few parenting skills if I had had her life experiences.

There is uncertainty over who his father is. We have recently sent off some of our son's saliva for ethnicity testing. We want him to have pride and knowledge of his heritage, but the uncertainty makes that hard. We hope that the results will give us more information so that we can help Zak understand his life story as he gets older.

We are trying to bring Zak and our daughter up to understand and see the value of all faiths. I find Buddhism very helpful and we occasionally attend a children's group at the local Buddhist centre. My husband is atheist/agnostic, but as a family we have also attended children's meetings at a local Quaker Meeting House. We want our children to have the opportunity to explore spiritual issues in accepting environments, where no one is going to say that any one set of beliefs is absolutely right or wrong – this feels all the more important due to Zak's heritage. We have a Muslim friend who has invited us to attend the mosque with her and her adopted daughter, which we will all do when Zak is a little older.

Zak is now a confident, outgoing boy. He loves to be the centre of everyone's attention and is skilled at making connections with almost anyone he meets. Needless to say, he has worked his charm on our family and friends who think he is fabulous. My brother, who himself was adopted, is especially fond of him and we expect that that relationship will become very important to him as he starts to understand what adoption means.

He already explains that he came out of Melissa's tummy but that his sister came out of Mummy's tummy, but of course he's still got a lot to learn. Parenting an adopted child of course brings extra challenges and responsibilities – I feel a strong sense of responsibility to Zak's birth mother. But I think adoption is also a great privilege. Zak has taught us a great deal and brought us all huge joy – we feel we're an extremely lucky family.

Chapter 13

TAKING IN THE CHILD, TAKING ON THE SCHOOL

It's the biggest outside challenge most adoptive parents and their children face: school.

While adoptive families try to heal the damaged trust of an adopted child, build emotional bridges and attachment, the wrong school and the wrong teacher can just as quickly undo all that careful work.

It grates with adopters, like a nail on a blackboard, when teachers or other parents wrongly try to group adoptive children into the same educational and behavioural box as all other children. 'Our children have come from the care system. They were in the care system because most of them have been neglected or abused or both. They have suffered loss, they have suffered fear, loneliness, violence, hunger and cold, some have suffered severe pain,' said one angry adopter, exhausted with the battle with schools who wanted to constantly compare their child with others.

While educators and standard setters look for ways to help the physically and mentally less able child, little or no training is given to teachers about how to treat the emotionally damaged children that come into their classrooms, instead, these already broken little people are often punished, excluded and marginalized both by their classmates and by teachers who just don't understand them.

The lack of teacher training on the effects of early trauma on a child's development has been a major problem for many adopters. 'We are all quite rightly outraged and full of sympathy when headlines scream of children dying at the hands of their abusive families. However, there is much less sympathy for the children fortunate enough to be "saved" who are taken into care or adopted and then act out their distress in anti-social or challenging ways,' said adoptive parent and educational consultant Anne O'Connor.

'Many of the behaviours shown by traumatized children in care are a direct (and rational) response to their experiences.'

Two of the most common reactions are a deep-seated lack of trust and a constant watching out for danger. Although a child might be forming secure attachments at home with his new family, his world can be broken apart in school where his special emotional needs are not understood. Too often teachers tell adoptive parents, 'We can't treat them differently to other children', so they get excluded from class for being 'naughty', held back after class for 'not concentrating or sitting still' and reprimanded for an angry response when they are asked to 'draw their family tree', 'bring in a picture of themselves as a baby' or 'write about their earliest memory'.

Forced into situations they can't deal with, they lose any fragile sense of self-control. 'I am not suggesting that all children in the care system or who are adopted will have problems. However, society does them and their families a disservice if we don't take into consideration the impact being brought into care has on a child,' said another adoptive parent.

An Adoption UK survey of nearly 500 adoptive parents (2011–2012) revealed that:[1]

- Adoptive children had needs requiring greater support services, with educational support being a particularly problematic area.

- Professionals – from social workers to school staff – need better training in early childhood development, how trauma can affect this development and about the impact of abuse and neglect.

- There needs to be improved liaison between educational and support systems.

---

1   E. Pennington (2012) *It Takes a Village to Raise a Child.* Banbury: Adoption UK. Available at www.adoptionuk.org/sites/default/files/documents/Ittakesa villagetoraiseachild-Report-June12.pdf, accessed on 5 August 2016.

- Adopters need better access to therapeutic, education and counselling services.

Before entering the minefield of education, Adoption UK suggests all adoptive parents should:

- research schools, meet school heads and explore their experience of working with adopted children

- ask how a school/teacher can support your child and what support mechanisms they have in place

- visit the school to gain a feel for the learning environment.

Once your child is enrolled, adoptive parents need to:

- establish a positive rapport with staff and encourage regular progress meetings

- be honest, explain how and why you need their valued help

- work with the school in supporting your child

- celebrate all your child's achievements

- have empathy with the school's targets, but don't be frightened to speak up.

Experiences of adoptive parents differ widely; a change of teacher or a change of school can make a significant difference to a child's overall development and happiness.

But don't panic inside or outside the home, says one seasoned adopter:

Things may sometimes seem awful but you can turn them around. Maintain a sense of humour. Stay calm. Pick your battles. Maintain firm, clear (calm) boundaries and don't let them be hijacked. Focus on creating a happy environment – against all odds!

Another adopter says that it is important to get across to teachers that the priority for adopted children is their emotional development:

This is more important than academic achievement: they need to develop and enhance their emotional intelligence before they can be expected to make academic progress.

Hopefully one day adopters won't have to fight the system, it will work for our children; it will acknowledge that 'carrying bags of trauma' will make it harder for a child to learn.

Understanding the child within

As a family, adoption has been a rocky ride. All through life's changes, there have been complex ramifications for our adopted son David.

It took a while for David to settle into his junior school and he often showed an inability to understand social situations and chose rough and unkind children to be with as he had a weak sense of self-esteem. He often ended up in trouble and not being able to fully understand or learn from his mistakes. David received support throughout junior school as he had missed so many years of formal education due to his severely neglectful and abusive past. His old scars, seen and unseen, continually affected his ability to just be, and he spends a lot of time being hypervigilant, worrying about food and viewing the world as so full of threat he would often struggle with the most basic tasks.

David spent many of his early years being very hungry and fending for himself, and this has led to his brain development being impaired so that he cannot link cause and effect in the way you would expect for a child his age.

By 11, David was still unable to choose appropriate friends without adult support. When David transferred to his local secondary, despite thorough liaison with the junior school his needs were not supported adequately and he was left to get on with it with disastrous consequences. Within two weeks he was with some friends who bullied him, stole his things and were violent and abusive towards him, David did not understand that these were not great friends and he slid into behaving inappropriately himself, stealing, lying, being late and with a complete disregard for his and other people's things.

Despite frequent meetings trying to explain David's complex needs and background, the school failed to take our worries seriously and offered no further support. It was only following several serious incidents of stealing and bringing weapons into school that we were offered six weeks on a self-esteem group and a termly meeting with a teacher/mentor. We felt this was totally inadequate and started looking for an independent school.

My feeling was that he needed to be in a small environment and in a school that recognized individual children and had a nurturing environment. One school was ideal with small classes, very good discipline and clear structure. They offered us a place and we achieved charitable grants to fund it. Without them, David wouldn't have had an education.

In fact, when he was 11 years old, I couldn't see any future for him at all.

Their ethos of valuing childhood suited David and allowed him to spend much of Year 8 building a fort out of old cardboard boxes and wood. The school supported David as an individual, though he had his ups and downs.

As I write this, I am feeling rather emotional as I look at my now 16-year-old young man sitting with his dad and little sister and just being. We have just heard he has gained the right GCSEs to do a wildlife ranger course at a local college. As I look at my son, a keen amateur wildlife photographer looks back at me, who has been sports captain at school for two years and holds several school records. David competes regularly in the local athletics team and has now found some really good friends.

He now texts me when he is unsure and needs some help with college, and college have agreed to support him. He has his own personal faith and a family who thinks he is the bee's knees. He could be all right, you know.

I wish I had chosen a different school

There is one image I will never forget from my son Owen's early days at his new school. I arrived to pick him up as usual and I waited and waited. When the final child and mother had been reunited and walked out of the playground, my heart sank. What had they done to my son? Why wasn't he here? Had they lost him? All kinds of absurd thoughts ran through my mind as the panic rose inside me.

I walked into school and to his classroom, my heart in my mouth. On entering, I saw two teachers standing with their arms folded and on seeing me one said, 'Well, your mum's here now.' I glanced in the direction she was looking and saw in the furthest corner, under a collection of desks, was my son curled up into a ball trying to make himself as small as he could.

My initial feeling was of shock, but when I looked back at these two women, they were obviously waiting for me to chastise this terrified little boy. I stood there for a few moments unable to say anything. 'What's happened?' I finally asked. A list of minor misdemeanours was reeled off with what almost felt like relish and the teacher concluded, 'We told him to wait until his mum came to get him.'

I was beyond furious. My son had been with me for just five weeks; to him I was no more his mother than the dinner lady who smiled at him each morning. At the time I was just another adult who he felt was very likely to disappear in a puff of smoke at any time. I can't remember what I actually said to Owen to help him come out from under those desks, but I remember the overwhelming pressure from those two teachers to punish him for his behaviour earlier that day.

If I had a time machine, the first place I would visit is that classroom at that time and I would give those teachers a piece of my mind about shaming my son. I would have then removed him from a school that was so petty that terrifying a four-year-old and threatening him with his new mum was seen as appropriate discipline.

Sadly, as a new parent with so much still to learn about therapeutic parenting – about what motivated my son and the help he so desperately needed to feel safe and secure – I did neither of those things. Today I still find it hard to forgive myself but I will never forgive those teachers. I felt confused, I felt let down, I'd gone into school just a few weeks earlier with my social worker to try to explain to these teachers about what would help and what would not help him in the classroom. I now know I should not have ignored the feeling I had during that meeting that they were more interested in tittle-tattle than the actual advice and strategies we were imparting.

However, if I felt confused and let down, how must it have felt for a four-year-old whose new lovely 'forever' mummy was shouting at him for some incident he could no longer remember? While I can't shake the guilt of those early months, I can, with hindsight, share some of my feelings about what makes a good school. Looking back on my original decision about which school, I know that decision was taken with the best intentions. I chose the local primary school, as opposed to an inner-city school which was close to work, where I could have picked him up and dropped him each day, because it was just that – local. I felt, and was advised by others, that if he made friends in the city 12 miles away, he wouldn't be able to socialize with them after school and he would have felt left out among the local children. But that reason proved to be completely invalid. If your child has an attachment disorder, they cannot make and keep friends. It wouldn't have mattered if his school was next door or across the local park, he didn't have any friends who called for him or invited him to tea. In fact, the absolute opposite happened. Because his reputation for being 'naughty' stuck so quickly at school, that was how he was seen in the local community, and both he and I were given the cold shoulder by some parents. A school further away would not have allowed that to happen and at least given us some space from that reputation.

But what would have improved things more is if I had gone to a school that was far more geared up to helping children with behavioural problems instead of just giving them general labels.

It is a huge regret of mine that I chose the local school. Sometimes I do wonder how things might have been different during what turned out to be some very difficult intervening years. Having the school on side, rather than it just becoming the site of another battleground where I had to make almost daily visits to try and sort out another issue, would have been so helpful as well as a relief.

Why not all children are the same

Before our three daughters were placed with us, we looked at all the local schools. Some were small, some were large. We researched Ofsted inspections and listened to the opinions of those around us. The school we finally chose was the largest in the area and it came highly recommended. It was known for being supportive of children with additional needs, so it seemed ideal.

After an impressive tour of the school and a meeting with the head teacher, we excitedly put all their names down. Little did we know how soon our excitement would change to frustration. It was a matter of weeks after placement that the new school year began. Louise, our youngest, skipped into her nursery class on that first day, straight past all those crying kids clinging to their mums, without a single backwards glance. Louise was just three years old, but she didn't need me. All the other mums said how brave she was and how proud I must be of her independence, but I knew the truth. Louise understandably began displaying some controlling behaviours; one of those behaviours meant that we'd had to resort to 'pull ups'. That was the first time I had a disagreement with school. However, it was to be the first of many over the coming years.

We quickly discovered that only the children with a medical diagnosis were classed as having 'additional needs'. Attachment, trauma, loss, grief, neglect are not diagnosable. So Louise was expected to be the same as all the other 'normal' children. In fact, it seemed there was more understanding and empathy for the children whose parents had divorced or separated. Louise had a nice, new, loving family with both of her parents, didn't she? So the loss and trauma that she'd suffered before being adopted had to have gone away now, hadn't it?!

But I know it hadn't; how could it? I know she isn't the same; her story is one of fear, neglect, terror and trauma. Her story is not the same as any other child in her class; in fact, her story is not the same as any other child in her school, not even her sisters, so how can she be 'the same'?

Louise wasn't brought into this world surrounded by love and hope; she was born into an environment of fear, violence and neglect. I don't just mean dirty clothes and a broken crib. I mean no love, no tenderness, no one soothed her when she cried, no one checked her nappy, no one fed her when she was hungry, no one kept her safe, no one gazed lovingly into her eyes so no one made her feel loved, worthy and cared for.

Then she was taken from everything she'd ever known and sent with only one of her many siblings to live with a foster carer who loved and nurtured her. Then she was moved to a new foster carer who was different, who looked after her physical needs but nothing else. She didn't really like this new life, but it was out of her control. She regressed. Then she was taken once more and sent to live with some new people a very long way away. She'd been adopted.

Louise's development is not the same as a typical child, she has not experienced the same things as a typical child, and her neural pathways have developed differently so her brain doesn't work in the same way as a typical child. Her instincts and impulses are different, she doesn't yet understand cause and effect, and consequences for a child who has lived like this have very little effect; she doesn't care if you take her toys away, she never had any as a baby anyway. She won't try to earn the stars on your reward chart because she already knows she's bad; in fact, she'll show you just how bad she is as soon as you get out that reward chart. She doesn't always hear what you say because her ears are busy listening for danger; she doesn't always make rational choices because inside she feels chaotic. In fact, sometimes she feels so chaotic inside that the only way she can make herself feel normal is to create chaos on the outside too.

So each year when Louise displays her difficulties in ever-increasing and unpredictable ways, her teachers inform me that their behavioural expectations for Louise are the same as they are for her peers. They then tell me that they will be using the shame-invoking reward chart system and behavioural management techniques that they've used for the last three decades. Each year I'm left with the frustrating task of trying to find a way to explain to a teacher why this is unreasonable and unsuitable. Adoptive parents are generally well trained and prepared for the difficulties their children could face in school and are given an understanding of how a child's early history can affect their development and behaviour. Sadly, while teachers spend around 33 hours a week with children, they receive little to no such training on the effects of early trauma and attachment difficulties. When they insist on treating them 'all the same', the fallout can be hard to manage.

Parents give virtual head teacher a lesson

Some time ago the county in which I live appointed a Virtual Head Teacher. Despite her job title, she was a real person and her role was to work on behalf of those children who can find it difficult to access mainstream education – disabled children, children with learning difficulties and children from cultural and ethnic minorities. However, buried in her job description was a baffling reference to another group – adopted children. In order to establish whether this had been an error, she found her way to the county's Head of Post-Adoption Support and together they advertised for adoptive

parents to come forward and to share the difficulties they and their children may have experienced in school.

There were no empty seats in the conference room. When the Virtual Head Teacher arrived, the atmosphere was crackling with expectation. She started proceedings by telling us about her long teaching career and her new role. She opened up the floor and a few nervous parents started to explain the challenges that they and their children face in school. There were accounts of inappropriate behaviour systems which shame the already shamed, exclusions which exclude the already abandoned and teachers who refuse to understand the impacts of early trauma, tagging children as 'controlling', 'lacking in focus', 'disruptive' and 'unteachable'.

The Virtual Head Teacher looked rather stunned and must have felt as though she and her profession were under attack. Then she uttered the words, 'All children are a bit like that, aren't they?' It was the spark that set the room alight. There were a few gasps from around the room followed by a long, long, painful silence. The Virtual Head Teacher shuffled in her chair and fished her pendant from her cleavage.

Then a man spoke up. He was confident, eloquent and angry:

> Our children have come from the care system. They were in the care system because most of them have been neglected or abused or both. They have suffered loss, they have suffered fear, loneliness, violence, hunger and cold, some have suffered severe pain. Raising these children is the biggest challenge which many of us will ever face.

We all nodded in agreement.

I spoke of my own family's experience, which resulted in months of searching for a school that had some appreciation of attachment and trauma. We found one eventually: an excellent village school in a different county, half an hour's drive from our home. The difference in our son is remarkable, but the travelling and the dislocation from our local community have come at some personal and financial cost. Amongst that roomful of parents, I was the only one who recounted anything like a positive experience.

Following the meeting a small working group was formed. We met over many months in dusty halls and cramped meeting rooms.

What grew out of our meeting was, not very excitingly, a form. However, education runs on systems and forms, so we knew we had to play the game by its rules.

The form is called the Education Plan for Adopted Children. It requires a meeting at the school between staff, a social worker and a parent, as a minimum. It lays out the basics of the child's early experiences, their moves into and within the care system, and their adoption. After this initial meeting, the Plan is produced and then updated regularly at follow-up meetings.

The system prompts discussion about how the child presents themselves, their fears, needs and challenges. It demands actions with clear answers. It informs the school and empowers the parent.

Of course, any system that is optional stands or falls on the willingness of those involved to make it work. It goes without saying it does not come with any additional funding. But it provides some authority and legitimacy. It says that parents are not seeing ghosts and that their children are not merely 'naughty' and badly parented.

Many of us know the trajectory that these children, if failed, can follow, so the stakes we are playing for are high.

If I were Queen of Education, I would develop and roll out a national Education Plan for Adopted Children with guidance notes and training for all teaching staff. It would save much heartache and distress, and taking into consideration the broader picture may even save money over the long term.

The right school

My son Daniel recently moved to a new school.

I could have done with more support in choosing his first school. I now know what questions I could have asked but I picked what I thought at the time was the best school for him. But I've since put Daniel in another school which has a lot of other adopted children.

Daniel's original school had a good infrastructure for supporting vulnerable children and he did benefit from that in his first year. He also had a brilliant class teacher who understood attachment issues, but by the second year everything changed. When the adoption order went through, the school still got pupil premium for Daniel, but because they had different legal responsibilities as he was no longer a looked-after child, they no longer saw his needs as a priority – I had not been expecting that.

Daniel's new class teacher wasn't interested in attachment. He just thought Daniel 'needed to pull himself together' as he was now in a happy home and so he should be like the other children. Daniel was being punished all of the time because of his handwriting and his spelling which was delayed – despite the fact he was good at maths and creative subjects. He got told off a lot in public.

The head teacher dismissed my concerns because of my inexperience as a parent so I'm glad Daniel moved schools. All of the teachers at Daniel's new school are trained in attachment and most of the support is provided in the classroom. I've also got to know a lot of other adopters.

I can see it from both sides

Choppies was two and a half when we adopted him. I took almost a year off work to look after him. As a college lecturer, I was fortunate that I could take that amount of time off and it helped us to bond strongly as a family and to develop crucial routines.

I went back to work when my son started nursery. Initially, it went OK but then suddenly we started to be called in to speak with teaching staff. They felt that he wasn't displaying the normal emotional and social skills compared to others in his age group. He would display what would be considered defiant behaviour and was unable to follow instructions and would be very needy. They attempted to use traditional strategies with him but they did not work. It got progressively worse as he was struggling emotionally and socially. You could see the regression in his behaviour from wetting his pants to sitting under the desk chewing his feet, while other children learned and played. Our hearts were breaking in what seemed like a futile effort to support his learning journey.

We did consider ADHD or Asperger's syndrome as many of the behaviour traits he displayed matched these conditions. We were left scratching our heads.

By Year 1 there was still little improvement to Choppies' emotional state. It was decided that he needed external specialist support accompanied by an assessment and that it was imperative to act now; otherwise his learning would be seriously impeded. Jointly as a family and school, we embarked on the process of involving social services and the educational psychologist. We were working as a team to support each other, with Choppies at the centre of our efforts.

I clearly remember his class teacher declaring, 'I'm going to work through this with you!' They sought our advice and we sought theirs. As a lecturer teaching young people who experience social, emotional and behavioural difficulties, I gained an insight into the world of trauma and its impact. I work with teenagers rather than primary children but I still have a wealth of experience, so together we brainstormed a positive way forward.

We employed many innovative learning strategies for him to use, like the use of fiddle toys in the classroom to act as a comforter. Both the class teacher and teaching assistant acted as his key worker and were always ready to share the day's experiences with us, be it the good, the bad or the ugly. Amongst other things we devised a mapping book which showed which situations he found stressful and where he did well. We scored behaviour and attitude and how he coped. It was a positive thing as he loved to see how he was doing and thoroughly enjoyed getting his stickers when we all agreed he had made progress.

We have regular meetings with his 'SENCO' (special educational needs coordinator) and his class teacher so see how he is progressing socially, emotionally and academically. Things are very good.

We adore the school and we have mutual respect. Choppies has just completed Year 3 and has reached all of the targets required for a child of his age.

I have a firm conviction that it should be an automatic right for learners with such complex needs to have a key worker to champion their cause. It's about accepting them at their point of need, giving them hope and a future, and walking that journey with them so they become all they are destined to be and can function successfully as adults.

I believe that there is a gap in training educators in this complex area of trauma. I hope one day all schools will address the need to work better with these learners.

Tactless teaching

When our daughter was in junior school, we were contacted when she refused to do her English work, which was to write about her earliest childhood memory! The class teacher was aware that she was adopted and attending play therapy, but couldn't understand why she was being so defiant. After talking to her, we suggested that perhaps she would be happier writing about a memory she had with us. 'Well, that's not really what we want,' replied the teacher. I told her she could have that or nothing.

This was one of the many incidents that caused our daughter a lot of distress and left us having to deal with her 'off the wall behaviour' at home. The situation could have been avoided. So could another time when her schoolbooks went flying across the kitchen because her homework was to draw her family tree.

I was contacted on another occasion as she was being continuously extremely disruptive in class and was having to be sent out of the classroom. The actual problem was a young male trainee teacher whose voice reminded her of one of her abusers, so when he was taking class she couldn't cope.

Keeping going

Dan was a year old when he came to us. His first primary school was in inner London. It was fantastic because they were used to dealing with children from chaotic, disrupted backgrounds. Dan was placed on the special educational needs (SEN) register in Year 1. By the time we left London when he was seven and a half, he had made enough progress to be taken off it. The teachers had created a good relationship with him, which meant that he wanted to go to school and do well.

We moved to North Somerset where Dan attended a small village school and was put back on the SEN register. When he was ten, he found it hard to cope with the pressure of SATS. The staff didn't know what to do with him as when he got frustrated he started getting into fights. He was probably also unsettled by the imminent move to secondary school. He would have been permanently excluded after the last, most severe fight had it not happened only two weeks before he was due to leave anyway at the end of Year 6. As it was, he was excluded for those last two weeks, which was a sad end to his primary schooling.

Dan's first year of secondary school was characterized by him being overwhelmed by anxiety and being unable to go in many days. His attendance was about 50 per cent during that year and it was partly because of what had happened at the end of primary school – it was shocking for him and so he was frightened about how he would cope at a much bigger school. The staff attempted to help him by saying that was water under the bridge, but he, showing a lot of self-awareness, said, 'What happens if that water comes around again?'

Towards the end of the year we, as Dan's parents, were threatened with prosecution by an education welfare officer because of Dan's lack of attendance. The officer didn't understand Dan's difficult start in life and how this was impacting on his capacity to manage school, which added to Dan's anxieties and ours. Thankfully, a social worker in the local adoption support team intervened and the threat of prosecution was dropped, and a senior education official actually phoned us at home one Sunday afternoon to apologize!

Dan had a better experience of secondary school in his second year, but as he hit adolescence, his behaviour both at school and home proved more challenging, with escalating outbursts of violence and destruction, which he wasn't at that point able to control. In numerous meetings with school staff we explained how his early trauma affected him in school. We arranged for Dan to be assessed by CAMHS and he was diagnosed with ADHD and executive function deficit.

When we felt we weren't getting the message across, we brought in an expert witness, someone with a background in teaching children with emotional and behavioural difficulties who then worked for a local adoption charity. He tried to get the school to understand what was causing Dan's problems but at the end of the meeting he said they just weren't listening.

We felt dismissed by the school staff as parents who were falling down on the job. As we had educated ourselves about early trauma and its impact on educational achievement, we found it very difficult when we were not listened to and not understood. We felt there was a total lack of empathy and understanding from most of the staff we were dealing with. I would have liked to have seen Dan moved out of the classes where he really struggled, liked to have seen him put into a small 'nurture' group so a designated member of staff could see how he was doing as a person. Having said that, Dan later told me that being sent out of lessons to a small unit within the school was not good for him; it just made him feel 'dumb'.

I also disagreed with the school's reward and punishment system – that kind of behaviourist approach has never worked with Dan. What always worked was a good relationship with his teachers. Unsurprisingly, the teachers who took the time to get to know Dan, were playful with him and found out what made him tick, had a much better relationship with him than those who took a more rigid stance. When Dan felt accepted and understood, he worked well.

A recurring pattern was that other kids would taunt Dan verbally and he would then hit them. There was one major fight which resulted in Dan being permanently excluded when he was aged 13. I was extremely shocked, hurt and angry on his behalf. It was deeply traumatic for him – and us – but for him it felt like further rejection. Dan briefly attended a unit for children with emotional and behavioural difficulties, but the same behaviourist approaches produced the same explosive outbursts from Dan, so we decided to home-school him for a year and a half.

It was stressful in terms of juggling things and I had to cut back significantly on work. Of course, being out of school Dan hooked up with other kids who were in similar circumstances. There were thefts, although never by Dan, so it was partly for the security of the house that I stayed at home. But it was also a relief not to be constantly dealing with the school.

At the time I felt Dan's school experience and being permanently excluded had severely limited his chances in life, but the picture looks a lot better now than it did then. There has been some excellent input from a specialist team at the local college, from the Prince's Trust and from a project for unemployed young people run by the Conservation Volunteers. We're very grateful for all of that.

For the last two and a half years Dan has been training with a wonderful local charity that works with teenagers and young people. He has a tutor who's relentlessly positive and affirming – just the sort of person Dan always needed.

Dan is now working part-time as an assistant coach in outdoor pursuits. His self-confidence has been built up and he's able to use his own experiences to relate to the young teenagers he's working with. Dan believes if he hadn't been permanently excluded from mainstream schooling, he wouldn't have got involved in alternative education, like that provided by the Prince's Trust, which he feels has benefited him greatly.

Dan, who is now aged 22, recently told me his secondary school was not right for him. When I asked in what way, he quoted something that he'd read: 'If you teach a monkey, an elephant, a giraffe and a fish to climb a tree, only the monkey will feel smart.'

Chapter 14

CONTACT IN ADOPTION

Contact with birth families is a constant focus for discussion and debate by social workers and adopters, with conflicting views on its strengths, weaknesses, short- and long-term benefits. Some adopters see it as a valuable link with their child's personal history, a bringing together, however painful at first, of the threads of a child's life, opening out discussion on a past that could otherwise haunt their child's future. Others find that it loosens the links they are trying so carefully to build with their children and just causes their children pain, confusion and inner conflict.

Contact can mean anything from meetings with the birth mum and family on a regularly agreed basis to a once-a-year letter from a grandmother at Christmas. Current thinking by most adoption authorities and charities is that some degree of contact is generally in a child's best interests, unless it is demonstrably clear that the children would not benefit from a continuing relationship of any kind. But adopters don't all or always agree.

'The idea that contact is a good thing for children and is in their interests is in my opinion complete rubbish. It was destabilizing our children and upsetting them every time we saw their birth mother and we eventually refused contact,' raged one adopter.

'I feel there needs to be a radical change in thinking in favour of the adoptive family unit to ensure that it is kept intact. Social services seem to forget that an adoptive family is quite different from a foster family and should be treated like a natural family which is what we are in law.'

But another adoptive mother who continued contact even though it resulted in her daughter pushing all behavioural boundaries said:

Contact does not create problems, it brings them to the surface, where they can be explored and hopefully eventually resolved. It would not protect my daughter to avoid these issues; it is my opinion that you cannot protect a child from something that has already happened, they need to make sense of it so that they can move on. Contact for us has been a hugely challenging but ultimately, I hope, a useful and rewarding experience.

Contact can be difficult for adopted families who have adopted more than one child from different birth families with different contact arrangements. 'We pulled out of a second adoption because there was a strong push for regular contact with the birth family,' explained one birth mother. 'We have no contact with our eldest son's birth family – and after discussing it with other experienced adopters, I had nightmares about all the problems it could throw up within the family and with our eldest son who is thriving.'

Some of the most positive contact meetings are between siblings, and adopters have been struck by the depth of bond between brothers and sisters, particularly when children from the same birth family are adopted by different families.

But one of the major challenges both adopters and social workers currently face is unplanned contact through Facebook and other social media. 'Hello' messages from long-forgotten birth parents and family members can drop unbidden like a bombshell into an adoptee's inbox at any time. Adolescents going through a bad patch can equally cruise the internet to see if they can find the birth family they have half forgotten. This unplanned contact can be shattering as birth families rewrite history for the confused child, claiming they were 'stolen', that they have 'always loved them', that the abuse that took them into care never really happened.

Contact plans are outlined for every child placed for adoption. However, Facebook and the internet have destroyed any safeguards. It is critical that children understand the importance of protecting their privacy online.

It is important to remember that under the adoption laws an adoptive parent can refuse contact with a birth family for their child until the child technically becomes an adult at 18, which is also when their own social work notes become available to them.

The other mother

I have always told our daughter Megan (our son Billy not yet being ready to acknowledge that we are not his birth parents) that parents have three functions in life; one is to bring children into the world, the second is to look after them and the third is to bring them up. Sometimes the parents cannot complete all these tasks for various reasons.

In this respect, our children are not so vastly different from children who have birth parents living with other partners. No one can ever deny that the birth parents will always be their other mum and dad, whether there is contact or not.

We started to foster our children, a girl, then six, and a baby boy of 11 months with a view to adopting them over seven years ago. There had been two specialist reports which both recommended that the children should not be returned to their birth mother. We had been assessed for adoption and assured by social workers that, although the formalities would have to be completed, we and the children would be a 'forever family'.

We were really excited on the day the children came to live with us, although it felt very strange to see their loaded suitcases and hold-alls in our house. The cases belonged to their mother. For some reason it took me two weeks to unpack them. I felt as though I was treading on someone else's toes.

The first few months were completely overwhelming. If we had ever thought we would have plenty of time to bond once the children came to live with us, we were mistaken. On top of almost daily visits from social workers and the health visitor, we had to drive them 25 miles to the nearest town for contact visits with their birth mother twice a week.

These visits were an emotional trial, just as we were starting to build attachments with the children. I had been permitted to meet the mother at an early stage, and it had been very important to me that she thought we were suitable parents for her two beautiful children. However, from then on we were completely excluded from the contact visits which were supervised by a family support worker to prevent the mother from attempting to undermine the placement.

I would leave our children at the door of the Family Centre to be met by a social worker who would whisk them away to the room where their birth mother awaited them. I would not even have time to give our baby a cuddle. I would then wander around town for two long hours feeling empty and aimless; suddenly, my status as their forever mum would seem diminished and unimportant. I physically missed the closeness with our baby son and worried about what he was doing. It felt like I was missing my right arm.

I would return to collect the children after their mother had gone, dreading that they would not want to come back with me because they would have been swamped with presents and sweets.

Their mother did not accept us as the children's new parents. She was tremendously influential with our daughter who was afraid that calling us 'Mum' and 'Dad' would offend her. She therefore referred to us by our Christian names during the contact visits. This must have been very confusing for our infant son, who had called us 'Mummy' and 'Daddy' with his very first words.

I remember the sickly smell of sweets during the car drive home from these visits, as we were regaled with tales of people we did not know who were present at the contact meeting. We were responsible for these children, and as emotionally committed to them as loving birth parents, yet we had no say in the contact visits at all.

It was clear that our daughter felt unsettled and confused by the contact visits. They reduced over the years to a frequency of every three or four months, but she would go through a couple of weeks of disruptive behavior, both at home and at school, following each visit.

Shortly after the children came to us, the mother had another baby. The child protection system at the time did not find sufficient evidence to remove him from her care because the baby did not have a record of physical or emotional abuse with his mother.

The mother then moved to a city many miles away from the remote area we live in, and where she had no history with the city's social work department. At our annual review by the Children's Panel, a decision was made to consider placing our children back with their mother instead of supporting proceedings for us to adopt them, because the city social work department reported that the mother was doing well with her new baby.

We were devastated. The shock and stress were huge as we contemplated the thought of the children we love, and had believed we would adopt, possibly being returned to the traumatic and damaging situation they had been removed from nearly two years previously. In the event it was decided that the mother had enough to cope with one child, so for the time being they could remain with us. We were therefore relegated to the status of foster carers rather than prospective adopters.

From this point, the mother's attitude changed towards us for the worse. She now had enough confidence to believe she might get her first two children back. With the help of a Legal Aid solicitor, she opposed us and our continuing plans to adopt the children. This would now happen for a further four difficult years.

Although the contact visits were much less frequent, they were as disruptive as ever; perhaps more so because they would stir things up after several months of smooth-running family life. Seeing Mum now was quite an event, especially as she brought the new baby brother the first two or three times. A lone family support worker found it impossible to adequately supervise two children, their mother and anyone else the mother had invited along. Our daughter reported that her mother would take her to the toilets to 'try on new clothes', then try to persuade her to make allegations against us, or tell her that she was going to 'get her back'.

As events turned out, the contact visits ended naturally. Despite the mother's opposition, we eventually managed to adopt the children. The mother had a further baby, and I imagine she realized that she could not cope with her first two as well. Visits became less and less frequent, and have now stopped altogether.

Our daughter is presently disillusioned with her mother's repeated failure to visit. She has had to cope with the knowledge that she was once her mother's only child, and now her place has been usurped by two other children, only one of whom she has even seen. She is adamant she wants no further contact with her mother, probably because she cannot face the hurt it would cause her. Of course, there may come a day when she changes her mind, and also when our son wants to know more about his birth family and asks to meet his mother.

I only hope that, if contact ever does start again, our children will be secure and mature enough to benefit from it. Over the years, I have become confident enough of our own place in the children's lives to realize that they regard my husband and me as their true parents, the ones who have given them the stable home, the love, the commitment and the time.

However, as their 'bringing up' parents we have to help them grow towards being happy and fulfilled adults. If this means that they will want to reunite with their birth mother one day, we will wholeheartedly support them,

It's OK to love two mummies

Five and a quarter years ago we were first introduced to our two little boys, brothers aged three and six. We had been told to 'expect the unexpected' and for me that was extreme hostility from the six-year-old Liam towards me as 'Mummy', although they chose to call us Mummy and Daddy from day one. Liam was strongly attached to his birth mum (who he was seeing once a fortnight until he moved in with us) and rejected closeness as betrayal of her.

My husband's work was very supportive and he was able to take six months' adoption leave. I stopped doing supply teaching and so we were both at home full-time. Liam latched on to his new daddy and even suggested to him that they take me to the beach and leave me there so he could get a new wife. I think he had his birth mum in mind! When I tried to speak to him about his hostility, he just said, 'I don't like ladies.'

The three-year-old, Josh, was very bewildered at first and would sometimes sit with his head on the floor saying, 'Go, go!' which was his way of saying 'No'. However, he loved to be cuddled and was very affectionate. He soon embraced us as his parents with warmth and affection.

But we had many battles with Liam, emotional and physical, over the early months and years as the boys continued to have contact with their birth family. A lot of anger surged to the surface in Liam. Strangely enough, it was often in the darkest times that a breakthrough was made. Like the times Liam was ill, feeling rotten and just wanting to be mothered. Or when, excluded from a family outing for bad behaviour, he stayed home alone with me and moments of real companionship followed as we shared activities and did something nice for the people he'd upset by baking cookies for their return home.

The day he got so mad that he urinated under his bed was another example. I discovered it while it was still warm and easy to identify. At the time it felt like the last straw. I'm sure he expected a row, but I felt all my energy and anger drain away; I just sat and looked at him and said, 'I don't know what to say or what to do.' After a few minutes I suggested he helped me to clean it up which he did conscientiously. Then I took him down to watch a recent documentary we'd recorded, thinking, 'It can't make things any worse.' It was about children moving on from foster placements to adoptive homes. The children put into words very articulately what Liam couldn't about their fears about moving on, their longing to be back to live with their birth families and their explanations about why this was not possible. 'He's just like me!' said Liam and, although he didn't want to talk about it afterwards, I think he somehow felt less alone.

Contact caused us real heartache as it involved a plane flight and the boys being whisked off by social workers to meet up somewhere fun with their birth mum and two older siblings. If was very hard to see them being driven off, and confusing for the boys, as the family were not able to be supportive and give the boys permission to move on. On one occasion, Liam's earring hole (not used for three years) had been reopened by his birth mother and sister, and a pink stud inserted – whilst being supervised by social workers!

We felt that face-to-face contact was too unsettling for the boys and jeopardizing the placement. It was like tearing a scab off a deep wound that is starting to heal. So contact has lapsed which has enabled us to have a more settled period. Whenever they want to speak about their 'other family' or look at photos, they know that this is OK.

I remember saying to Liam after a difficult emotional struggle, 'It's OK to love two mummies. You've got room in your heart to love us both.' I'll never forget his reply: 'I've only got a wee heart.' He cried as he struggled to work out which one of us he loved the most.

As we look back at this turbulent period with a little distance, we can see that the boys have brought to our family a tremendous loyalty, affection and 'difference' which has enriched our family. It can be refreshing and helps us look at life from a different perspective.

The long road to formal adoption was completed after five years with our day in court. Liam said as he came home from school that day, 'Hi, proper Daddy! Hi proper Mummy!' which kind of summed it up really.

Strengthening bonds

Our recent arrival, five-year-old George, sobbed hopelessly in the back seat of the car, causing me to pull over so my husband Simon could hop into the back and comfort him for the rest of the trip home.

We had just enjoyed a happy, sunny day in Legoland, meeting with George's half-siblings for the first time. It was his first meeting with them for several months, and since moving in with us. We hung back and enjoyed observing their interaction; their love for each other was obvious, and George was relaxed and refused to let go of them for the entire four hours that he spent with them. It was interesting to see his features reflected in their faces, and it convinced us that we'd made the right decision to agree that he should have contact with them at least twice a year, so long as they were not a negative influence in any way.

Because they both have unfettered contact with their birth mother, George's half-siblings still do not know where we live. Steve and Susan are 12 and ten years older than George and had been his prime carers during his first two years, and were in care with him for the next two, before George was moved to a more appropriate setting for a four-year-old.

We felt it would be grossly unfair to deprive him, or them, of the chance to see each other. After all, they had provided our son with vital nurturing which was a lifeline during a traumatic time for him at the most crucial time of his development. We credit them with enabling George to express empathy and to love and be loved, imperfect though their parenting skills had been. Clearly their birth mother had done a good job at nurturing them both, before the demon drink intervened.

With impeccable five-year-old black-and-white reasoning, George found it hard to comprehend why we hadn't adopted all three of them. Over time, the parting when we made contact gradually became less traumatic as the penny dropped for George that Steve and Susan were not going to disappear from his life and, although George has inevitably made different bonds within his adoptive family, we have continued to see Steve and Susan sporadically during the last nine years.

Steve, who was doing well when we first met him, working for a painter decorator and saving up to pay for driving lessons, is doing less well, living with his and Liam's birth mother, and losing his driving licence (due to a drink-driving incident). He does not respond to our calls at the moment, but we hope he will get in touch soon and get his life back on track. We saw Susan recently, after a gap of a year. She is hard-working and reliable, and likes to work outdoors. But life is precarious for her. She lives in bedsit land with a one-eyed, three-legged dog she rescued called Princess who she adores. She has very low self-esteem which makes her vulnerable to exploitation by unscrupulous employers. I am trying to find her a mentor through the 'leaving care' team within social services, and am also trying to help her find her a better job.

We have all benefited from Steve's and Susan's sporadic presence in George's life; he is delighted that we take an interest in his siblings, and loves us all the more for understanding their importance to him.

I recognize that every adopter's situation is different. However, if it's appropriate to maintain some level of contact with innocent siblings, grandparents and others, I recommend it as a good way to provide a sense of continuity. By acknowledging and respecting their previous meaningful relationships, we can only strengthen our own bonds with our children.

Open hearts and open minds

The first information we had about our children's birth families came from social services. We had nothing else to base our opinion on, especially as we never had the opportunity to meet them.

There is a danger, it seems to me, in some cases of placing us, 'the rescuers', on a pedestal of goodness, whilst the birth family can easily be portrayed as the 'bad ones'. The child sits in the middle of this. The juxtaposition that is created doesn't really help anyone, least of all the child or young person who has been adopted.

Maybe as new adopters and then somewhat younger, these thoughts did not occur to me. Possibly I was happy to be judged as the superior one, stepping in to save the day. However, some years later and with the benefit of experience, not to mention the lasting effects of secondary trauma, I have rethought things.

Like two estranged parents in a divorce settlement, our distance from one another surely isn't helpful to the children. I feel in the next few years I should be doing more to help try to build or at least establish some kind of relationship, not least for the sake of the children. I'm not saying for one minute that we will all become friends and skip off in to the sunset together like one big happy family. This isn't an episode of *Long Lost Family*! But an exploration of the distance between us could at least be considered, because if it is just fear that drives us apart, then that can be overcome.

In our case our children are from different birth families and so they come with different histories and have contrasting views on how they would like the future to look. Each story has its own complications and the outcomes will be different.

I for one, though, am going through an experience of reframing my views on how the future will look for us with regard to contact. One statement from an adoptee stuck in my mind at a recent conference when she said that she would have preferred a stepped approach to contact and that going from 'zero to one hundred' at age 18 was overwhelming.

A mother's contact dilemma

'It's awful for at least two weeks after the children get their (twice-yearly) letter from their birth parents. They're upset, their behaviour gets worse and they feel completely confused. Every letter says, "We love you, we think about you every day and miss you lots." The children feel bewildered. What they read simply doesn't chime with what we (have to) tell them about their early life and why they were adopted.'

The words of my friend ran through my head when unexpectedly I received a cheery email from our letterbox coordinator, saying that our youngest daughter's birth father, John, via his probation team, wanted to start writing to our children.

Until that point, John had not been part of the equation for many reasons. I write once a year, on behalf of our children (who came to us at 16 months and 11 months and who are now seven and six), to their birth mother, Julie, who has recently read the letters having previously not responded.

John and Julie have been together since before our eldest child was born, but John isn't her birth father, though he is the birth father of our youngest child. 'He's really keen and very enthusiastic,' said the email ('Great,' I thought); 'It could work really well' ('It could,' I thought); 'he's not the birth father of your eldest child' ('I know,' I thought); 'but he's lived with them both' ('He hasn't,' I thought) and 'he's "happy" to write to them both' ('What!' I thought).

As I scrolled down the email, I was eagerly anticipating some thoughts and considerations about the children. I felt sure there would be some advice and insight into how they might be prepared; what would be done to support John in understanding his role and commitment; information about why this initiative was John only, despite the fact that he was still with Julie; how we as parents could be supported to help prepare the children; what had prompted John to initiate this request now. It was disappointing to find nothing.

Maybe we, or rather the (four) adoptive families we know well who have letterbox contact, are just unlucky. Their letterbox contact was established from the outset of the children being placed with their adoptive parents. Apart from the blindingly obvious no-go areas ('Here's our address should you ever want to visit us'), it seems as if the birth relatives can write pretty much what they want. There's no 'monitored or supported' regard to the changing needs of the children and the fact that they need a consistent 'story' that resonates with and acknowledges what their parents have to tell them about their early life to help them understand why they were adopted.

There's been much recent debate about how we as adoptive parents talk to our children about their early life history and that trying to protect them by 'sugar-coating' the reality could create even more problems. To me, it seemed essential that from the outset any letter was well thought through and must not avoid the 'elephant in the room'.

The elephant in the room is the complete disregard of the birth parents' role in the children's early life experiences and subsequent adoption and the children's permanent family status. In our children's best interests, I felt some things had to be a given. The first and subsequent letters had to acknowledge that the birth parents couldn't look after babies and children, which is why the children were adopted by parents who could keep them safe and who they would always be with. That would never change. Their mummy and daddy would always be their mummy and daddy, and the birth parents were pleased and happy about this.

I wanted to make sure that professionals were involved to support and liaise with the birth parents to explain this. As parents, we were more than receptive to the letterbox idea. While they're still young, it's something over time they would take for granted and accept as the norm. I felt sure that the professionals I asked for advice and support would be in complete agreement.

My thoughts from the outset have been about how we work together to ensure that establishing letterbox contact is done in a way that will help and support the children. All concerned need to support and reinforce consistently the reality of the children's life story so that they can make sense of their early life, much of which is difficult. I feel that I was, and possibly still am, at the mercy of two prevailing assumptions: first that contact from birth parents/relatives is 'good' and second that I, as an adoptive parent, would naturally panic about it and that my questions and concerns were a way of shying away from something I'd rather not deal with. Neither of these is true.

Apparently, I (and my children) faced a Hobson's choice. Have I thought that if I don't agree to this letterbox contact, then the birth parents could approach my children by social media anyway? Of course I've thought about it. The catastrophic effects of unregulated contact via social media could not have escaped the attention of any adoptive family. It's something that we as parents are already talking and will continue to talk about with our children, but for goodness sake, just now, they're seven and six.

The process can't simply be: birth parents decide they want to write; send email to adoptive parents suggesting same; adoptive parents say great, let's get on with it.

All adoptive parents have to support, therapeutically parent, communicate difficult issues and at the same time help their children to feel loved, secure and safe.

Social workers did eventually have a meeting with the birth parents and their support workers, to talk about some of these issues: the importance of the children's not the adults' best interests; the ongoing commitment; the shared story; the issues around birth parentage and how they could be explained.

The birth parents were generous enough to acknowledge that they hadn't thought about many of these things. So far, I feel sad and disappointed that the complications they hadn't considered have meant that they haven't written yet, but I hope this will change with the right support.

Birth parent dropping out of contact

Our adopted daughter Sara is nine years old and has been with us since a baby. We have had good direct and letterbox contact with her birth mother from the beginning.

The birth mother has grown up a lot since she had our daughter and has subsequently had another child who has stayed with her and is now has 18 months old. We met our daughter's birth mother and her sibling a year ago.

However, in the past couple of years, the birth mother has not really done the letterbox. We have some sympathy with this as it is hard with working and having a small baby. Now she is not replying to any texts or phone calls from the contact supervisor who has worked with us and her for years. It doesn't look like direct contact will happen this year. The contact supervisor has told her she will never be 'forced' to have contact, but she won't reply to offers to come and discuss things.

But my daughter doesn't understand. I'm not sure we do either. Contact supervisor says it's sometimes hard for a birth parent to stay connected when they have another child. Or maybe she feels guilty or fearful that now our daughter is older she will start asking 'difficult' questions.

I'm coming to your birthday party

We have had intermittent contact with members of my elder daughter Izzy's birth family throughout her adoption – but it has always gone through me and my husband until this year. My daughter will be 18 in May and she received a message saying her elder brother and grandma will be coming to her party. We don't live in the UK and she was really upset by this message, as I was.

She was upset because she has felt that her brother has little to say to her in recent years and grandma has not been in touch for some time.

I was annoyed because I felt it was a not too subtle message that at 18 she was now theirs again and there was no need to ask me. However, they overlooked that at 18 my daughter can make her own decisions and after all the fallout from the message – which she had to cope with – she sent a message back saying her brother was welcome to come and visit but not on her birthday as that was to be a family event and that she wasn't sure if she wanted to see grandma at all.

She has had no reply – but this event seems to have really helped our daughter to become more comfortable with being adopted and she has spent a lot more time with her wider adoptive family saying she wants to belong to them as well as to us.

I now really feel that the contact was never helpful for her and thwarted her attachment in some ways.

Our second adopted daughter has had a very closed adoption. I wonder what will happen when she hits 18?

Chapter 15

ATTACHMENT ISSUES

A recent study by Adoption UK[1] revealed that new adopting families should be the focus of intensive health and social services in the way that new birth families are. 'It found that becoming an adoptive family is even more challenging than becoming a birth family because new healthy bonds of attachment must be made and old, unhealthy patterns of attachment must be replaced or reshaped,' reported the study.

Attachment disorder – when neglect and abuse causes a child to distrust everyone around them – digs deep into the resources of patience and unconditional, unremitting love that adoptive parents need to give to an unattached child.

The battle to gain the trust of a damaged child can often take years. 'Imagine how terrifying it is for a child when a prime source of safety, his birth father or mother, is a source of terror,' says Dr Dan Hughes, a psychologist who has made a study of attachment disorder and written a number of books about its cause, effects and how to rebuild attachment. He has created his own model for adopters trying to rebuild primary links of trust with their children – PLACE: create an environment which is Playful, Loving, Accepting, Curious and Empathetic.

Secure attachments provide a safe base for a child, reducing fearfulness and stress as they learn to trust that their needs will be met. Experts believe that neglect can have as profound an impact on a child as abuse. A child doesn't need to have a conscious memory of a trauma or a loss to be negatively affected by it.

---

1   A. Bell (2012) 'Exploring the Support Needs of New Adopters.' Research study of 455 Adoption UK members, report published in Adoption UK's magazine *Adoption Today.*

'This all paints a very gloomy picture, but please don't forget that our children have many strengths and survival skills,' said Anne O'Connor, an adoptive parent and specialist in attachment issues:

> They have a lot to teach us about resilience and the plasticity of the brain which enable them, in the right environment, to re-learn many of the things that were denied to them in their early life. In the process they will communicate their needs to us in the most powerful way they can which is through their behaviours – many of which will be challenging and tiresome.

Attachment is a challenge all adopters face to one degree or another and deal with in different ways.

A labour of love

Rob is the father of four birth children and three adopted children, one of whom has significant attachment problems.

'They just need a lot of loving and they'll be OK.'

Many of us adoptive parents have encountered this persistent view of hurt children. We may even have thought it ourselves. Hopefully, our adoption preparation will have pointed out that things aren't that simple, but at the same time there is truth in the statement: love is incredibly powerful.

However, giving love to hurt kids can be frustratingly difficult. It's not so much our ability to love that is the problem as the children's ability to receive it.

Most children are offered a constant and consistent stream of love by their birth parents in the early months and years of their lives. They learn that being loved is fantastic and makes them feel great. They learn how to receive it and how to handle it. They learn that they deserve it and expect to be loved.

But many adopted children didn't come into a world where they were immediately immersed in love. It wasn't offered consistently and unconditionally. Sometimes it wasn't offered at all.

The result is that they view love as something alien and treat it with deep suspicion. They don't recognize it, don't know how to handle it, think that they are not worthy of being loved, feel uncomfortable with the strange feelings that it provokes in themselves and suspect that it's a tool for adults to use in controlling them. They may also be wary: whenever they've been loved before, they have been moved on. As they see it, as soon as love started to blossom, the adult discarded them. Worse, they may see letting someone love them as being the signal – or even the reason – that their placement is about to break down. Love results in their heart being broken. Love, to them, can't be trusted.

If our children desperately need to be loved but find it so hard to accept love, then what can we do?

Therapist Holly van Gulden, adoptive parent, well-known speaker and author of a number of books on adoption including *Learning the Dance of Attachment* and *Real Parents, Real Children: Parenting the Adopted Child*, talks about offering hurt children love in a form that they can accept. For instance, they may find a full, face-to-face hug to be frightening. Instead, they need some sort of touch that is less intense which they can cope with. Our son could only accept a hug facing away from us. Even that could be too hard for some children; they may not be able to accept more than a fleeting ET-like touching of fingers.

The same is true of presents. Present giving often involves exaggerated gestures, 'Look what I've got for you!' excitement and glitzy wrapping paper. If giving them a present in such a 'normal' fashion results in meltdown and the gift being destroyed, you'll need to find a different way of doing it. The aim is to find the level that they can accept and then to slowly, gently and sensitively increase the intensity and closeness as the children become able to accept it.

Getting it wrong can have spectacular results. Give a gift too overtly and you may quickly be presented with rages and the gift smashed to pieces. A treat can be sabotaged with appalling behaviour. Cuddles that are too intimate will be broken out of, possibly violently.

The other aspect of giving love is that children normally ask for it. Where there are no requests, I easily forget that my children need me to do these things to show them that they are loved. And where they do make requests, I find it difficult to tell the difference between what is a request for love and what is an attempt at controlling. For instance, is the incessant demand for me to push my son on the swing a cry for quality time from me? Or is it that he doesn't really know how to play and is getting me to do it for him? Or is it that he feels that he's being in charge if he's got me doing things for him?

When he asks my wife for a cuddle, does he really want one? Or is he getting in first to stop someone else from getting one? Or is he getting close so that he can stick his elbows in to injure her; another punishment for his birth mother, projected on to my wife?

All of this calls for as much sensitivity as you can muster. It's yet another part of the endlessly fascinating and frustrating job of helping a hurt child to overcome their trauma.

Timing

This summer we were lucky enough to have one of those well-timed holidays where I saw my daughter in a fully relaxed state for the first time in seven years. We had fun.

But I well remember early days with our daughter when fun was overwhelming and scary. Her self-esteem was non-existent and she was a bundle of anxieties and hypervigilance. For some children, having fun is a totally alien experience and they need to be introduced to it gently. They need to play at much younger games than their developmental age.

When we were away this year, our ten-year-old spent some time unloading and reloading a full-sized car trailer and manoeuvring it around the garden. This was like the two-year-old activity of enclosing and transporting, putting objects into bags, trains, etc. This was her favourite activity for two days and then she stopped. At two, when she should have had access to these sorts of toys, she was in a very unstable physical and emotional environment and probably did not explore this form of learning.

Of course, there are very many of us who have huge concerns about our children's academic achievement and what this might mean in terms of their future prospects, career and ability to be self-sufficient. It is my belief, however, that it is vital to address the child's stress levels. A much stressed child will be using all their survival strategies to cope in a hostile world (as they perceive it). This does not allow them to learn easily. When you are focused on survival, the human drive to learn does not come into play.

This makes me wonder whether some of my daughter's learning difficulties stem from her focus on survival and consequent neglect of the early developmental tasks and ideas explored through play which help to build intellect and reason. If I am right, then her increased attachment and security should lead to a sea change in her ability to take on new knowledge and adapt to new situations.

Whatever the outcome, it is my belief, as stated in Daniel Goleman's book *Emotional Intelligence*, that the best predictor for a successful and confident adult is a happy, confident and emotionally literate child.[2]

Getting the right help

Simon had always been happy at school, enjoying the social side and respecting his teachers. However, academically he was not making much progress at all in literacy, and the teaching methods prescribed by the National Curriculum to get spellings and times tables to stick appeared as effective as pouring water into a bucket with a large hole in it.

So when Simon hit Year 6, at the age of ten, I reflected with despair on what would happen when Simon left the nurturing environment of primary school and hit secondary school. To my surprise, the solution to our dilemma turned out to be to hire an ex-young offender to mentor Simon under the guise of Simon-sitting every time we went out.

Charles responded to an ad that I placed in a local newsagent's window. Hoping to attract a male, I advertised for preferably a 'football mad teenager to coach a ten-year-old boy who is allergic to doing homework with parents'.

Our son, Simon, moved in with us at the age of five and we adopted him at the age of six. His early years were traumatic and his experience of female authority figures during this time was poor. He was taken into care at the age of two when his mother (a violent alcoholic) was imprisoned for child neglect and abuse. Social workers were well-meaning, but ineffectual, and for two years allowed him to be bullied in care by his reluctant foster mother (imagine a three-year-old being told they are stupid every time they ask a question). This foster carer also allowed teenage foster children to bully

2   D. Goleman (1996) *Emotional Intelligence: Why it Can Matter More Than IQ.* London: Bloomsbury.

Simon emotionally and physically. So, not surprisingly, we inherited considerable baggage with our charming boy. His attachment disorder means that Simon can be very controlling, and both verbally and physically abusive towards me, his mother.

Foetal Alcohol Syndrome as well as dyslexia impact on his learning. And when he arrived, our focus was on nurturing, playing and building a relationship with him; learning Maths and English stayed in school. One glimmer of light: he was happy for me to read to him every night, something that hadn't happened before he moved in with us.

We met Charles in a local coffee shop the day after he responded to my ad. Aged 23, he had an impish charm and ready smile, and I could see him being a hit with kids, and although he was nervous with me, he was upfront about his previous misdemeanours and the fact that he had been homeless in the past. When I inquired about his motivation to go straight, he said that the birth of his son (at the age of 17) had been the driver. He wanted to be the father that he hadn't had. Charles had split from his son's mother, but takes an active part in his son's upbringing. He informed me he had spent the previous couple of years working with Harrow Social Services, mentoring 'clients' in their young offenders' unit, young adults coming out of the care system and autistic children too. He handed over his full disclosure CRB Form, so I was able to see that there were no reasons why he should not work with children, and a CV.

Charles was an immediate hit with Simon; we'd return home to find homework and reading completed, without much of a fuss, and none of the emotion that we experienced. Charles demonstrates that early setbacks can be overcome; Simon can't play the sympathy card. Charles' respect for me began to rub off on Simon as he relaxed and started reading regularly to us at home, which has had a fantastic effect on his reading level.

Simon has recently started at secondary school and has settled in well with the support of a Statement for Literacy. The level of trust between us and Charles is such that, in June, Charles and his son moved into our house for a few days while I accompanied my husband to a conference in Las Vegas, the first time we'd been away together for six years. This had the other advantage of Simon seeing first-hand how hard life is when you become a teenage dad.

Holding hands

When Jamie moved in with us, he'd immediately latched on to Louise (my wife) and made it very clear that he didn't want me to do anything in the way of care. He wanted her to put him to bed, do his bath and all the rest. If we were out and he had to hold someone's hand, it had to be hers.

It was quite a privilege when, on Father's Day – this is over a year after he moved in – he actually gave me a fleeting hug: the first ever. I'd love to say that opened the flood gates, but unfortunately they were still rare after that.

And then I took Jamie and his siblings for a walk on the common. It's a large meadow, really, with a few cows grazing on it. The grass was about knee-height to me and thick with pollen. Jamie, as ever, rushed off here, there and everywhere and you could see where he was as the pollen swirled behind him like a vapour trail. When we got to the bottom, near the stream, he came back complaining that his eyes were itchy. I was a bit shocked when I looked at him as they were vibrantly red and massively swollen. Here was a classic case of hay fever. And so we turned round and headed back towards the car. After a while, I felt a hand slip into mine, which wasn't unusual, but this one felt a bit odd. I didn't recognize the feel of it. I looked down and it was Jamie! To me, this was absolutely immense. It was such a huge thing because there was so much behind it.

Kids, so they tell you, communicate their thoughts, beliefs and feelings through their actions. For over a year now Jamie's actions had been telling me, 'I don't trust you. I think you're dangerous. You're scary. I don't want you around.' And now he had voluntarily put his hand in mine. This signified such a huge shift in thinking. Suddenly, this one action was telling me a whole new inner world. 'I have an emotional need for comfort at the moment. I have this need and I can't meet it myself. It's possible that someone else could actually meet my emotional needs. Physical contact with another human being brings me comfort. This huge, male person may be able to bring me comfort. I am willing to trust him enough to make myself vulnerable and put my hand in his.'

It's taken me some time to recognize the magnitude of some of these thoughts. Take the one about physical comfort. Babies typically learn at an early age that physical contact with another human being is wonderful. They spend so much time up against their parent's bare skin, which prompts a surge of comforting chemicals to be released, that it's second nature to them. A child who's been neglected and not had that experience over and over and over may not know that. Why should they know that that sort of contact is lovely when they haven't had it?

That Jamie had learnt this was, to my thinking, a really big step.

Bracing for the storm

It's now 18 months since our little boy John, now four, came home. Everyone commented initially on what a happy boy he seemed and what a great job we were doing, but we were braced for the storm that had to be brewing. We understood too much about what had happened to him to believe that he could actually be as content as he seemed.

Somewhere along the way he became very anxious, agitated, hypervigilant, angry, demanding, manic and controlling. We can't pinpoint when it happened but there was a gradual realization that these states of being had arrived and not gone away.

We started to read more about attachment issues and therapeutic parenting and talk to social workers for advice. Analysing behaviour and discussing strategies became a full time occupation. It's fascinating and heart-breaking.

We've received a lot of post-adoption support. We attended two Theraplay courses relatively early on and a post-adoption worker has also stayed in touch with us and visited the house to talk with us and do further Theraplay with our son. Just because he is now adopted, we haven't been abandoned.

We've also remained in touch with some of the adopters we met during the Theraplay classes. We all need people in our lives with whom we share an understanding. Adoptive parents have to actively seek those people out.

Mostly, our son rages at us and tries to control us. He finds it very, very difficult to do as he's told. A 'no' to him presents a challenge. He will do the thing anyway, or something random and destructive, and then he will rage at us for stopping him. We have to hold him tight and restrain him so that he can't hurt us, himself, the dogs, or otherwise do damage. He needs very firm boundaries and we need full body armour!

The nice bits: physically, he is thriving. He eats and sleeps better than he ever did in foster care. He's growing. He's learning. He loves us and we love him. He uses us like furniture in that wonderfully comfortable way that kids do with their parents. He climbs all over me and tells me that he loves me, that he likes me, that I'm his best friend, that I'm beautiful. He is very sociable. He is funny and clever and beautiful. Watching him grow and change makes me proud. I feel like a mum. I have a son.

Everything changes when you become a parent. Our son is different and we have to parent differently. Friendships are mostly remote these days and some, I think, are lost. We're not very available, babysitters are not an option for us, adult conversation before 7.30pm (when he goes to sleep) is difficult and after 7.30pm is often unwelcome as we're tired and have so much to do. Our conversation is also very limited. We don't do much and our son is all-consuming. We also often sound negative. When we join in with conversations about parenting or our son's development, we come away feeling like we've tried to convince people of how terrible it all is. We haven't. That's not how we feel. We just don't feel heard very often when we describe the way things are and then we feel a need to come up with examples to counter those platitudes ('All children do that', 'Oh I know what you mean'). I think we've become a bit socially difficult! I hope that we can re-establish more of a balance at some point down the line.

For now, I'll settle for managing to read a bit sometimes (I used to be an avid reader) and short bursts of intensive exercise as many times a week as I can squeeze in. The latter is my lifeline. As are other adoptive parents. It's been a hell of a journey so far and we've barely started! Would I change anything? No. Well, except the times I've lost my patience and shouted at our hurt and confused son. I wish I could take those back. That's a parent's lot, I believe: constant guilt. And we adoptive parents are more challenged than most so we're bound to get it wrong sometimes, but the pressure is on to make up for so much damage done to them by others

For years we waited to have a family. I worried and I hoped and I experienced profound disappointment. We have one now. I don't have to wonder and regret. I feel proud to be an adoptive mum and

I rarely feel sad about not being a birth mum (I thought I was going to be seriously lumbered with that grief for life). Life is rarely how you expect it to be. Once you get your head around that, all sorts of things become possible. What we have is strange and difficult, but it suits us.

I loved him but I didn't like him

I love my children and have been willing to go through hell for them; here is a tiny bit of our story. I hope it will inspire, not disillusion.

I had been a social worker for ten years and felt I would be able to cope with most difficulties I was going to encounter as an adoptive parent. My son, Ralph, was three and my daughter, Hera, was two when they came to us; they had endured dreadful abuse and neglect in their early years. My son was lovely and charming but had violent tantrums. I can't remember my daughter smiling at me for the first year. Ralph took up all the space in the house, leaving little room for Hera. I was exhausted and all my emotions seemed to be running at full blast: ecstasy or despair but nothing in between.

Right from the start I had difficulties with school. By Year 2 Ralph was being bullied by classmates and isolated by teachers. We moved him to a different school where at first he appeared to cope.

But as he got older, the problems increased; I began to dread the trips to the playground, the dark looks from other parents and the approach of his teacher. I was the bad mother of the naughty boy. Meanwhile, at home things were getting worse; by the time he was aged eight, Ralph was becoming more and more violent. He appeared to have no idea of danger, and no interest in relating to me in any other way other than screaming, hitting and yelling abuse.

I loved him with all my heart but I didn't like him; he seemed to be using every means possible to make me reject him, yet it was also very apparent that he needed me. I went online and came across Family Futures Consortium. I talked to the manager, Alan Burnell, and he informed me that Ralph had attachment disorder and explained developmental trauma. For the first time in years I began to feel some optimism.

The first thing I did on returning home was to contact social services; I hadn't done it before because, having been a social worker,

I felt I was admitting to failure. Ralph started having therapy from the post-adoption unit and it did appear to make some difference. The therapist also saw Hera, because of her relationship with Ralph and because I was concerned she was too good! I watched as this apparently happy child curled up in a ball in the corner of the room. She expressed her feeling of not feeling part of our family; Ralph's behaviour was taking up all the space and energy in the household.

I started to absorb all the information I could on developmental trauma and attachment disorder. I tried to explain the condition to his teachers and gave them all the information I could. They are busy people and didn't read it. I got the feeling they thought I was an inadequate parent looking for excuses for her naughty son. After 18 months of therapy, Ralph's behaviour appeared to be improving although he was still having violent outbursts, and could be very abusive.

He moved on to Year 5; I arranged to talk to his new teacher, explained the behaviours she would encounter, why he would exhibit them and some possible ways to deal with them. Her intentions were good but she was unwilling to change her teaching style. His behaviour in and out of school started to disintegrate rapidly. The work that had been done in therapy was undone. He began to be sent out of class and seemed to be spending more time at home than at school. It soon became clear the only resolution they wanted was for Ralph to leave the school. I had to find an alternative fast. I had concluded that the only solution for Ralph was special school provision. Thankfully, I lived in a reasonably enlightened authority and managed to get Ralph into a special school, for children with high-functioning autism and behavioural difficulties. It worked!

Within a couple of months Ralph's behaviour improved radically. His outbursts became less frequent and of shorter duration and violence. For the first time in seven years I didn't have to explain myself to others, and could relax.

He stays at school a couple of nights a week and, finally, after years of being squashed in a corner, Hera has space and time with us. She has become happier and more confident and can trust us enough to misbehave! Ralph and Hera's relationship with each other has also improved. I cannot begin to express the joy at positive things Ralph's teachers have to say at parent meetings – and I no longer see Ralph's future as prison.

Apron strings

For those of us with attachment disordered children, the 'normal' process of cutting the apron strings is anything but straightforward. In fact, establishing some apron strings, some form of attachment, can seem a lifetime's work. There has to be something to let go of! And after the blood, sweat and tears (literally) that I'd put into creating conditions in which my damaged daughter could finally bond with me, she has now reached the age where I should be encouraging her to stand on her own two feet.

If I'm honest, I don't want to. I want some return for my efforts. I want some more of the wonderful 'mummy-ness' I've got at last, of being the person she turns to without hesitation because she trusts me to be there for her. But she's nearly 18, engaged and working!

Naively, I'd assumed that the long-awaited and painfully won bonding was the end of all our troubles. Once again, however, the discrepancy between chronological age and emotional age rears its head. How do we explain to a fiancé, a man she loves in an ordinary young adult way and with whom she has a normal young adult relationship, that there are just some things she needs a mummy for, a mummy's knee and a mummy to wipe away the tears? Thankfully, he's a very understanding guy. And what about work? I can't go in to talk to the boss as I did to her teachers. Yet the adultness of work responsibilities sits uneasily on the shoulders of the little girl she is in some respects.

Once again, I've had to sit down with her and work out some ways of handling her 'different-ness'. And I've had to give myself a good talking to and remind myself to be thankful that we got to a position that many adoptive parents only dream of…having some apron strings to loosen.

Finding someone who understands

'Is the adoption going to break down?' said the voice at the end of the phone. It had never occurred to us in the almost ten years since placement that such a thing was even a possibility. Tom was our son 'as if he had been born to us', but we were at our wits' end, at breaking point, and had run out of people and places to turn to.

Tom came to us at just over seven months old. We were overjoyed. I remember thinking surely there would be no issues of remembered parents or foster carers – he would think he had been with us forever. Of course, we never hid the fact of his adoption from him and although we never actually sat down to have the 'You are adopted' conversation, he always knew that he was adopted and that it was no big deal.

But at almost ten years of age we still felt like we were parenting a three-year-old with behaviour to match. We had never expected to be hit, kicked or bitten by our child. We had never expected him to do this to other children. Why did he never learn? Why was he making the same mistakes over and over again? Surely we should be able to get him up and dressed and out in the morning without constant battle and rages? And if only he would let us give him a hug.

I had read every parenting and attachment book you could think of. I'd investigated ADD, ADHD, autism, you name it. The GP, child psychologist, school nurse and educational psychologist had all had a go. The school inclusion officer had been involved too. I'd been on every training course I could find. I am a fixer but this one had beaten me.

Home life was like walking on eggshells with an unpinned grenade in your hand. School was even worse and I jumped every time the phone rang and felt sick every day when I went to collect him.

Then I went on a course entitled *Learn the Child* by trauma specialist Kate Cairns. It was brilliant – this was the kind of information that every teacher and childcare professional should know. This was why Tom was struggling at school. This was what was behind his behaviour. This was how he was feeling inside! Maybe, after all, we were not totally alone in this situation. It could have been our son that Kate was talking about!

I asked her, with tears in my eyes, if she offered therapy to children in our area. Although she didn't, she put me on to an organization now called Integrate Families which operates in the north of England. We went for an assessment and finally someone understood. We kept hearing 'That's not OK'; 'You shouldn't have to put up with that'; 'Adopters never give up but it's taking its toll on you and your relationship'. They had heard it all before. They understood and, what's more, they actually cared and wanted to do something about it. They wanted to help us. Not just Tom but us.

We had massive problems to overcome. But we trusted them and couldn't wait to get started. We were elated to feel that we had finally found people who knew what we were facing and knew how to help us on the road to recovery. I contacted school and let them have the report. Thud. That was me crashing back down to earth. They didn't agree with it: they thought we were being sold down the river; they thought we should get a referral from school to an NHS psychologist rather than going private.

I found myself trying to justify myself to them and feeling guilty and disloyal. I hate bad feeling, but thankfully I found my voice on this occasion and we started therapy. We went to therapy sessions every Wednesday. At first our son would not talk. He hid under cushions, curled up like a baby, ran out of the room, hurt us right there in front of the therapist. We moved on to him hiding in a tent designed exactly for that purpose and tapping out 'one tap for yes' or 'two taps for no' in response to questions. Sometimes he would pass notes out and we would pass them back in.

Just being with someone else in these situations who could see first-hand but from a professional point of view what was happening and then explain it to us in terms of his brain and his feelings really helped, and we were shown how to help and what to do to restore a shaky equilibrium. We were being taught how to be therapists. And Tom was being taught about his feelings and his brain and helped to understand how he felt and why he felt that way. None of us needed to hide any more.

Two months later we could see a difference. We understood, Tom understood and the emotional temperature in the house was down ever so slightly. We were having some good times – three months later we were able to relax just a little and even have a bit of fun.

Now it's over a year later and we are into our second year of therapy, attending just once every three weeks. Post-adoption support has closed our case, although we are free to contact them at any time.

We envisage finishing therapy in summer just before our son starts secondary school. I have managed to get a Statement of Special Educational Needs (SEN) for him – I had no idea I could request this as a parent, believing the school had to request this. I dread to think where we would be now without this.

We have been in a very dark place without hope or help for too long. Adopters need to be made far more aware of potential problems and where to turn if or when they occur.

When lessons are not learned

We adopted our daughter Emily at 14 months old; she was an only child and initially all went well. When she was around 18 months old, we started to go to a weekly mums and tots group. This is where we now know, looking back, that we saw the first signs of attachment issues. We got the awful looks, glances and tuts when my daughter wouldn't share or would push another child.

Thinking of Super Nanny and toddler tantrums, we started putting her for a minute on the 'naughty' spot – we later learned how wrong this was! Aged two and a half, Emily started three hours a week at playgroup. We thought this would help her social development away from mum and get her ready for playgroup. Again, how wrong we were! This environment caused several issues that our daughter wasn't ready to cope with.

Following advice from a behaviour specialist and health visitor, we looked at another school. It had a better environment, was a smaller group with a strict routine and our daughter had a key worker – we only know now how vital this was.

Eighteen months on, we decided to move house just prior to Emily starting full-time school in order to get more space, something which we thought at the time was the best for us as a family. But again with hindsight this was not the right decision; a new house meant a new school.

The issues and the meetings started in the first school term. Emily began pinching, kicking and spitting, initially at the other children. She then began picking up swear words from others. After a year of meeting over 30 types of professionals, we met one social worker who introduced us to a specialist course about attachment issues. We learnt how vital routine, permanence, structure and the same person/carer within set environments are. We began to understand the reactions of our daughter are the 'flight or fright' reactions, and while we may never know the reasons for them, we learned we just needed to be there for her and hold her. The 'naughty spot' changed to 'time in' together.

Despite our best efforts, our daughter, aged just five, was excluded for a period of time. After several meetings with various professionals, it was agreed she needed routine and structure.

Year 1 arrived. Stand-in teachers and lots of student placements caused more incidents. Speech and language therapists, the local authority, inclusion officers, psychologists, educational social workers, social workers, support workers, governors of the school, GPs, child psychologists, paediatricians, CAMHS appointments, head teachers, year teachers, health visitors, behaviour specialists, school nurse... they have all been involved. Then we get told this mainstream school doesn't have the resources.

We are then advised to see other schools and perhaps an assessment centre – despite us stressing that change is the worst thing for our daughter!

We agreed one of us would home-school and would have to walk out of work. We have decided home education is the only way to provide our daughter with the routine and stability she needs. If our daughter was in full-time foster care, she would have automatically got this additional funding for school to obtain the necessary resources. We are aware of foster families not adopting children due to this loss in funding.

I feel the system has failed our daughter. She had three foster care homes within her first 14 months of life; then we find professionals are not properly trained in attachment issues; then we learn the right resources are not available. If we had this information from day one when our daughter was 14 months old, we wouldn't have subjected her to most of these environments and situations. Lessons are not being learned. It is damaging our children.

We need to learn and invest from day one with the love, time and care they need. There should be a system for professionals to meet, discuss, meet, discuss, meet, discuss, meet, discuss...

There is a gap in knowledge within schools about attachment – and not just attachment issues arising from adoption but for all children.

Chapter 16

BREAKDOWN

It's a nightmare scenario – the one no one wants to think about – the thought of a child that you have nurtured going back into institutionalized care because it's the child or your other children, the child or your marriage.

Like all tragedies, it happens for a number of different reasons. There might be an unrecognized problem that doesn't go away as everyone thought it might, but grows until it becomes unbearable. It can be as complicated and sad as an adoptive parent asking for a little respite from the traumatized child in their care and finding that instead of receiving support they are judged unable to cope and the child is removed permanently. It could be as simple and devastating as the local authority changing its mind: the child you fostered with a view to adoption is to be reunited with his or her birth mother.

For many it's a long and agonizing process spanning a number of years as they try unsuccessfully to include in their family a child who just doesn't want to be a part of it. Some children have such deep-rooted problems as a result of their past that they are hard-wired against developing permanent close relationships and are unable to be a part of a family.

They are so deeply damaged, so severely traumatized by all that has happened to them that they test and test – not just until they find a firm boundary – but until you break.

The first national study into adoption breakdown was published in 2014. Researchers from the University of Bristol analysed national data on 37,335 adoptions over a 12-year period to show that 3.2 per cent of children move out of their adoptive home prematurely.[1]

The research showed that adoptions were more likely to break down if a child was placed once they were over the age of four and that most breakdowns occurred during the teenage years, when the risk of disruption is ten times greater when compared with children under the age of four.

Professor Julie Selwyn, head of the Hadley Centre for Adoption and Foster Care at the University of Bristol, said: 'The disruption rate was lower than we expected. The reasons for that became obvious when we met the families, whose commitment and tenacity was remarkable in very testing circumstances.'

Their analysis of the breakdowns showed that prior to being adopted, of adoptees whose placement broke down:

- 91 per cent had witnessed domestic violence

- 34 per cent had been sexually abused

- 97 per cent had mental health problems

- 25 per cent had been diagnosed with autistic behaviour.

In 80 per cent of cases, breakdown happened following violence and crime.

'We had not expected child to parent violence to feature so strongly in parental accounts of challenging behaviour,' said Professor Selwyn. 'Young people were mainly violent to their mothers, but fathers, siblings, pets and in one case, grandparents had also been assaulted.'

Society makes its own judgements of adoptive parents who are having problems with an adopted child. The adopter often finds a lack of sympathy from friends and even family outside the adoption world, who have no real understanding of what goes on behind closed doors and little sympathy. They have the view that you have 'chosen' the child and take the 'you've made your bed and you must lie in it' approach.

---

1   Department for Education (2014) *Beyond the Adoption Order: Challenges, Intervention, Disruption.* London: Department for Education. Available at www. gov.uk/government/publications/beyond-the-adoption-order-challenges-intervention-disruption, accessed on 5 August 2016.

Even some social workers appear to criticize rather than support the adoptive parent. Although they will do everything in their power to return or keep a child with his or her birth family, the same rules don't seem to apply to adoptive families.

One adoptive mother, traumatized by the breakdown of a placement, said:

> My first advice to other adoptive parents in the same situation might be: avoid the social services if at all possible, they operate with a blaming model rather than a helping model when it comes to childcare cases.
>
> When things go wrong you feel very isolated, and the isolation doesn't help one bit.

Talking to others in a similar situation and accessing adoption helplines can give adopters the lifeline they need to find a way through the dark nights, depression and unbearable challenges they are facing.

But, as when anything else in life goes very badly wrong, days, months and even years can be filled with regrets.

The dark side

When Hannah and her husband, Jonathan, had two boys placed with them, they struggled to get what they felt was appropriate support and the boys were removed only a few months later. Hannah shares their experience to encourage other prospective adopters to look very closely at support plans from the outset.

We have joined the ranks of disheartened prospective adopters who fell short of an invisible benchmark some adoption teams seem to use as a way to decide which adopters deserve more resources and investment – or not.

This is the 'dark' side of adoption that hardly anyone likes to talk about

On a fateful October day over three years ago, we went to the meeting thinking about a future family. We were excited about this new stage in our lives and got a great support worker who we respected. By the time of the approval panel a year later we felt more than ready. The panel approved us as prospective adopters for up to two children. Our confidence was sky-high.

Right away we were told about two siblings, the eldest being older than our preferred age range of three to six years. We felt a flutter of nervousness but felt confident in ourselves and in our adoption team who couldn't have been more helpful at this time. Within six months we had been approved.

Introductions were a time of non-stop activity. Before we knew it, our children were home and we had our first week putting a routine together (which, for consistency, mostly followed their usual routine), agreeing on boundaries and generally going through those awkward initial days where we were all finding ways to come together as a family.

We enjoyed a few weeks of play and family fun, helping them as they got to know the area, the neighbours and potential new friends. It was also a time of adjustment: for us, in becoming parents to two older children with their individual personalities; for the children, to realize being in a family was different to foster care. And there were the regular supervisory visits.

We were tested daily, with behaviours that revolved around control (in particular with mealtimes, bedtime, television, bedwetting). There were tantrums that became markedly aggressive from our eldest and a love–hate sibling relationship that could go from laughter to anger to crying in seconds. We were managing these to our best ability, though we were constantly analysing and reflecting on our actions.

Things got harder when school started. The controlling increased, together with some aggression. Our confidence was slipping so we kept asking for additional help such as family therapy; then our support worker was replaced. We were still struggling with the adjustment to being parents. At that time, the right encouragement and understanding may have helped us find our way. We worked hard to maintain a calm environment, and show love and affection in all ways.

We felt, knowing our lack of experience, our adoption team would meet us halfway and provide us with additional support. Unfortunately, it was not felt that we needed this kind of support. By the third month we were bonding with our youngest, but our delight was clouded by our struggles with our eldest. The promised additional help came in the form of therapy sessions just for us; however, within a month it was clear they weren't working as they were intended. Again, we asked for something more family-oriented.

A month later a meeting was arranged...but this was in fact a platform for the support workers to discuss their concerns. They listed the things that they were unhappy and uncomfortable with, things that had already been discussed. They referred to the poor bonding with our eldest as proof that things weren't working as they should. Everything seemed to be our fault. In the face of such a seeming lack of constructiveness, our confidence nose-dived.

Over the next few days, we found ourselves unable to recover our spirits. We felt that we couldn't go on with the placement as it was. Our eldest boy was unhappy and had been since the move, but we were bonding with our youngest son and he was thriving and we wanted to do whatever we could to maintain our placement with him. We presented various suggestions. We tried to remain hopeful, though felt a sense of dread. We were summoned to a meeting where we heard it had been summarily decided to end our placement with both of our boys.

There was no discussion, no alternative suggestions for maintaining the placement. Within the week the boys were gone and we were left in our empty house. Only five weeks later a disruption meeting was arranged. At the meeting we felt under attack by the team.

We're unlikely to see the full report, but the summary says enough to make it impossible for us to ever consider adopting again. It even makes me wonder why we thought adoption was right for us. From one perspective, it's a masterpiece of diplomacy that appears to work hard to highlight our failings while the agency's actions seem inconsequential by comparison.

Knowing all this, if I could go back in time, I'd return to that October day three years ago and stick to reading my book on the commute home...instead of the newspaper that started a hopeful conversation that ended in despair. And, if I did go ahead, I'd be very insistent about defining every aspect of support I could access, in writing.

Adoption may not be right for everyone, but without the right kind of help and support it can go wrong for anyone.

Enough

One year ago almost to the day, I made the decision that I could no longer continue caring for my eldest adoptive daughter, Lizzie.

We had been struggling to keep going for a number of months and the future looked impossible. So what made something inside me scream out 'enough'? Bizarrely, it was the respite that we had arranged that allowed a part of me to feel free and sing again. For a week we didn't need to be hypervigilant; we didn't need to lock our bedroom door to feel safe at night; we didn't need to check behind us before we went down into the cellar to ensure we weren't locked in, and we could allow the cats to roam freely knowing they wouldn't be harmed. But, most importantly, we could relax, start to be ourselves again and not be constantly barraged with anger and hate. We began to feel slightly human and could laugh and enjoy our other adoptive daughter. But then the time came for Lizzie to come home and we approached the day with dread.

Her anger and hatred started as soon as we were away from the public eye and I felt everything closing in around me again. I felt I was becoming someone that I did not want to be. I was emotionally shut down and dissociated from my eldest daughter. I disliked this side of myself as well as feeling guilty that I was just unable to reach her or had the emotional capacity to continually forgive the things she did and said.

The day I said 'enough' I felt my anger rising and wanted to hurt her and end all the anguish of the last year. She met my eye and I could see the challenge in them. I could not win and so to survive I must admit defeat. 'Enough.'

We had tried every strategy we could think of. We'd followed advice of adoptive parents, carried out training and read books about attachment. We were out of ideas, emotionally exhausted and changing into people we did not want to be. Worse still, we just didn't have the emotional strength to parent and help our youngest daughter as much as we wanted. She also has special needs and needed us to be able to therapeutically parent her too.

I do hold the local Child and Adolescent Mental Health Services (CAMHS) partly responsible, especially when we said so clearly how desperate we were and how close to disruption we felt. They offered Ritalin, a diagnosis of conduct disorder and a reassurance that some children test and test until they feel safe. Others, such as Lizzie, may test until they know where the cracking point is, in the same way that a structural engineer will test a bridge's strength by knowing when it breaks.

Once I had made the decision that we could no longer care for my eldest daughter, I went even further into mental shutdown and shock for weeks.

You see, we saw it in our daughter's eyes when we said, 'No more.' We saw the relief and lifting of her mood when she realized she would be moving on again. We recognized it as validation that it was the right decision, that the emotional closeness to us for her was just too scary. We saw it in the smiles as she packed her bag, more excited by the new clothes she'd just been bought than any concern that she was about to leave what we had sold to her as her 'forever family'.

Our eldest daughter's old respite carer when she was in foster care made contact with social services and offered to care for her. We should have been thrilled perhaps, but they lived over 300 miles away. At 1pm on the deadline day the team leader rang to say that he had a meeting with his legal team and they would start care proceedings if we did not collect our daughter from school at the end of the day and she would be taken to her old respite carers.

The world felt like it was falling in. We didn't pick her up from school.

I miss Lizzie's infectious laugh, the silly games we played and the rare moments of vulnerability she showed when she was able to give and receive love. It is then that I question myself and sink into a pile of self-loathing.

But when I look at our youngest daughter and see how she has blossomed, I know we made the right decision. Suddenly, we can see her needs and help her with them. We can carry out all the strategies and theories we've read about and help her. She misses her half-sister but she knows that she will always see her and trusts us that this will happen.

My relationship with my partner is more loving than before as I have emotional reserves and we don't spend every evening wrestling Lizzie to bed or talking through strategies for the next day's battle. Our family home is happy; it is built on loving relationships and trust. It is in this environment that our youngest daughter is now able to grow and love freely.

I failed to parent one child. This failure will haunt me forever. But the choice was to continue and risk both children's futures and our own, or sacrifice one.

Siblings should not always be together

We adopted Joe and Rosie in 2001 when it was seen, by the courts, as important to keep siblings together. Their birth family asked that they were placed for adoption together. In Rosie and Joe's case, it was not the right decision. The trauma they experienced before birth and in the months living in their birth family has resulted in them being left with big muddles.

By being kept together, they are a constant reminder to each other of the trauma they experienced, and parenting them both has been a challenge.

In March 2014 Jack and I had to make the hardest decision of our lives. Joe's constant attacks on Rosie resulted in my husband and I deciding it was unsafe that he remained living with us and he is now accommodated in residential care under Section 20 of the Children's Act.

We would never have envisaged being where we are now, back in 2001. Everything was exciting and new. We were full of hope that Joe and Rosie would have a brighter future. We had plenty of love to give and were hopeful that we could make a difference after the tough start they had both had.

Jack and I have always stood up to challenges and have worked hard since 2001 to get Joe and Rosie's needs recognized. Rosie did not choose to be Joe's sister or to continue to live with him and now she needs help to heal mentally before Joe can return home.

Joe also needs help to heal mentally before he will be able to accept Rosie's love and ours. Jack and I lost our way a bit for a while with all the stress and pressure placed on us, but we've never given up hope that one day Joe and Rosie will be able to live together without Rosie being attacked by Joe.

Why weren't we told

We have been married for over 20 years, are both in our mid-forties and have worked full-time since leaving school/college. A few years into our marriage, following several attempts at fertility treatments, we made a decision to take a different direction with our lives.

Over several years we thought about adoption and finally applied to our local authority for an adoption pack. We attended the preparation days and began weekly meetings with our social worker. After eight months we went to the adoption panel and were approved unanimously for up to two children aged up to four years.

Two days later our social worker rang and said that having attended an exchange the previous day, she had identified a possible match of two little boys – brothers, one aged 18 months and the other three years. She told us that the older child had been physically injured but there was no other information as they had been removed at that point.

We decided to go ahead. Introductions went well and we felt like we'd won every lottery in the world. We spent the next few days rushing round buying everything – Mothercare must have loved us. I'd left work and transformed the house ready for our new family.

At the end of August the children moved in with us and the first few days went well. It took us by surprise how easily we adapted from having no children to suddenly having two! The children slept and ate well, and taking the older child to nursery for the first time is something I will never forget – such a special moment.

The children's social worker and ours came to the house alternately every week and at one of these the children's worker talked about a criminal injury award and brought a letter from the birth grandmother in which she talked about the father being in prison.

We had started to see a change in the older child very early into the placement. He would be very aggressive towards his brother and would scream hysterically at bath times and bedtime, and would physically withdraw if we tried to cuddle him.

Sometimes he would look so sad and completely shut down so you couldn't reach him at all, and I'd find him sitting in his bedroom staring at the wall holding the hands of his teddy. We were so worried and asked and asked if there was something they weren't telling us, but no one replied to our calls or emails.

We went to see a child psychologist who told us we must ask to see the court files. By this time the older child, who suffered from breath-holding episodes, was having about six per day. These were very distressing and frightening to witness and we were always terrified that he wouldn't come round. Again we asked what was behind this and were told nothing.

Things came to a head in December at a review meeting. The older child had made a sexualized comment and we asked if there was a possibility he had been sexually abused. Again no answer was given. At this meeting we said that unless an assessment was done we couldn't commit to the placement as we felt that there were things we weren't being told.

A month later there was a meeting of the professionals at which they agreed to fund an assessment. They also agreed to allow our social worker access to the children's files. She rang us as soon as she had read the files and asked to come and meet us.

The information we were given was completely devastating. The birth father had been to prison for violence and the birth mother had admitted taking crack cocaine throughout the pregnancy and suffered from learning disabilities. She had regularly been admitted to hospital with injuries following violence in the home which the older child had witnessed. Our social worker had not known this information. We were and are completely devastated. To hear this information, whilst explaining most of the behaviours we were seeing every day, left us with the most awful decisions to make. The children had been in our home for six months.

We were absolutely desperate. I cannot describe how we felt – I think we both knew that the decision to end the placement was the only one, but our hearts were breaking. We spoke to very close friends, parents, and no one came to a different view. We made the most difficult decision of our lives to end the placement and within days the children were removed.

We have no idea how the boys are, and the pain of each day is at times unbearable. The independent reports which were commissioned after the ending of the placement have stated that the placing authority made a conscious decision to withhold certain information from us. How do they justify that?

The independent reports, at our request, have recommended that adoption procedures change at both authorities and that full information be disclosed. We have since received a letter from the placing authority apologizing for our distress. We only hope that the children receive the support and help they have been denied up until this point.

The guilt we feel is overwhelming.

Chapter 17

WHO AM I? TELLING, TALKING AND NEEDING TO KNOW MORE

Once upon a time, telling meant making sure your child knew before they could talk that they were adopted and just as special as born to children but different in that they had another set of genetic birth parents. They would be told little else.

But today a full package of good and bad information – a life story book – is given to adoptive parents as material to share with their children as and when appropriate. There are no rules about what the book should include and how it should be compiled. Adoptive parents are given no guidance on how to use the book – it is left to their parental intuition.

Adoptive children are forever part of two families – the one they were born to and the family that adopts them. Current opinion by adoption authorities is that a level of ongoing contact between adoptees and their birth families is, in most cases, beneficial. Many adoptions today are therefore, to some degree, open adoptions where an adoptee has some ongoing contact with one or several members of their birth family; this contact ranges from a yearly letter to regular face-to-face visits. But, with or without contact, an adopted child's life story book is a vital link to their earliest years and to understanding their journey into care and finally finding a 'forever family'.

Adopters have found that the life story book 'builds a bridge back to that huge part of [the child] that we didn't see and it is her/his main link to her past'. It also 'opens the door for the children to ask questions and talk'.

The adoption charity Coram said that they had learned from adults they supported as children that a key to identity formation for many of them came once they acquired a real idea of their life from the very beginning.

The 'national minimum standards in adoption' focus on the importance of life story work and state that it should 'represent a realistic and honest account of the circumstances surrounding the child's adoption'. A life story book should provide the contexts and explanations for, as well as evidence of, the child's history.

It should include a range of mementoes from photographs of their birth family, hospital bracelets, medical information, birth certificate and maybe even a lock of their baby hair. Some also include letters from extended family members. They should also include photographs and memorabilia from their time in foster care.

Adopters should also receive – usually before or shortly after adoption – a 'later life letter'. This will include more intimate and in-depth information about a child's early history and birth family, and will be written by the child's social worker. The purpose of this letter is for information within it to be a resource for adoptive parents to use when talking to their child about their background and history, and for it to be given to an adoptee later on in their childhood or as a young adult, at a time deemed appropriate by the adoptive parents.

Research by Coram showed that a lack of information about their past can prevent children from addressing unresolved feelings.[1] Gaps in their life story narrative were frustrating for adoptees and for some children a source of speculation and fantasy. Coram concluded that:

- Life story books are a powerful resource when done well but useless and potentially damaging when not.

- Story books are tools that children return to in the present and in the future – research shows that this was particularly true when children approached adolescence and questioned their identity.

- A life story book is more than just a book and should contain photographs and other memorabilia.

---

1   D. Watson, S. Latter and R. Bellew (2015) 'Adopters' views on their children's life story books.' *Adoption & Fostering 39*(2), 119–134.

Adoption UK supports the suggestion by Coram that adopters get involved in helping children develop their life story book so it becomes a record of a child's life pre- and post-adoption life, connecting the two.

It is ultimately an adopted person's journey to live with at least two families in their hearts and minds: their birth family and their adoptive family.

Finding my identity

I'm adopted. Although my life is private, my emotions that tie me to my adoption are not. I believe that the emotional process I have experienced will not be dissimilar to most adoptees out there.

I was born in Malaysia, look Asian yet have a very clear neutral English accent. Often the combination of my accent and my appearance prompts curiosity, which leads to probing questions such as 'Where do you come from?' The majority of the time I reply by saying, 'I'm from Scotland', which is true I am a British citizen with white Scottish parents.

But I can tell by certain expressions or stares (people are puzzled or disbelieving) that the uncertainty comes from my ethnicity. If doubted by strangers and asked where I come from, I could answer with some hostility, which is what I instantly feel like doing as I'm made to feel different and stand-out simply by their judgement of me.

I'm grateful and proud that I'm adopted and I know I should embrace my uniqueness. By confronting my feelings towards my own adoption, I've come to realize my parents didn't hold a racial or cultural prejudice. They wanted a baby to love and to complete their family. A baby that had stark black spiky hair, small eyes and a round, podgy face! I don't call my parents 'adoptive', I never have: they are my mum and dad. I've lived such a varied, incredible life full of love, support, opportunity and experience. I'm so very thankful. Nonetheless, at times I felt I had to put on a façade in front of my family and friends, as I didn't want them to know the entirety of my feelings towards my adoption.

Although I knew I was adopted from the age of around five years old, my parents didn't really initiate an adoption chat and, possibly as a consequence, I hardly raised questions about my birth family; I didn't want to appear ungrateful or offensive.

Slowly, I started to feel disconnected, disconnected from a sense of self-identity, not knowing where my foundation of character or personality came from. During my formative years, I was so preoccupied with being a self-obsessed teenager I didn't think much about my adoption, let alone any of the tough emotions that comes along with it. Being adopted was an occasional thought; soon it became a daily reminder and eventually it consumed me. I had countless questions I needed answering: 'Is my birth family alive? Where do they live? Are they healthy? How am I similar to my birth mother? Will I find them?' A sort of depressive state hit me at 16 years old; I felt isolated and lonely. I recognized that this was the first indication that my adoption was affecting me.

Fortunately, my parents realized the significance of knowing my ethnicity (where I came from) and I was able to visit the hospital where I was born and my hometown with my mum for a few days. Just being surrounded by parts of my 'past life', I felt some sort of untraceable connection. This was the start of my emotional journey of discovery.

I wish I'd had the courage to talk to someone, or had contact with other adoptees that were going through the same internal struggles. I wish Mum and Dad had sat me down and told me everything and showed interest in supporting my emotional identity needs earlier. I do appreciate it is tricky to figure out what may or may not be going through the mind of an adoptee (which would depend on their own circumstances), but realize this: as soon as you decide to adopt, it's not just about you and your needs anymore, it's about the family as a unit and the awareness/consideration that your adopted child has a history (and possible ethnic issues) you need to confront.

Honesty is the key. Be as open as you can; tell your child that they are adopted and be prepared to talk to them about it.

Adoption is about kids' needs too

I think adoption is an amazing thing and I'm really pleased it gives children the life and family they deserve. I have good parents, a good life, brothers and sisters I love and I've had the best upbringing possible.

Yet I still find being adopted really hard to deal with. I have parents and I know they're mine, but I also feel like I have others somewhere. I don't belong to them and they have nothing to do with me anymore, but I still feel like they are my parents to a certain extent. And I feel like I have more brothers and sisters somewhere so it's often hard to ignore these thoughts and just enjoy the life I have.

It's weird for me to think about my biological parents because I've been told they're not safe. I've heard about things that happened to me and my siblings as a child and for that I hate them, but I still don't know them and I don't know why they did what they did.

Being adopted only really started to bother me recently. Why did I have to be? Why couldn't they keep me? Why did it take so long for anyone to want me? I woke in the night crying because I felt I wasn't wanted or good enough for them.

I'd cry because I didn't know who my birth parents were and was too scared to meet them. So I spoke to a few people and specialists. They didn't help. I was always asked what I wanted to know and what I'd ask my parents if I could meet them. I don't know. I just want to know who they are. I want to decide for myself if they'd have been OK or are OK people. I want to decide if the right choice was made or if I should have stayed with them. I don't want everyone else to make these decisions for me. I'm not stupid and I'm not a child anymore. I know I was with my birth parents for the first three years of my life, then another three years being moved around and given to different people. A lot happened in that time. In those six years what happened made me who I am, and I don't remember any of it.

When I was adopted and even now, 12 years later, I often think what if my siblings and I had gone to someone else? What if we didn't go to anyone, or what if we were still with our biological parents? What if we'd gone back to them? What if we'd never left them: what would our lives be like?

Now that I'm older and know more about what is going on in my life, I think it would be better. I wouldn't be a working-class girl who could do the things I can do, but I wouldn't be as confused. I'd know who I was, where I came from and why I behave the way I do. I'm 19 and I've only just realized why I push people away from me. It's because I can't trust people.

But there are other things too. Why do I get scared of things I shouldn't be scared of? Why can't I do things which should be easy? Will I ever know?

When I was little, I'd imagine another me on the other side of the world wishing for my life. I'd always think I should be the other girl without the family; that I should be the one wishing for one. And I'd always feel bad because I felt I had what someone else should have, not what I deserved.

I still don't feel like I deserve this family yet. I know there's nothing I can do about it. My adoptive mum always told me that I deserve it. She says I didn't ask for anything I got and that I didn't do anything wrong. Neither did other kids who still don't have parents. I'm always trying to accept that my life is good and I belong with the family I have, but all I can do is try and it doesn't help much. I want to go and learn about my birth family. I'm old enough now but I'm scared. What if I get hurt again? What if I'm told I wasn't wanted? I guess I have this life anyway but no one wants to hear their parents didn't want them.

Or what if it's the opposite? What if they did want me? What if they still do, then what? Do I start a life with them or do I hurt them and say I have parents and a family I'm happy with? Anything could happen and I don't like the unknown when it's this kind of stuff.

I'm pleased adoption works for people and I'm pleased it gives people a better life. But I can't be the only person who is unsure about who they are and where they belong. I can't be the only person who feels unwanted.

Biting the bullet**

Ellie was two and a half years old when we adopted her. For a while things continued very positively and every few weeks we would reflect and say, 'Look what she has achieved.' At home she was always the little girl with curl (when she was good...), even though sometimes I noticed that we did not seem special to her and she appeared to love everyone. She found close relationships difficult and hated any change of routine. In front of others her self-control was perfect, while with us she could change from Jekyll to Hyde in a split second. As she got older, her tantrums gained momentum and she could be violent. She had 'letterbox' contact with her mother but the letters contained little information other than 'I love you, I miss you.'

By the time she was nine, her tantrums had become public as well as private. Ellie didn't care who saw her when she was in a rage and I was at my wits' end. I felt it was time to bite the bullet. I knew what I was going to say could backfire but I felt so defeated that I was willing to take that chance. Looking at the years ahead, I knew that I couldn't carry on like this. I had turned from being a bouncy, positive 'the bumps are what you climb on' type of person into an emotionally exhausted wreck, never knowing when she was next going to blow.

I explained that while onlookers might overlook a toddler having a tantrum, people seeing that type of behaviour from an older girl might report me to the police or social services, thinking that I was possibly an abductor or at least mistreating her.

I explained that she was a very intelligent girl with a lot of choices – bright at school and with a supportive family, she had the potential to be whatever she wanted to be. If her behaviour continued in this vein, we were at risk of outside intervention, over which we may have no control. We may lose our choices – she may lose her choices.

Next (and how I battled internally over this) I began to discuss her early life, and told her that while her birth mother loved her, her birth mother also had choices and had not always made the choices which were right for both of them.

I explained that we could get out her files and read what had happened – and that it might not be a nice story. She listened to and digested that information. The next day we read her file together. (I did miss out a couple of the worst bits.)

It was magical, as if a spell had been broken. How long would it last? Our 'little girl with the curl' disappeared. The 'very, very, good' became pleasant, down-to-earth good, and when she was bad she was no longer over the top. And so it has continued. Her guilt seems gone, for now at least. She has stopped cuddling strangers.

Most importantly, she no longer pushes us away, and our relationship has progressed and deepened very much as a result.

It is now a year since that night – a night when I reached the depth of despair and which proved a catalyst in our relationship. As time goes by, I am regaining my optimism and feel that any further setbacks — which must surely come with the teenage years — may possibly prove easier to deal with.

Last week Ellie told me, 'I'm really happy. I like myself now.' I have never seen Ellie looking so relaxed over such a sustained period — she now looks like a 'complete' child and says that, for the first time, she feels like one too.

Open hearts and open minds

Adopter Mary reflects on how she listens to her adoptee.

Sometimes we may think we are listening as parents, but are we really open to what is being said, especially if what is said does not sit comfortably with us? I like to think I am a good listener, but we need to do more than just listen — we need to ask the right questions.

As adopters, we regularly cry out for greater adoption support. This usually falls on deaf ears, but at least we can find a platform from which to speak; our children's voices are seldom heard at all.

The importance of life story work is a key theme for adoptees. I have always encouraged my children to explore their life stories and take an active part in redesigning their life story books so that they felt ownership over their story rather than it being a book given to them as a complete story, written by a stranger and at one point in time.

Instead, it needs to be an evolving document that keeps pace with their age and understanding. This involvement in compiling their story is, I believe, a positive step, but this isn't enough. After all, the stories are still too often about things that were done to them and not in their control.

Chapter 18

TRACING AND
SOCIAL MEDIA

For many adoptees there comes a time when talking and wondering about their birth families is not enough. However traumatic their history, they want to meet their birth parents. Sometimes the search is prompted by a need to find their physical roots, sometimes it's instigated by a need to try to make sense of what happened in their traumatic past, and sometimes the search isn't instigated by them at all. Under legislation passed in 2005, birth parents have the right to seek out their adopted children once they reach 18.

For those who do succeed in finding their birth mother or brothers and sisters, a meeting can provide the pieces that always seemed to be missing in the complicated puzzle of their lives. It can be positive for all involved in the adoption triangle, but it can equally be traumatic, stirring up unpleasant memories and undermining the strong new roots an adoptee has built with his or her new family. It can also be confusing for young adopted adults who are not ready to or who have no wish to unpick their past history and meet their birth family.

'Adopted children, because of their past, are often emotionally much younger than their actual age,' said one adoptive mother. 'And in any case no parent stops being a parent when a child suddenly reaches the age of 18.'

One of the biggest dangers in recent years is that meetings between adoptees and their birth parents, once so carefully orchestrated by social workers and others, have now become impromptu. Social media means that often, with just a few facts, anybody can trace almost anyone.

An angry teenager, frustrated by some incident at home or at school, starts searching for someone else who will maybe 'understand them'; another teenager cruising on Facebook can suddenly find a message pop into their inbox: 'Are you my brother/sister/son/daughter?' Sometimes it's a careless posting online of a picture or comment by a friend, sister or brother that opens this Pandora's box.

A 2013 report published by the USA-based Donaldson Adoption Institute on the impact of the internet on adoption concluded that social media and other elements of modern technology are having 'transformative' effects – positive and negative – on adoption policy and practice and on millions of people's lives, while raising serious legal, ethical and procedural concerns that have yet to be addressed.[1] The report found:

- Finding birth relatives is becoming increasingly easy and commonplace, with significant institutional and personal implications, including the likely end of the era of 'closed' adoption.

- A growing number of young adoptees are forming relationships with birth relatives, sometimes without their adoptive parents' knowledge and usually without guidance or preparation.

Adoption UK has produced social media guidelines for adopters to use with their young children:[2]

- Ensure children and young people understand the importance of protecting their privacy online. Almost all social networking sites provide privacy tools to ensure that users can manage who they choose to interact with. Encourage children to keep their personal information private and be responsible publishers.

- Assume everything is public unless you make sure that it isn't.

---

1   A. Whitesel and J.A. Howard (2013) *Untangling the Web II.* New York: Donaldson Adoption Institute. Available at www.adoptioninstitute.org/old/publications/2013_12_UntanglingtheWeb2.pdf, accessed on 5 August 2016.
2   Adoption UK (n.d.) 'Social networking.' Available at www.adoptionuk.org/resources/article/social-networking, accessed on 5 August 2016.

- Be careful with personal information – as soon as a person posts personal information to the internet, he/she has lost control over who will see it and how it will be used.

- Depending on your child's age, consider the use of parental controls such as filtering.

- Remember that social networking and interactive sites can be accessed through mobiles.

The good, the bad, the different

Our adoption experience is in the middle ground, I guess. Not all good. Not all bad. While the children were small, our life was pretty much like everyone else's, apart from minor skirmishes with education! But as they grew, so did our problems.

Trouble at school expanded to become complete disengagement with education, which has taken our son a further ten years to shake off.

Our daughter, who always demonstrated very controlling behaviour, became absolutely impossible as a teenager. Social media enabled her to trace her birth family without our knowledge when she was 16, and that commenced four years of Hell. The police featured in our lives, as did social workers, the job centre, the medical profession, adoption counsellors (all pronounced useless by our daughter) and numerous fly-by-night 'friends', most of whom only lasted a few weeks. All of her friends from school melted away, unable to cope with this maelstrom, leaving just my husband and me to pick up the pieces – which we are doing, very slowly. She still has no job or education. But at least we are talking.

Social media has made life impossible for adopters.

Who am I?

I have always been curious about my past. It troubled me through my teens, I shelved it through my twenties and I contemplated it through my thirties.

I had always promised myself that I would trace my birth mother when I finally arrived at 'myself'. By that I mean when I arrived at a place in my life when I was completely comfortable with who I was – when I was not looking to fill a void or searching for something unattainable – hence 40ish – a strong, confident, self-assured mother of three. The time was right.

My personal journey of discovery was a whirlwind – taking no more than six weeks from start to finish. It is important to consider that for 40 years I had thought about this woman, contemplated many different scenarios, experienced a broad spectrum of emotions – some full of hate – 'she must have been a prostitute' – some full of hope and romantic notion – 'soft, sweet mother who made one mistake and would have kept me had she been able to' – private thoughts, private hurts, private hopes.

Adoption provides a comforting shield of anonymity – and to step out from behind this is like stripping your soul bare – making you incredibly vulnerable and very alone. Personally, I do not believe there is a bigger rejection in life than to be rejected by your own mother, the one person who is supposed to love you unconditionally. The reasons for the rejection are immaterial because the pain remains raw. I also believe that being rejected by your mother leaves you with a subconscious sense of never quite being good enough. This is why I also believe that in order to have the emotional strength and rational reasoning necessary to go on this journey, it is imperative that you have arrived at yourself.

The initial process was straightforward. I contacted my local authority, spoke to the adoption team and completed a form requesting information and my birth name. After a couple of weeks I was given an appointment to visit social services and meet an adoption social worker. I duly went to the appointment, unsure of what to expect. I was taken into a room and given a piece of paper with my original birth name on it. I already knew my mother's first name; something my adoptive father helped me find out when I was 15. It was a strange moment, as I had lived my life with one name, yet here was evidence that I was in fact somebody else. I left with this knowledge, went straight home and used the power of the internet to my full advantage.

My surname was the key. I was born in Reading – something I had always known. I grew up in the Berkshire area and always had a hunch that my birth mother was in the county. I traced the surname under the electoral register – and found a match. Rightly or wrongly,

I asked Dawn, an older friend of mine who lived in the area, to drive to the address. In hindsight, this was not a considerate thing to have done, but I was on a mission and I desperately needed answers. Dawn visited the house and rang the bell. A woman answered. Dawn asked her if her name was Janice – it was. She then told her that she had a message for her from Alison (my birth name): 'Would she meet me?'

Dawn called me and said, 'Do you want the good news or the bad?' I said both. Dawn then told me 'The good news is you will age well! The bad news is she will not meet you.'

I was outraged. I was only looking at this from my point of view. I did not really consider how she might have felt. I was only thinking about myself and what I was hoping to achieve. At the same time, I also searched on Friends Reunited. I contacted two people with the same surname asking if they were connected to my mother. In a strange turn of events, they both replied.

It transpired that one was my half-sister – born one year and one day after me. The other was my mother's half-sister, who was a single woman with an adopted daughter. My half-sister, Jude, was incredibly helpful. We emailed for a few days and then decided to brave a phone call. I must stress that it was brave on her part. She had grown up with my mother and had always thought she was the eldest child of three. A couple of years beforehand, two other women had made contact with my mother – earlier siblings. Jude had already had to come to terms with the fact that she was no longer the eldest child, but third in a line of five. After my contact with her, she had to come to terms with being fourth in a line of six – very tough. It raised hard questions for her about my mother, secrets from the past, etc.

My mother had six children with five different fathers. She asked for the first three to be adopted, one after the other, and kept the other three. Apart from blowing any romantic 'mother' notions right out of the water, I was determined not to be judgemental. Jude and I talked and she was instrumental in persuading my mother to meet with me. Jude also emailed me photographs of my grandfather and herself, but not of my mother. The physical resemblances shocked me – something I had never experienced before, as I don't look anything like anyone in my adopted family.

Meeting my birth mother was a surreal day. I had arranged to pick her up from Twyford station on a Saturday morning in December. I had begun the process in November and by December the meeting was actually happening. I drove into the station and immediately recognized her standing there clutching her handbag – stoic yet apprehensive. I had no photo of her but she was easy to spot. I drove up, wound down my window and asked her if she was Janice and she got into my car. In that one split second 40 years of wondering was finally over. Strangely, she seemed familiar, or maybe I just wanted her to be. We drove to a local pub in a village where I had lived for most of my twenties. I was comfortable on home turf. We sat and had coffee, and I asked her to tell me her story – determined to accept her for who she was.

My mother admitted she had lived in fear of being traced. Her life was quite a sorry tale – she told me that I was the third child she had had adopted. She gave birth to me in the hospital and just left me there. She had been a wild teen. She had spent time at a Magdalene Convent/Institute – sent there, aged 16 (one child already adopted), by the court as her own mother could not cope with her and her father had left home. She had married four times and was beaten and abused by at least one husband.

She looked me in the eye and told me she had no idea who my father was and that she was ashamed to have to tell me that. Touchingly, she had brought a box of black-and-white photographs in an old tin that she wanted me to have: photos of her as a baby, of her parents and of her other children.

The meeting lasted three hours. I listened intently. I did not interrupt – I let her tell me her story. I told her at the beginning of our meeting that I was not there to judge her but I would only accept the truth. I also told her that I had requested my file from Berkshire Social Services. She gave me insight into my medical history, which was helpful for me and my own children. I gave very little away about myself and she did not really ask about me. Throughout the meeting I felt emotionally numb. It was a day I had thought about for so long unfolding in front of me, in which I was playing a part yet feeling so detached. We both looked awkward in the photograph that we asked someone to take of us. Then I needed to go. I felt overwhelmed and just wanted to run away. I dropped her back at the station and we exchanged mobile numbers and text messages. I drove to Dawn's house, a safe haven, and digested the day.

One week later I met Jude in Covent Garden. We spent the day together. She too had brought me a tin of photographs. She had a daughter and gave me a card with the words 'To My Sister'. She very much wanted to be a part of my life. This is where things began to get complicated for me. I grew up with an adopted brother and sister – so I already had a sister. My 'adopted' family loyalty started to feel compromised and my head was spinning from a week of revelation. I also received my file from Berkshire Social Services in an impressively short time. There were numerous notes in the file about my foster carers before I was finally adopted; letters from my adoptive parents (my adoptive father died when I was 19 and it was strangely comforting to see his familiar handwriting in the file).

There was also clear evidence that my mother knew exactly who my father was. I was devastated. I had promised not to judge in return for honesty. I challenged Janice about my father again and she refused to tell me about him. She had lied to me after 40 years and even with so much water under the bridge she still could not tell me the truth.

I have concluded that this knowledge was her power – the only element of control she had left after the adoption of her first three children, and if that is the case, I understand. However, I went looking for the truth and could not accept anything less – and for that reason I severed my contact with her. I also severed contact with Jude, as she wanted a sister – a role I was unable to fill. I feel very guilty about this fact, as Jude was instrumental in helping me achieve my own goal and I couldn't return the favour.

Was it worth it? Honestly, I am not sure. I flung the lid off the proverbial Pandora's box. I examined the contents. I mulled them over and I slammed the lid back on – throwing away the key. That is how it felt for me. I had the luxury of doing that because I am adopted. I stepped out of the shadows, I found what I was looking for and I stepped back into them. Janice and Jude remain exposed. Is that fair? Probably not. I was one of the lucky ones. I had a privileged childhood and, as a mother myself, I have nothing but respect and admiration for my adoptive parents for giving me and my siblings a chance in life.

Tracing my birth mother gave me the missing piece of my personal jigsaw – and I am grateful for that. I no longer have to wonder where I came from. However, what I have learnt is that 'adoption' is not the scapegoat for life's ups and downs. Who I am is my responsibility. It is determined by how I choose to live my life, my thoughts and beliefs, my actions, my choices. The answer to that question can only come from within me.

Meeting my son's birth mother

When I first enquired about my son Daniel 21 years ago, there was no question of any contact with his birth parents, a married couple who had been unable to accept a child with Down's syndrome and just wanted to put this painful episode behind them.

On approval six months later, I learned it was the father who felt he could not cope and the mother had been faced with having to choose between her marriage and her son. Whilst I felt that I would have made a different choice, I could sympathize with her dilemma and was grateful that their decision had given me the chance of a family. A few months later whilst waiting for the adoption order, I was told that the mother wanted to write letters to me and Daniel.

When the letter arrived, the one for Daniel proved to be very sensitively written, explaining that he needed a special kind of love that she was unable to give him, but that she would always love him. During the next few years Ruth and I corresponded around once a year and she always seemed delighted to get my news, especially when I told her that Daniel had a little brother, Matthew, also with Down's syndrome. Then, when Daniel was six years old, the letters stopped coming and mine were returned with 'not known at this address'.

For years I wondered what had happened. I felt I had lost a friend and Daniel had lost the chance to get to know his birth mother, but there was nothing I could do except wait and hope she got back in touch. As Daniel's 18th birthday approached, I wondered whether this would be the time Ruth would make contact, as she had spoken in one of her early letters of a hope that she might meet him when he was grown up.

Putting both Ruth's maiden and married names in the search engine of my computer gave no useful results, but in her last letter she had told me the name of the business and the state where she lived in America (Ruth is American, her husband is English, and they were living in the UK when Daniel was born). It seemed highly unlikely that she still worked there 16 years later, but a quick internet search soon gave me the address I needed. For some months I hesitated until Daniel mentioned his birth mother of his own accord.

Composing the letter was far from easy as I needed to give enough information for Ruth to realize who I was but without anyone else guessing her secret. Sending the letter, I had little hope that it would reach Ruth but within three weeks an ecstatic email arrived. Ruth said she had moved and had not given a forwarding address to social services because she was finding contact too painful, but in recent years she had wanted to receive news of Daniel. I explained to her that Daniel could email on his return from college. In the meantime I sent her photos and forwarded some of Daniel's emails to me. By the third email Ruth was already talking about flying over to visit.

One of my concerns was that Matthew would feel left out. When he saw Daniel reading an email from his birth mother, Matthew asked wistfully if he could have one from his birth dad. The question prompted me to try to trace Matthew's birth parent as well. Under the contact agreement with social services, I had written to Matthew's birth parents each year until his 18th birthday but they had never replied, even though I had often said I would love to hear from them. Since the parents' surname was unusual, a quick internet search soon gave me their business address so I wrote to them. Unfortunately, their reply showed that they were clearly upset that I had traced them and could not face contact, although they did respond to my request for some up-to-date photos of them.

From a young age, both my sons have known that they were adopted and have seen their life story books with pictures of their birth parents and foster parents, but they have not really questioned why their birth parents gave them up. All I have said is that they needed special care because they had Down's syndrome and their birth parents felt unable to give them that care which made them very sad, so they asked a lady to find them a new mum and she found me, which made me very happy.

Ruth's first letter to me confirmed that she was still married to Daniel's father who still felt unable to have any contact with Daniel himself but respected his wife's need to deal with the situation in her own way.

When I told family and friends that I had contacted my son Daniel's birth mother and that she was coming all the way from the US to visit us, they could understand why Daniel felt happy and excited but expected me to feel differently. 'I'm surprised you are not jealous,' my sister remarked, especially as my jealousy of her as a child had blighted her childhood. It certainly felt a little strange to see Daniel type 'Dear Mum' in one of his emails to Ruth and to help him choose a birthday card with 'Mum, you're cool'.

Yet I remembered how many years I had longed for someone to call me 'Mummy', and Ruth had waited much longer because after Daniel she had no other children. They say that jealousy arises from insecurity, but I knew that Daniel had more than enough love for two mums. Being a single adopter can be a lonely experience and it was good to be able to share stories and photos of Daniel with someone who was really interested.

On the morning of Ruth's visit, Daniel was full of excitement. At last the doorbell rang and the next minute Ruth and Daniel exchanged a long hug. It was a beautiful moment. For the rest of the day we sat and talked while I showed Ruth all the photo albums and videos of the school plays. The following day we took Daniel swimming and then went for a tour around his college.

I was concerned about the effect of this visit on Matthew but he coped very well. Ruth was sensitive to the situation and made sure she included Matthew, bringing him a present chosen with as much care as the one brought for his brother.

She spent five days staying nearby in a local bed and breakfast. Understandably, Ruth was dreading saying goodbye to Daniel but he made it easier by not getting upset at the parting. He really enjoyed her visit and looks forward to her emails and seeing her again one day, but in the meantime he is getting on with his life.

It is now four months since Ruth's visit and we have just celebrated our son's birthday. Although Ruth was unable to be with us in person, for the first time she was able to send Daniel a present and talk to him on the phone. When I first started searching for Ruth, I knew I was taking a huge risk of causing further hurt, but the outcome has been better than I could ever have imagined. (Fiona Barrington has written her autobiography *Not Your Normal Family*.[3])

---

3   F. Barrington (2008) *Not Your Normal Family*. London: New Generation Publishing.

Facebook contact helped my daughter to move on

We had always been open with our daughter Heidi about her past and had ensured that she had a good life story book as well as photo albums and other stuff from her birth mum. And for years we had annual letterbox contact, exchanging a letter and photos. For a few years I had encouraged Heidi to write her own letter to her birth mum, which she did, but as it never contained much news, for the past couple of years I wrote on her behalf.

Early in July of last year Heidi received an iPhone from my husband. I was not happy about this and within three weeks we found she had logged on to over-18s dating sites and she was receiving messages from men who wanted to meet her! We took the phone away from her and gave her the use of an old analogue phone on the days we needed to contact her!

Heidi, now aged 15 years old, went to pony club camp in August where she was injured and concussed for 15 minutes when her horse fell. She was given a CAT scan at hospital and discharged, but since then she has had difficulties remembering simple things and problems with school work. The doctors have assured us that this is normal and it may take up to a year for her brain function to return to how it was before the accident (which she still can't remember).

Five days after the accident, Heidi made contact with her birth mum through Facebook, but I didn't find out until five weeks later. I am also on Facebook and saw that her birth mum had commented on a photo of Heidi. I was gobsmacked to see her birth mum's name on Heidi's page and wondered just how she had found Heidi. When I asked Heidi, she said that it was her that had contacted birth mum. By this time they were texting each other and arranging to meet up!

I felt like I'd been hit with a shovel. My husband, who rarely shows his emotions, broke down when I told him over the phone. What was most surprising was that a year before I had encouraged Heidi to meet birth mum as she wasn't in the best of health. Heidi had refused and weeks before she had made Facebook contact I had written birth mum our annual letter and got Heidi to sign it! So why was she able to do messaging but not write her a letter?

We contacted our local social services office and our social worker contacted birth mum to try to stop Facebook contact and text messaging. She also arranged for Heidi to see a social worker to talk about setting up a face-to-face meeting in the future. Heidi was very emotional when she met with the social worker. Heidi also told her adopted brother that she wanted to go and live with birth mum. So all of our lives were being turned upside down.

We tried to remain calm and be supportive, and contact with birth mum was arranged for October half-term week. Heidi wanted me to accompany her. The day arrived and we met up for coffee at a nice countryside park. The meeting lasted for just over an hour. Heidi and birth mum hardly spoke, while the social worker and I kept the conversation going. Heidi is very shy at the best of times and birth mum didn't really know what to say. We took some photos, had big hugs and the contact ended.

A couple of weeks later, Heidi said that she didn't really want to see birth mum and contact, messaging and Facebook had all ended. It was quite sad and difficult as birth mum had made friends with several of Heidi's friends through Facebook, and to Heidi it felt like she was stalking and interfering with her life. Heidi doesn't use Facebook anymore.

However, the end result has been fantastic. Heidi has worked really hard for her mock GCSE exams, and she knows what she wants to study now and what grades she needs. She acknowledged how much she had upset her brother. She now appreciates all that we have done and the sacrifices we have made for her. Heidi even wrote us a letter apologizing and thanking us.

Staying safe in a virtual world

Be very careful about what information is out there. Although we did not use Facebook, information placed on it by other people still meant we could be traced by my son's birth family.

My son, aged eight, had face-to-face contact with his two brothers and letterbox contact with his birth parents and was adopted outside their local authority to avoid accidental meetings. During direct contact with his brothers, he let slip his new surname, and this enabled his brothers to track down photos of our family on Facebook, posted by friends which the brothers recognized from the contact visit.

They passed this information on to their birth parents who found our address on 192.com. Then the phone calls started. It caused a lot of trauma.

Contact photos put up publicly

Our children's birth mother put contact photos on her Bebo sites. We had sent her the photos in good faith and she promptly scanned and uploaded them and named everyone in them.

To be fair to her, she genuinely did not realize she had done anything wrong. In fact, it was she that told our social worker that she had done this during a conversation about the next contact session. She was extremely surprised at the hoo-hah it caused and did (eventually) take them off again – but only after we threatened to call off contact.

Our main area of concern prior to this was that the birth family did not understand the finality of adoption and seemed to regard it as a long-term version of foster care, and in our opinion this episode clearly demonstrated this.

Our local authority has subsequently updated its contact/photo terms and conditions to include the internet.

Assuming that my son's birth family is no different to many others, then I think that similar things may easily happen.

Just go away

My daughter, D, who is now an adult, told me yesterday that her birth mother had been texting her (she got her number from her siblings). D hates her birth mother and has told her so, but her birth mother is trying in her own sad way to cause trouble between my daughter and her siblings, telling lies, etc. That's bad enough but she is also trying to sell D a sob story, but D said to me, 'Mum, she forgets I was with her for seven years. I don't forget how evil she was.'

Her birth mother has been telling D that she is just like her. D exploded and told her she was nothing like her – she is not a child abuser, druggie, etc. My daughter was very upset and just wants to be left alone to live her life. To add to the mix, my oldest adopted son naively texted his birth mother, though she accepts she is to blame for all his problems. This really upset D.

I have advised my daughter just to delete her birth mother from her phone and Facebook, but understandably there is an element of curiosity and, I suppose, control that has stopped D from doing this. I feel really upset that D, who has made such huge progress in the last couple of years, has to deal with this torment.

This contact is toxic and damaging to D's self-esteem and mental health. Sadly, all this brought back a nasty memory for D who thankfully spoke to me about it. I just wish this blasted person would go away and leave us alone.

Our children are still vulnerable

My family has been blown apart by the intervention of social services with birth contact. My sons, 18 and 19 years old, were told by a social worker, in the street, in a totally unplanned meeting, that she had received a letter from a birth family member, and this was 'good news'. This was all done on my youngest son's 18th birthday. It was because they were 18, they were now deemed adults and were told they no longer needed their parents' consent, and therefore could do what they wanted. We had never encouraged them not to find birth family themselves, but the eldest had wanted to do it when he was ready – the situation I feel was forced upon them, and us as adoptive parents; we were not even informed so that we could support them.

I am currently in discussion with social services about their conduct, and because we were still being dismissed, I got my MP involved who rattled a few cages and they sat up and listened, for a while at least.

My eldest son is very confused by everything, birth family are laying guilt trips on them, and social services seem more keen on supporting the birth family than us as adopters, and the ones caught up in the middle are our children. We have been totally left out and dismissed. I don't know of any parent who gives up caring just because their child turns 18.

I hope my situation is not the norm. Nobody prepares you as an adopter for the lack of involvement once they turn 18.

I will not ignore my children. I have put a lot of love and support into giving them a secure upbringing, but unfortunately legislation changed in 2005 so that now birth families can make contact, whereas previously it was up to the adopter to make the first move. Unfortunately, the legislation and certainly the social services individual we have endured has not looked at the bigger picture and the needs of the children – who they class as adults. We know that even at 18 they are vulnerable, especially adopted children, and that they need that extra care – but hey what do I know – this individual purports to know more about my children than I do!

I am still pursuing my quest to improve things for others whose children turn 18 as I believe adopters have to be included in any decision about contact – we are still their parents, whatever age they are.

An adoption inheritance

I was born in the late 1960s to an 18-year-old unmarried mother who had concealed her pregnancy for six months. I was relinquished for adoption and placed with my mum and dad when I was about four months old.

My dad was a school teacher and my mum was at home. They also adopted another baby girl who is 18 months younger than me. I was always aware that I was adopted and that this meant that I was special and chosen. On the whole we were a happy family. My dad was around a lot and my mum was fun and lively.

Sadly, when I was seven and a half our mum died of cancer. I was devastated Nowadays we understand more about grief, but then nobody understood why we were angry, anxious, not sleeping. At that time being adopted really did not figure in how I felt. I had lost the only mother I could actually remember, though in reality it was the second mother I had lost.

My father remarried and he and my step-mum had two birth daughters. When my step-mum had the babies, I began to understand that they were different; they looked like their parents. With my teenage years came gradual understanding that being adopted meant that there was someone 'out there' who had given birth to me.

After university I started to search for my birth mother. It took me a number of years on and off and I finally met her when I was 30. It was amazing and wonderful to meet someone I was related to by birth, someone who looked like me. Luckily, my birth mother is a lovely person who has become a good friend. Her family welcomed me and my partner. I feel I have two families.

As an adopter, I wouldn't want my children to go through the 'not knowing' that I went through. It did affect my teens and twenties; I felt that part of me was missing. I am partly made up of a birth inheritance and partly an adopted inheritance. I have been influenced by both families through genes and experience. I think some of my personality traits and abilities are probably genetic, but many of my values and attitudes come from my adoptive family. I am much closer to my sisters in my adopted family than to my birth mum's sons.

I personally resent the view held by some professionals and adopters that 'all adopted people are damaged'. Yes, we may all be at risk of attachment problems or the effect of developmental trauma, but many adopted people live happy, successful lives. I do know of adoptees who suffered a lot before they were adopted and have been very hard to re-parent and will probably always have significant problems; I am not naive but would ask that we are seen as individuals.

As my partner and I moved forward to adoption, all our families were supportive. We were fortunate enough to adopt two children separately who were under one when they were placed. They both have direct and indirect contact with their birth families and we fully support this.

Adoption has been my only experience of family life. I do not feel that is a negative thing to say, that's just how it is.

Whose children are they?

Three years ago one of my adopted daughters requested through her social worker that she wanted contact with her birth mother before she turned 18. We went through social workers and the meeting took place in the social worker's office. Next thing we knew, the girls and their birth mother had exchanged mobile numbers and were in contact. We tried to keep control and keep it light, so we invited their birth mother and her current partner to their 18th

and the six of us celebrated together under our watchful eye. Since then the girls have gone to their home on a regular basis.

For the last two Christmases we have been left sitting on our own, whilst our daughters have been with their birth family. All the hurt and anger has built and built until last week one of my daughters went there without me knowing. It has taken me a good three days to calm down and try to look at all my feelings and rationalize why I am feeling so mad about it all.

Although my daughters, after meeting their birth mother for a few months, were able to read their notes about their past, they went straight to the birth mother's home and she denied anything had happened. As she has not been, as I see it, honest about their past, I cannot in my mind feel they are truly safe with her, although I know this was a long time ago and she has now moved on with her life.

We are going to meet her tomorrow. I cannot force her to tell them the truth of what happened when they were small. I am hoping if she will, I can then accept her integrity and hope we can have closure and move forward.

I must say as soon as my daughters were 18 we did seem to lose all rights.

We have, on a positive note, brought both girls up to be stable young women, one with a family of her own now and the other at university.

Chapter 19

THE BIRTH MOTHER'S STORY

They are the third and essential part of the adoption triangle – the birth family. They are often regarded with unsympathetic disapproval: they have 'given away' their children or had parenting skills that were so inadequate and/or abusive that their child had been removed from them. Their vulnerability, sensitivity and the emotional attachment they felt for the child from whom they have been parted, however poor their parenting skills or however logical their decision, are disregarded.

But they are in many circumstances victims: of circumstance, of the society in which they live, of violent and sexual abuse and addiction. And whatever their history, however traumatic the circumstances of a child coming into care, the birth parents cannot and must not be forgotten.

One adopter writing on the Adoption UK forum said:

> It's not about them being part of your family. My son's birth parents are not part of our family. But they do exist and whatever your feelings about them, your children may want to know about them in the future. They may not want to know more than the basic facts. But you don't know. I think it is one of the hardest parts of adopting – coming to some sort of accommodation that these people do exist, whether we like it or not.

Our birth parents are responsible for our genetic make-up: the way we look, our allergies, physical weaknesses and strengths, creativity. The nature-versus-nurture debate is ongoing, but no one denies that nature plays a strong part in the make-up of our lives. Nothing can change that. But it is still, more often than not, an uncomfortable relationship – if there is a relationship at all.

'Adoptive parents generally see us as a possible threat,' said Doreen Ward, a founder member of the Natural Parents Network (NPN). 'And the birth mother is full of fears that she is inadequate and not as good as the adopters. There is a lot of fantasy, envy and jealousy on both sides. But that shouldn't be. You both love the child and you are connected because of the child.'

She believes that fantasy and fear are made worse when birth parent and adoptive parent know nothing of one another. 'Fears vanish and the sense of being different diminishes once you meet.'

But sometimes you never meet. 'The adopted child wants to protect the adoptive parent who has brought them up, so they are kept out of the picture and often not told about meetings between children and their first mothers,' said Jean Robertson-Molloy, chairman of the NPN. She said that both in the past and today birth mothers never forget the trauma of the decision. Some go on to have more children, to create new families; others are so traumatized that they can't conceive a second time.

However, increasingly in today's adoption world, some openness in adoption is the norm – even when it is limited to letterbox contact once a year.

'I have letterbox contact with my two oldest children who were adopted when they were five years old and eight weeks old,' said birth mother Angela, who made a revolutionary turnaround in her life after having to face up to the trauma of her children going into care and, despite her efforts to challenge the order, ending up being adopted.

'Knowing I had that contact, helped me to pull myself together, to finally leave my abusive partner and start again.' She moved to a different area, completed training as a lawyer, remarried and now has a five-year-old daughter and maintains a good relationship with her older son's birth mother. 'When she writes to me she always says "your children" when talking about the children. I cannot tell you how much that acknowledgement means to me. When I write back to her I always say "our children". Because they are our children.'

In the past it was always expected that birth parents would disappear and get on with their lives – good or bad. But birth parents don't disappear. And today birth parents have as much right to contact their birth children when they reach 18 as children have a right to find and contact their birth family.

'In this day and age, there will almost certainly come a day when curiosity takes over and my daughter looks for her birth mother on Facebook,' said another adoptive mother. 'If we are talking about her all the time, and I don't vilify her (she was very young, emotionally damaged and prioritized drugs and alcohol over her daughter), it might feel more natural for her to share that contact with me, rather than everything being secretive. She then can't look back and blame me for "ruining" her relationship with her birth mother.'

However traumatic the circumstances are that bring a child into care, many birth mothers suffer a lifetime's sense of loss and constantly want to know whether their child is well and well cared for.

'When adoption becomes the option, the birth mother is taken over: having her child adopted is usually a decision made for her not with her,' said Doreen. 'That is not healthy and is why many birth mothers end up feeling angry and victimized. It is not good to feel a victim. It is better if they feel a part of what is happening and partly responsible for it.'

My daughter's baby

I am an adoptive mother and have been a member of Adoption UK for many years.

What follows may be a distressing read but I would like to say that I do not ever regret having adopted my two children. I treasure the memories of their childhood, and still enjoy a close relationship with one of them.

My adopted daughter Ellie, then aged 19, fell foul of the child protection system when pregnant with her first child. Discrepancies she gave to a midwife about her medical history when she attended an antenatal appointment caused her to be referred to social services who decided to instigate child protection proceedings. She had previously told a doctor that she had had a dramatic adolescence with the usual problems that we associate so much with that age group. Now she was denying (in truth) most of the things she had previously said. Without our knowledge, social services accessed confidential records under the child protection legislation.

I was astounded to receive a phone call from a social worker to inform me that a child protection conference was taking place and it was highly likely that my daughter's baby would be taken into care at birth! She had accessed records of our CAMHS sessions that I didn't even know existed and greatly exaggerated the seriousness of my daughter's problems. I could not reason with her. At the time, I thought she must be some kind of rogue social worker – surely, this was a huge mistake.

An initial child protection conference took place two weeks later and the social worker's report contained damning information which was not only incorrect but also made subjective assumptions about my daughter's difficulties – such as that she must have attachment disorder and therefore would not be able to bond with her baby!

My daughter did have some emotional and behavioural problems, but she is also a very warm, caring person – brilliant with babies and young children. Whilst I was concerned that she had become pregnant before achieving any kind of economic stability, I respected her choice to go ahead and fully believed, and still believe, that having her own baby would bring out the very best in her.

The report also claimed that as we were not deemed to be assertive with our daughter, and because we disagreed with the social worker's assessment, we would not be able to protect her child from her. This was based on one sentence in the CAMHS notes from three years previously, 'parents not assertive', and a meeting following the social worker's phone call at which my daughter became angry when we discussed the discrepancies she had given about her medical history. Naturally, my daughter was distressed – she was being told that she wouldn't be allowed to keep her baby.

Because we remained calm and did not admonish her for her behaviour (she just walked out of the room and came back in when she had calmed down), we were ruled out as supporting or alternative carers. There were 12 social work and health professionals at the conference, only one of whom – the midwife – had met my daughter. The anxiety we felt was unbearable, but it must have been far worse for my six-month-pregnant daughter. We did our best to draw attention to the inaccuracies in the report and to explain misunderstandings, to no avail. A child protection plan was made. There were further meetings including a meeting chaired by a legal officer at least half my age whose demeanour was icy and rigid, rejecting all our attempts to rectify significant errors. The meeting agreed that a care order would be applied for immediately after the birth of the baby. My daughter – now seven months pregnant – was absolutely devastated. What would that kind of anxiety do to the growing foetus inside her?

The above is just a snippet of our story. A very protracted court case followed and we fought very hard to keep our grandchild in the family. Sadly, we lost. In trying to find out how to help our daughter and ourselves, we accessed 'forced adoption' websites with stories which echoed our own. We were dismayed to learn that our chances of success in challenging the local authority were almost zilch. This was a shock! We considered ourselves to be respectable members of society. We were approved as adopters, and had undergone the detailed personal assessments which that entails. How could this be happening to our family? I discovered that it was and is happening to families, quite innocent of any actual or suspected future abuse, up and down the country.

I find some of the blogs on forced adoption websites somewhat reactionary in the language they use, but then, if you have had your own child taken away from you, how can you avoid being emotive about it?

Adoption is both a lifeline and a minefield. We need to see all sides.

Angela's story

My name is Angela. My eldest two children were adopted 12 years ago. This is my story.

I grew up in a household where mental and physical abuse were the norm and, struggling to cope, I began self-harming at the age of 11. I continued on a self-destructive path, becoming involved with drink and drugs in my early teens.

My first serious boyfriend very quickly became my husband – I was only 19 and the marriage barely lasted 18 months – at the end I was left homeless and penniless and so depressed that I attempted suicide. Due to the quick thinking of a friend who found me, I was resuscitated. My Catholic mother disowned me and has never spoken to me since.

On release from hospital I moved away, got a job and started a new life, hoping to leave my problems behind. My relationships with men were always complicated by abuse and I bounced from one disastrous relationship to another. One of these relationships resulted in my first pregnancy. The father of this unborn child left me.

Shortly afterwards, I began a new relationship. This was my first real taste of domestic abuse. He was controlling, manipulative and violent. I had such little self-respect that I felt I should be grateful that he was prepared to take on another man's child. After a really serious beating, I stabbed him in self-defence and I was arrested for attempted murder. The only way I could secure bail was to agree to leave the area. I lost my job, my home and any support that I had.

After a few false starts I managed to sort myself out in time for the birth of my son. I accepted a plea bargain from the prosecution, had the charges reduced and was given probation. I found a house to rent and returned to work as a paralegal and began training to be a solicitor. Life was good, at least on the outside. But the pressures of being a single mother, working and studying full-time, put a huge strain on my mental health and I began drinking again and self-harming in secret.

Then I met 'him' – the man who would eventually destroy me. At first he was charming. He had had an abusive childhood and struggled with drink and drug addiction, but had sorted himself out and was working. We seemed to be kindred spirits and I fell helplessly in love with him. My friends tried to warn me but I didn't listen. Within six months I was using drugs regularly and eventually had a complete breakdown and was unable to work. I spiralled into drug addiction and my son suffered. My GP recommended I speak to social services in order to access the mental health services that I desperately needed. Within weeks my son was in care.

Without my son, I lost all motivation and was under the complete control of my partner: he told me what to wear, what to eat, what music to listen to, who I could talk to. I wasn't allowed out on my own. I became a recluse and a total mess. Social services kept telling me I had to sort myself out if I wanted my son home, but never offered me any help. They kept moving the goalposts; no matter how much I did, the social workers always wanted more.

I then found out I was pregnant. He was furious. He insisted I have an abortion. He told me I wasn't fit to be a mother. I couldn't go through with the abortion. I sorted things out enough for my son to come home four weeks before the birth of my second child. I was still on the waiting list for psychiatric help.

Things went wrong from the minute my second son was born. He had colic and cried constantly. My partner hated it. I used to hide upstairs with the baby, terrified of what would happen if I couldn't keep him quiet. I became very ill and ended up using drugs again. When my son was six weeks old, I haemorrhaged very badly and had to be rushed to hospital. My partner refused to care for the children, so I discharged myself and within an hour of arriving home he was dragging me by my hair and throwing me down the stairs as the baby was crying. He broke my thumb, cracked my ribs and battered me black and blue. I phoned the police and went to court for a restraining order.

Social workers told me that my children were now on the 'at risk' register as I had failed to protect them. Over the next couple of weeks the police failed to arrest my partner, failed to take photos of my injuries and failed to stop him coming into my house. I had to ask social services for help around the house as my injuries made everything very difficult. They provided someone to help me who kept a list of all the jobs I didn't do. This was eventually used against me. No matter how hard I tried, I couldn't keep my partner away. He would walk past the house and spit on the windows, throw paint up the wall, pour rubbish on the path and over my car. He threatened me and the boys.

I couldn't take any more. I walked into social services and begged for help, sobbing on the floor. The following day they took my eldest son from nursery and my ten-week-old baby from my home. It was two and a half weeks before I got to speak to my son. He was destroyed. My happy, bubbly, carefree little boy was quiet, ashen-faced and withdrawn. My baby boy was so quiet they took him to hospital only to be told he was fine; it was just the shock of being taken from his mum.

My partner came back and the abuse escalated. My mental health plummeted. I was suicidal but I fought to have my boys returned. A full psychiatric report ordered by the court stated I needed a minimum of 18 months' therapy. This was considered too long for the boys to wait and I was told on New Year's Eve that they wouldn't be coming home. They were being adopted. The report said it was not a case of if I would commit suicide but when. Six weeks later I took a massive overdose of pills; a neighbour phoned an ambulance.

By the time I reached hospital, it was thought too late to save me. Social services attempted to get my boys to the hospital to say goodbye but a snowstorm prevented them. They told me if I fought and got better, I could have the children back. Three weeks later I walked out of hospital and went to a refuge where I was given help to understand what had happened to me.

When I contacted the social worker, I was told that they had lied; there was no chance of me ever getting the boys back. I was told if I stopped fighting them and agreed to the adoption, I would be allowed continued contact with the boys until an adopter was found. They said I could help choose the right family, meet them and there could be a proper 'hand over'. I didn't really have a choice.

After this, at each contact session my eldest son would say, 'They haven't found me a new mam and dad yet so I still get to see you...' After a couple of weeks I received a letter saying that after consulting a child psychologist it was no longer felt appropriate for contact to continue. There were concerns that my son would resent the adopters and blame them for stopping contact. I was devastated but more concerned about my son. At the next contact session, as soon as I walked in my son said, 'Mam, you better sit down, I've got some bad news.' Once I was sitting, he said, 'Not this week but next will be the last time you ever see me.' They had told him. He was five years old.

On 2 July 2004 I said goodbye to my sons in a conference room while a social worker looked on. I was instructed not to cry and to make it as easy as possible for my boys. No matter how hard I tried, I couldn't help it. I held my children and I cried. I feel it was better for them to know I was sad that they were leaving than have them believe that I didn't care. I was promised postbox contact twice yearly, maybe more. One of the last things I ever said to my eldest son was 'Mammy will write very, very soon'.

At the end of the session I carried my boys to the car, strapped them in and kissed them goodbye. I pasted a smile on my face as they drove away, out of my life forever. As soon as they were out of sight I collapsed. My children were gone and I would never know if they were happy or safe.

Thankfully, my solicitor put me in touch with a charity called After Adoption. After almost two years of fighting, I finally received a letter from my sons. It was handwritten by my eldest and contained loads of beautiful photographs. The spark was back in their eyes! They were happy and healthy but most of all they were safe.

Knowing that my children were happy, combined with the help and support of the charities I was working with, gave me the strength I needed to finally walk out on my abusive partner and I never ever went back.

I moved away and started my life all over again. I met a wonderful man who is now my husband and we have a beautiful daughter. It has been a hard road. I still suffer flashbacks and panic attacks. It has taken seven years for me to be able to trust my husband won't hurt me, but together we have found a way through and are happy.

My sons are now 13 and 17 and live in Australia. They write to me and I have as good a relationship with them as the situation allows. Their adoptive parents are amazing and have kept me a part of their lives which means the world to me.

I hope that eventually they will want to meet me.

Letter from a birth mother**

Dear Mr and Mrs Wakefield

I just wanted to say thank you for supporting Natalie in her decision to find me and to reassure you about my own reasons for wanting to meet her.

I can remember reading an open letter in a woman's magazine from a woman who had given up her baby for adoption years earlier and hadn't ever seen him again. She said that she was 'grateful' to the couple who had adopted him for 'bringing him up for me'.

I don't agree with that: you brought Natalie up for her and for yourselves and made a far better job of it than I would have given my situation. She is your daughter, it was you who sat up in the night with her, comforted her when she fell over, treasured her first crayon pictures from school and all the other million and one things that make a family. You are her mum and dad.

I am looking forward very much to meeting her, not because I want to see my 'missing' baby, not because I want to call myself her mother, but because I gave her to you from love. I have never forgotten her and I want to meet the young woman she has grown into and, if she wants it, to become friends with her.

I have never forgotten, either, how very kind and understanding you were to me all those years ago, and please believe me when I say I would do nothing to hurt you now. All I want is Natalie's happiness, and if that means including me in her life as a friend, that will make me happy also.

I suppose what I am saying is that I am not hoping to have my missing baby back, I am hoping to make a new friend of this person who is so very precious to you and that I will bring a new and happy dimension to her life but not replace what she already has.

I do hope this makes sense. I'd be lying if I said I didn't love her, even though I haven't met her yet. I've loved her since before she was born, and time and distance do nothing to change that. But loving means letting go and I did that 24 years ago, and I don't intend to try to 'take back' now. Thank you for your care and compassion all those years ago and thank you for understanding now. You are very special people.

My son and his mum and dad**

I get upset that someone else is calling my son their son. I have often wondered what the word 'adoption' really means to the parties of the adoption triangle. To the birth mother it means losing all her parental rights, but it cannot mean that her child does not exist any more. To the child it seems to mean that he or she has a new family and a new name, but still has a genetic history that adoption cannot change. To the adoptive parents it seems to mean that they are the parents of children who come to them with an extra package – their past.

After 32 years of ill health, I approached my son's adoptive family because I did not know what had happened to him; among other things, I often wondered if he was still alive. If he had died, no one would have taken the trouble to find me and tell me.

When I had my family of two more children, they did not replace my lost child. He will always be the special individual that he is.

I know that in my son's heart his adoptive mother is his true mother and the feelings he has for me are different. We love each other but more like a brother and sister or aunt and nephew. I am great friends with his parents and they welcome me with open arms every time I visit their home. Our son still lives with his adoptive parents because they are all happy together and they are his true family. I would not destroy what they have created for each other; that is sacred. I am grateful for that, and I feel privileged to see at first hand the bond they have with each other. If I could have only known that years ago, my life would have been a lot better.

Despite this wonderful reunion, I still cry for my lost baby. I have lost 32 years of his life, but I try to make sense of all of this by saying to myself that I gave those years to his parents. Because they have welcomed me with open arms, I cannot begrudge what they have together.

It is six years since I made my approach to them, and at the time I did feel a lot of guilt. Looking back, I wish my intermediary had done a better job when he approached my son's adoptive family by offering them counselling. Three years after the reunion, my son's mother went ahead and got some counselling for herself. Adoptive parents do suffer in silence when adopted children and their birth families are in touch with each other. I am sure that if all parties of the adoption triangle received counselling at this crucial time, a lot of questions could be answered, which would mean a little less heartache.

USEFUL RESOURCES

There are many organizations, regional, national and international, dealing with different aspects of adoption. Here are links to some of the better-known and established organizations in the UK. Some international resources are listed at the end of this section.

Birth parents

Natural Parents Network www.n-p-n.co.uk

A self-help organization offering non-judgemental, confidential and independent support to those who have similar experiences.

Family Rights Group www.frg.org.uk

Established in 1974, by a group of lawyers, social workers and academics concerned about how families were treated when social services were involved with their children. They work with parents in England and Wales whose children are in need, at risk or are in the care system, and with members of the wider family who are raising children unable to remain at home, and advocate for parents whose children are subject to child protection inquiries.

Lesbian and gay adoption

New Family Social www.newfamilysocial.org.uk

The UK network for LGBT (lesbian, gay, bisexual and transgender) adoptive and foster families.

Sparklypoo www.sparklypoo.com

Books by Carolyn Robertson for adopted children and same-sex couples: *Two Mums and a Menagerie* and *Two Dads*.

Prospective adopters

Adoption UK www.adoptionuk.org

Providing support and forums for adopters and those thinking of adoption of all kinds. Adoption UK publishes the *Children Who Wait* magazine. It offers the benefit of peer support, using a deeper level of understanding from experienced adoptive parents, enabling adopters and prospective adopters to benefit from those further along the path of adoption.

Coram www.coram.org.uk

Coram is committed to improving the lives of the UK's most vulnerable children and young people. 'We support children and young people from birth to independence, creating a change that lasts a lifetime.' Coram Adoption has one of the highest placement success levels in the country.

Family Futures www.familyfutures.co.uk

Their mission is to improve the lives of children who have not been given the best start in life – by finding them new, secure families; by working with families to help them parent traumatized children differently; and by providing leading-edge training and development to parents and health care professionals – to create happy family environments for today, tomorrow and beyond.

Post-adoption support

Adoption UK (see above)

Adoption Plus www.adoptionplus.co.uk

An adoption agency which offers an adoption placement service, a developmental trauma and attachment therapy service, and a training and conference service.

After Adoption www.afteradoption.org.uk

After Adoption is an independent adoption agency working throughout England and Wales to help all those affected by adoption. From placing children with adoptive parents to supporting birth families and reuniting families separated through adoption, they work with all groups of people affected by adoption.

The Adoption Social www.theadoptionsocial.com

A social networking site run by adopters.

The Open Nest www.theopennest.co.uk

Offers post-adoption support and therapy. They aim to address the gap in the provision of specialist peer support services to adopted children who have anxiety and trauma-related behaviours and in doing so support families in a meaningful way.

PAC-UK www.pac-uk.org

The Post-Adoption Centre (PAC) was founded in 1986 in response to changes in institutional and social attitudes to adoption. Legislation permitting adopted adults to trace their birth parents acted as a catalyst for greater societal and professional awareness about the lifelong grief, trauma and guilt experienced by all parties in the adoption process. PAC provides counselling and therapeutic support to all parties in the adoption process – namely, birth mothers, adopted children and adoptive parents – and to professionals working with them.

PAFCA www.pafca.co.uk

Parenting Advice for Foster Carers and Adopters (PAFCA) is a website which regularly posts updated articles and information for adopters.

POTATO https://thepotatogroup.org.uk

POTATO (Parenting of Traumatised Adopted Teens Organization) is a support group and website formed by adopters who are parenting teens.

Family Futures 020 7354 4161 www.familyfutures.co.uk

As well as finding families for children, Family Futures offers post-adoption support and parent mentoring.

The Cambian Group www.cambiangroup.com

Cambian provides specialist behavioural health services for children and adults in the UK and works with over 140 public authorities.

Books

Caroline Archer and Christine Gordon (2006) *New Families, Old Scripts: A Guide to Language of Trauma and Attachment.* London: Jessica Kingsley Publishers.

Caroline Archer and Christine Gordon (2012) *Reparenting the Child Who Hurts.* London: Jessica Kingsley Publishers.

Dan Hughes (2012) *Parenting a Child with Emotional and Behavioural Difficulties.* London: British Association for Adoption and Fostering.

Ann Morris (1999) *The Adoption Experience.* London: Jessica Kingsley Publishers.

Bryan Post (2009) *The Great Behaviour Breakdown.* Palmyra, VA: Post Institutes & Associates.

Tracing

Adoption Services for Adults

www.adoptionservicesforadults.org.uk

An independent agency offering support to adult adoptees looking for their birth families.

The Family Records Centre

www.familyrecords.gov.uk certificate.services@ons.gsi.gov.uk

This site, provided by the FamilyRecords.gov.uk consortium, will help you find the government records and other sources you need for your family history research.

Transnational and transracial adoption

Transnational and Transracial Adoption Group

www.ttag.org.uk

This group is coordinated by and for transnational and transracial adoptees. Their purpose is to facilitate networking and contact opportunities for adoptees 'while recognizing, respecting and valuing each individual's diverse adoption experience'.

International resources
US

Child Welfare Information Gateway

www.childwelfare.gov

Kinship Center

www.kinshipcenter.org

Pact, an Adoption Alliance

www.pactadopt.org

Canada

Adoption Council of Canada

www.adoption.ca

Canada Adopts!

www.canadaadopts.com

Australia

Australians Caring for Children (ACC)

www.accau.org

Fostering and Adoption Services

www.childprotection.wa.gov.au

GLOSSARY

www.192.com – a search facility on the web helping individuals to trace people and their addresses.

ADD or ADHD – there are three types of attention deficit disorder, or attention deficit hyperactivity disorder, as it is more commonly referred to. These types are: inattentive, hyperactive-impulsive and combined. A child with ADHD has serious trouble paying attention to the extent that they become a distraction at home or in the classroom.

adoption order – a court order which makes the child legally part of an adoptive family and legally ends a child's relationship with their birth family. It is a permanent order, lasting for the child's lifetime. It cannot be changed once it has been made.

adoption panel – an adoption panel must be set up by each adoption agency to advise on decisions relating to the adoption of children. The panel has two main jobs:

- to consider the suitability of people who want to adopt children
- to match a child who has a plan for adoption with suitable people to adopt him/her.

Adoption Support Fund – The Adoption Support Fund (ASF) has been established because many families need some kind of therapeutic support following adoption and too many have struggled to get the help they need in the past. The Fund became available in 2015 and will enable adopters to access the services they need more easily in future.

Adult Learning Disabilities team (also described in some areas as the Community Learning Disabilities team) – the team is usually made up of a mix of social workers, community nurses, therapists, psychiatrists, clinical psychologists and other experts and administrators. They offer services to anyone over the age of 18.

After Adoption – After Adoption (www.afteradoption.org.uk) is an independent adoption agency working throughout England and Wales to help all those affected by adoption, from placing children with adoptive parents to supporting birth families and reuniting families separated through adoption.

ASD – Autism spectrum disorder (ASD) is a condition that affects social interaction, communication, interests and behaviour.

Asperger's syndrome – one of several previously separate subtypes of autism now often referred to as autism spectrum disorder (ASD). Asperger's syndrome was generally considered to be on the 'high-functioning' end of the spectrum.

attachment disorder – defined as the condition in which individuals have difficulty forming lasting relationships. They often show nearly a complete lack of ability to be genuinely affectionate with others. They typically fail to develop a conscience and do not learn to trust. They do not allow people to be in control of them due to this trust issue. This damage is done by being abused or physically or emotionally separated from one primary caregiver during the first three years of life.

autism spectrum – see **ASD**

CAMHS (Child and Adolescent Mental Health Services) – specialist NHS services. They offer assessment and treatment when children and young people have emotional, behavioural or mental health difficulties.

care proceedings – this is when children's services asks the court to look at a child's situation and decide if that child needs a legal order to keep them safe. A child's social worker will do this if they think that a child cannot remain safely at home.

celebration hearing – the final formal court hearing when adoption certificates are handed out to the adoptive family by a judge. Families often make this into a special day out and invite grandparents and godparents and give their adopted child/children presents. It marks the official moment of adoption.

child protection legislation – the UK's four nations, England, Northern Ireland, Scotland and Wales, each have their own child protection system and laws to help protect children from abuse and neglect. Each nation has a framework of legislation, guidance and practice to identify children who are at risk of harm, and take action to protect those children and prevent further abuse occurring.

children's panel – in Scotland under-18s who commit a crime, or are abused or neglected by their parents, or are in almost any kind of serious trouble, will probably find themselves in front of an appointed 'children's panel' who, along with other interested parties – social workers, teachers, relatives – sit around a table to discuss the child's situation and decide what should happen to that child.

conduct disorder – a serious behavioural and emotional disorder that can occur in children and teens. A child with this disorder may display a pattern of disruptive and violent behaviour and have problems following rules.

Coram – one of the UK's first children's charities. Coram's mission is to develop, deliver and promote best practice in support of the most vulnerable children and young people. Their work includes finding adoptive children, upholding children's rights, providing practical support to vulnerable parents, providing education about the risks of drugs and alcohol, and supporting isolated young people.

developmental trauma – this is the result of abandonment, abuse and neglect during the first three years of a child's life that disrupts cognitive, neurological and psychological development and attachment to adult caregivers. Developmental trauma, a new term in the field of mental health, has roots in developmental psychology and traumatology. Developmental trauma is inflicted on infants and children unconsciously and most often without malicious intent by adult caregivers who are unaware of children's social and emotional needs.

Disability Living Allowance (DLA) – a tax-free benefit for disabled children and adults to help with extra costs because they are disabled. It is not based on a person's disability but on the needs arising from it – for example, if you need someone to help look after you. From 20 June 2016, Personal Independence Payment (PIP) replaced DLA for people aged 16 to 64 years.

disruption meeting – this takes place to discuss the next step to be taken when an adoption or foster placement irretrievably breaks down

Down's syndrome – a genetic condition that typically causes some level of learning disability and characteristic physical features.

dual heritage – a child or adult who has parents from two or more different ethnic or cultural backgrounds.

dyslexia – a common learning difficulty that can cause problems with reading, writing and spelling. It's a 'specific learning difficulty', which means it causes problems with certain abilities used for learning. It is not a learning disability, as dyslexia does not affect intelligence.

dyspraxia – a form of developmental coordination disorder (DCD) and a common disorder affecting fine and/or gross motor coordination in children and adults. It may also affect speech.

executive function deficit – an inability to plan, organize and complete a set task.

Family Futures Consortium – a London-based adoption agency for children aged 3+ which also offer post-adoption support services and a variety of training courses.

foetal alcohol syndrome disorders (FASD) – these are the effects on the development of the brain of a child whose birth mother abused alcohol during her pregnancy.

Form F – the detailed form social workers fill in about prospective adopters or foster carers. Completed with the prospective adopter/foster carer, it details aspects of their family and life. Completion of Form F is at the centre of the process of becoming a prospective adopter

full disclosure CRB form – this is the Criminal Records Bureau check. This has now been replaced with the DBS (Disclosure and Barring Service) form which essentially does the same thing – checks whether the applicant is suitable to work with, foster or adopt children. All adopters have to be CRB-checked.

Integrate Families – the National Centre for Child Trauma and Dissociation, it offers adoption support and training.

introductions – this is the early part of the adoption process after an adopter has been formally linked with a child and before the adoptee comes to live with them. There is then a further period, often a year or more, before the child becomes legally adopted.

IVF – in vitro fertilisation.

key worker – the social worker assigned to your case.

LGBT – lesbian, gay, bisexual and transexual.

letterbox coordinator – the person ensuring that letters from an adoptee or an adoptive parent are sent to members of the adoptee's birth family and visa versa. There is usually an agreement as to how many times a year there will be letterbox contact, if any.

life story book – an album of photographs and information about an adoptee's early life before adoption. Many adopters see the value in continuing the life story book so that the child can trace their route from their birth parents through to their foster parents and then to their adoptive parents, creating a whole history connecting their past to their present.

matching introductions – see **introductions**

National Curriculum – the National Curriculum sets out the programmes of study and attainment targets for all school subjects at all four key stages.

Natural Parents Network – a UK-based, self-help organization for natural parents and relatives who have lost children to adoption.

non-violent resistance (NVR) – an innovative form of systemic family therapy, which has been developed for aggressive, violent, controlling and self-destructive behaviour in young people.

Ofsted – the government's Office for Standards in Education, Children's Services and Skills. It is a non-ministerial department.

Prince's Trust – a youth charity that helps young people aged 13 to 30 get into jobs, education and training.

Ritalin – a central nervous system stimulant. It affects chemicals in the brain and nerves that contribute to hyperactivity and impulse control.

SATS – Scholastic Aptitude Tests are a series of educational assessments, colloquially known as SATS, which are used to assess the attainment of children attending maintained schools in England.

school inclusion officer – a person employed to promote inclusiveness and support school effectiveness so that all pupils, irrespective of their individual backgrounds, circumstances or difficulties, are able to derive the maximum benefit from their learning.

Section 20 of the Children Act – under Section 20 of the Children Act 1989, children and young people can be 'accommodated' with the consent of those with parental responsibility. If the young person is 16 or 17 years old, they do not need the consent of those with parental responsibility in order to be accommodated by the local authority. A local authority may also provide accommodation to anyone between 16 and 21 years old in a community home if they consider it necessary to safeguard or promote that young person's welfare. Any person who has parental responsibility for a child may at any time remove the child from accommodation provided by or on behalf of the local authority. If the young person is 16 or 17 years old, they can leave the accommodation without parental consent. Section 20 is based on cooperative working between the local authority, the young person and his or her parents because the court is not forcing the child or young person to be looked after.

SEN register – if a child is on the SEN register, it means they have a special educational need. A special educational need is defined by the 2014 code of practice as, 'A child or young person has SEN if they have a learning difficulty or disability which calls for special educational provision to be made for him or her.'

SENCO – a special educational needs coordinator (SENCO) is a teacher who is responsible for special educational needs at school.

Statement for Literacy – this examines a child's ability in terms of reading, writing and verbal communication.

Statement of Special Educational Needs – this document sets out a child's SEN and any additional help that the child should receive. The aim of the Statement is to make sure that the child gets the right support to enable them to make progress in school.

Theraplay – a child and family therapy that has as its goal enhancing and building attachment, self-esteem, trust in others and joyful engagement. The principles underlying Theraplay are that, in healthy relationships, there should be natural patterns of playful, healthy interaction between parent and child.